MW01292270

FUMBLE
· · · · · · · · · · · · ·

FUMBLE

· ·

Bear Bryant, Wally Butts, and the Great College Football Scandal

JAMES KIRBY

· · · · · · · · · ·

HARCOURT BRACE JOVANOVICH, PUBLISHERS

SAN DIEGO   NEW YORK   LONDON

To Barbara

Requests for permission to make copies of any part of the work should be mailed to: Permissions, Harcourt Brace Jovanovich, Publishers, Orlando, Florida 32887.

"The Story of a College Football Fix" by Frank Graham, Jr. is reprinted with permission from *The Saturday Evening Post* © 1963 The Curtis Publishing Company.

All photographs courtesy of AP/Wide World Photos

Library of Congress Cataloging-in-Publication Data
Kirby, James, 1928–
    Fumble: Bear Bryant, Wally Butts, and the great college football scandal
    1. University of Alabama—Football.   2. University of Georgia—Football.
    3. Bryant, Paul W.   4. Butts, Wallace, 1905–   .   5. College sports—United States—Organization and administration.   I. Title.
GV958.A4K57   1986   796.332'63'0976184   86-4738
ISBN 0-15-134143-5

Design by Julie Durrell

Printed in the United States of America
First edition
A B C D E

· · · · · · · · · · · · · ·
ACKNOWLEDGMENTS

MY FIRST DEBT is to the late Bernie Moore, commissioner of the Southeastern Conference, for employing me to attend the 1963 trial of *Butts v. Curtis Publishing Company* and to advise the conference concerning it. He opened his files to me, shared his suspicions and wanted as complete an investigation as the circumstances permitted.

When I mustered the time and resolve to complete the public record on this subject, my first encouragement and technical assistance came from Marvin West, then sports editor of the Knoxville *News-Sentinel*, now national sports editor for Scripps Howard in Washington. He also wrote two supportive columns which made it impossible for me to turn back.

To Dean Kenneth L. Penegar of the University of Tennessee College of Law, I am indebted for both tangible and intangible support and for his patience in awaiting its published fruits.

Law students Alice Woody and James Bradley deserve special mention for hundreds of hours of tedious work as research assistants.

At Harcourt Brace Jovanovich, I owe special appreciation to: William Jovanovich for his personal attention to my book proposal and his unhesitating boldness in joining an effort to tackle football's "living legend"; to Peter Jovanovich, who inspired a reorganization of the manuscript that greatly improved it; and finally, to editor Jacqueline Decter for dedicated assistance of the sort every law professor should have when writing for the public.

Finally—for reasons understood by them—I am grateful to my wife and to my mother.

KNOXVILLE, TENNESSEE
March 1986

. . . .
CONTENTS

Eight pages of photographs follow page 120.

1

. . . .

Up from Moro Bottom

NOVEMBER 18, 1961. It was a balmy fall day at Birmingham's jam-packed Legion Field. The Crimson Tide of Alabama, ranked number two in the nation, was on its way to Coach Bear Bryant's ninth straight win of the season and his fourth victory in as many years over Georgia Tech's Yellow Jackets.

The Tide's defense was awesome. Led by linebackers LeRoy Jordan and Darwin Holt, it had allowed only 22 points all season. The last three opponents had been held scoreless.

By early in the fourth quarter, the game was well under control, more one-sided than the 10–0 score indicated: Tech had only crossed midfield once and had been held to under 30 yards rushing. The Tide again stopped Tech in its own territory and was about to get the ball back in good field position on a Yellow Jacket punt. Billy Richardson was back to field the punt for Alabama. One of his blockers was Darwin Holt, a senior from Greenville, Texas. Leading the Tech players covering the punt was halfback Chick Graning. Richardson signaled for a fair catch at the Alabama 31-yard line. Graning was racing toward him about ten yards downfield when Richardson made the catch. Holt then crashed his forearm into Graning's face, beneath his mask. Graning fell backward, unconscious. Holt ran to the sidelines.

The partisan crowd fell silent as Graning was carried off the field on a stretcher. No penalty was called. The incident drew little attention in Sunday's account of the game.

Then the extent of Graning's injuries became known. The Georgia Tech team physician called it the worst facial injury he had ever seen in athletics. His full diagnosis was reported in *The Atlanta Constitution*: "(1) fracture of alveolar process (facial bones); (2) five missing front upper teeth and the majority of remaining front teeth broken (will eventually lose other upper teeth); (3) fracture of nasal bone; (4) fracture of right maxillary sinus and sinus filled with blood; (5) fracture of right zygomatic process (bone beneath right eye); (6) cerebral concussion; (7) possible fracture of base of skull."

Atlanta sportswriters were indignant. They ran pictures of the heavily bandaged, swollen-faced Graning in his hospital bed. Jesse Outlar of the *Constitution* studied films of the game and accused Holt of an intentional late hit. He demanded that Bear Bryant dismiss Holt from his squad. When Southeastern Conference commissioner Bernie Moore announced that the conference had no rule covering the incident and that there was nothing he could do about it, Outlar responded with an open letter to the presidents of the member universities, demanding that they give the commissioner power to force a coach to dismiss a player in such a situation.

Wire services picked up the story. Headlines on the incident competed with the news that the game had vaulted the Tide into first place in the national ratings. Associated Press quoted Bryant as saying that Holt "came to me after the game and was all torn up and said that he had hit the Tech boy. He said he didn't know why he did it. He said he wanted to apologize to Graning. He was all torn up about it."

Holt told UPI that the blow was "an accident." He said that he did not know it was a fair catch because he never looked back at the ball carrier on a punt (a fact confirmed by the films). "I hit Graning with my forearm in an attempt to block him," Holt said, adding that he was trying to block Graning by putting his forearm on the Tech halfback's chest, but his left arm "slipped" and struck Graning in the face.

Georgia Tech coach Bobby Dodd wrote private letters of protest to Bryant and University of Alabama president Frank Rose and said publicly that they were "the only people who can do anything about the situation." Dodd also said "serious consideration" would be given to severing ties with Alabama when their series with Tech came up for renewal. (The following January, Tech announced that the series would not be renewed after the 1964 game.)

Bryant, who had been judged "the most controversial coach in America" by *Time* a month earlier, took the offensive. He called in the press, showed the game film, and pointed out that the Tech team was guilty of more infractions than his. The Alabama press rallied behind Holt and Bryant.

But the incident wouldn't go away. Furman Bisher, sports editor of *The Atlanta Journal,* had visited the Alabama campus four days before the Tech game to watch Bryant's team practice. Bisher's observations and the Holt-Graning incident itself formed the basis of his article in the October 20, 1962, issue of *The Saturday Evening Post:* "College Football is Going Berserk." Noting an alarming rise in the number of football fatalities in 1961, Bisher charged that deliberate efforts to knock opposing players senseless were increasingly a part of "coaching intent." Forearm blows of the sort used by Holt against Graning were cited as a deadly weapon condoned by some coaches. The Penn State athletic director was quoted as saying, "Tacklers seem to be under instruction to maim the ball carrier rather than merely bring him down."

Bisher quoted Auburn coach Ralph Jordan as saying his team was taking up "this new hell-for-leather, helmet-busting, gang-tackling brand of football." The reason? "Since Bear Bryant came back to Alabama, it's the only kind of game which can win."

Unless it was true, the article was libelous. It accused Bryant of teaching brutality to his players, of virtually encouraging them to commit criminal acts. In early January 1963, Bryant sued for libel in federal district court in Birmingham, naming Bisher and the *Post*'s parent company, Curtis Publishing, as defendants.

This was not the first time Bear Bryant had come under attack in the press, nor would it be the last. His was a career charged with challenge, peppered with controversy, and motivated by a fierce determination to win.

Paul William Bryant was born September 11, 1913, on a cotton and vegetable farm in the flat country of south-central Arkansas, in a community called Moro Bottom. Named for Moro Creek, "metropolitan" Moro Bottom consisted of six families spread over a two-mile area. The nearest town, Fordyce, was seven miles away.

Childhood was difficult for Bryant. He was the eleventh of 12 children born to Wilson Monroe and Ida Kilgore Bryant. As far back as he could remember, his father had been disabled by high blood pressure and lung problems and was unable to work. By the time young Paul was big enough to help his mother on the farm, his older brothers had all left home, and the responsibility for the tougher chores fell to him. Though his sisters pitched in with chopping the cotton and milking the cows, he had to do the plowing, haul water for the livestock, and drive the wagon on his mother's daily peddling trips across Moro Creek to Fordyce.

Bryant despised those trips; he had to be up at four o'clock in the morning every day to hitch the mules to the wagon. In winter the ride was bitterly cold despite the heated bricks his mother would put in the wagon. He even dreaded accompanying his mother to his uncle's place in Fordyce for a hearty meal after her rounds were over; his ignorance of proper table manners made him feel self-conscious.

This is not to say that Bryant was a shy child. On the contrary, he craved attention. When he was very young, it was his mother's attention he demanded. If he wanted a dipper of water, he insisted that Mama, not one of his sisters, bring it to him, and he would hold his breath, turning blue in the face, until she did. Switchings by Mama for pranks and stubbornness might have caused painful cuts, but they also brought him that much-needed attention.

School was the scene of many of Bryant's attention-getting antics—and more than his share of whippings. In their one-room schoolhouse, he and his classmates used to laugh at their teacher, a woman, when she administered punishment. But then she was replaced by a husky former football player, who used a paddle with holes in it. The new teacher raised blisters on Bryant's rear for causing a ruckus by putting a turtle in a girl's desk. Bryant threatened to come back and whip the teacher when he grew up, but he never did.

Even church was not immune from Bryant's mischief. He once threw a cat through a window into a girl's lap during a revival meeting. His reward: a lot of attention—and another of Mama's whippings.

In his autobiography, *Bear*, Bryant writes admiringly and gratefully of his mother; she was the dominant force in his life. A tall, handsome woman, she had a presence and appearance that belied the hard times she had endured all her life. As the family breadwinner and disciplinarian, his mother naturally played a greater role than his father in molding his character. Bryant says little of his father beyond mentioning his physical disability and religious beliefs. Both his parents were members of the fundamentalist Church of God and disapproved even of motion pictures and smoking. In deference to his mother's convictions, Bryant never smoked in front of her until the final years of her life. Neither of his parents ever attended a football game.

When Bryant was about 13, his family moved to Fordyce, and he enrolled in Fordyce High. The school turned out to be the right place at the right time for him. It was there that he was first introduced to football, and in 1929 and 1930 (his junior and senior years), the Fordyce team was Arkansas state champ, quite an achievement for a town of 3,600.

Ike Murry, a teammate on those winning squads and later Arkansas attorney general, recalled his first impression of Bryant:

"I first knew Bear when he stumbled into . . . Fordyce High—
and I mean stumbled. He was the awkwardest country boy I'd
ever known. Country. I mean rural, real rural."

But the awkward country boy came into his own in the next
few years. As a senior he played first-string end on offense and
tackle on defense, winning all-state honors at tackle. Football
gave Bryant's desire for attention a new outlet. Teammate Murry
said of Bryant's style:

> Bear was a showman, even in those days. Crowds loved
> him. He never caught many passes. His best play was
> when he went downfield to block a halfback. We played
> on a field half grass, half dirt. Bear would rumble down
> and put a rolling block at that halfback. I don't think
> he ever blocked him, but he'd always raise a cloud of
> dust, kicking and scrambling around the guy's feet. The
> crowd would roar. People loved it.

The Fordyce team and Bryant's play caught the attention of
Arkansas scouts for Coach Wallace Wade of the University of
Alabama. Wade's offer of a football scholarship was eagerly accepted by the upward-bound showman from Moro Bottom; he
jumped at the chance to be the only member of his family to
attend college.

Bryant was six feet, three inches tall, weighed 190 pounds,
and was still growing. He had come to be called "Bear," but
not because of his resemblance to the animal. It was Bryant's
teenage showmanship that earned him the nickname that stuck
with him for life. He recalled the incident in an interview that
was published in *The New York Times*: "It was outside the Lyric
Theater. There was a poster out front with a picture of a bear,
and a guy was offering a dollar a minute to anyone who would
wrestle the bear. The guy who was supposed to wrestle the bear
didn't show up, so they egged me on. They let me and my friends
into the picture show free, and I wrestled this scrawny bear to
the floor. I went around later to get my money, but the guy with

the bear had flown the coop. All I got out of the whole thing was a nickname."

At Alabama Bryant pushed himself relentlessly, driven by "that fear of going back to plowing and driving those mules and chopping cotton for fifty cents a day." A solid, dependable lineman, he made the all-conference second team in his junior year and played the end opposite Don Hutson on the unbeaten Alabama team that upset Stanford in the 1935 Rose Bowl. As a senior he broke a leg in midseason but endured the pain and went right on playing.

Bryant's leadership qualities now began to emerge. He was president of his class in his freshman and junior years and president of the varsity letter club ("A" club) as a senior. He was elected to Omicron Delta Kappa, the national honorary men's leadership society.

As a student he was less distinguished, however, failing to graduate from college with his class. Fordyce High, in its football mania, had not been demanding of its athletes in the classroom, and Bryant arrived at Tuscaloosa short on the credits necessary for admission to the university. Under the looser standards of that era, he completed the required course work at Tuscaloosa High while receiving financial aid from the university and working out with the Alabama football team. Bryant did not receive his college degree until 1939, his third year as an assistant coach at Alabama.

An achievement at Alabama of which the big, unpolished lineman from Moro Bottom was especially proud was winning the hand of Mary Harmon Black, the daughter of a prominent Birmingham judge. A campus beauty queen, she was chosen Miss University of Alabama in 1935 and was "just about everything a girl could be at Alabama in those days." She even had the ultimate campus luxury in the thirties—her own car.

They were married in 1936 and lived in Tuscaloosa while Bryant worked as a junior assistant coach. In 1940, Coach Red Sanders of Vanderbilt offered Bryant a job as his first assistant. Seeing the position as a step up, Bryant readily accepted the offer. Before telling Mary Harmon of his decision, he asked her how she felt about living in Nashville. She gave him 30 reasons against it and "nearly died" when he announced that he had already taken the job. Bryant felt that a coach's first need was a wife who could endure being neglected. He always praised Mary Harmon as an ideal coach's wife.

Bryant's stay at Vanderbilt was cut short by the outbreak of World War II. During the war he served in the navy and helped coach the North Carolina preflight football team. Appointed head coach at the University of Maryland in 1945, he quit after one year because university president Curly Byrd fired one of Bryant's assistants without consulting him and reinstated a player Bryant had fired for training violations. The Bear felt that if he tolerated such interference, it would ruin his standing with the players.

His next stop was Kentucky, where he racked up an impressive eight-year record of 60-23-5, including a 1951 Sugar Bowl victory over one of Bud Wilkinson's Oklahoma powerhouses. But in 1954, he took what appeared to many to be a step down by leaving Kentucky for Texas A & M. The reason for this surprise move, Bryant would later admit, was personal jealousy; he could no longer work in the shadow of the legendary basketball coach Adolph Rupp. As he put it, he was tired of being given cigarette lighters for winning seasons while Rupp was receiving Cadillacs. Apparently, the two were too much alike. When rumors that Rupp was retiring proved false and he signed a new contract instead, Bryant made up his mind to leave.

Bryant's first year at Texas A & M was marked by two major episodes that typified the extent of his will to win. Before the season began, he took 117 scholarship athletes to a remote boot-camp training site. Within ten rugged days, all but 28 were either kicked off the squad for failure to satisfy Bryant or quit from their inability to endure his incredibly demanding practice sessions.

The drills began early and were repeated all day, regardless of blistering heat or driving rainstorms. Cross-country runs in full gear generated dozens of dropouts or "quitters," as Bryant called them—gasping young athletes who had barely enough strength to return to camp and head home. One of Bryant's favorite tactics was to rout the players from their double-decker bunks for nighttime calisthenics after they thought their day's work was over.

Most of the quitters left after the camp had finally settled down for the night. Suitcases in hand, they sneaked quietly from the Quonset-hut barracks, then moved hurriedly down the dirt road toward Junction, Texas, to catch the next bus for home or college. Sometimes they were watched by the taciturn, leather-faced Bryant standing silently in a darkened alcove, smoking his Chesterfield and smiling knowingly.

One of those dismissed by Bryant for not hustling was an all-conference center. The other five centers came to plead with Bryant to give their teammate another chance. Bryant knew the purpose of their visit and, before they had a chance to speak, stood up, shook their hands, and dismissed them in turn, saying, "Good morning, gentlemen, good-bye, good-bye, bless your hearts, good-bye." Quite a penalty for attempting to aid a friend, but it promoted the sort of unquestioning discipline that Bryant demanded.

On Sunday Bryant took the squad to church—after a full early morning workout. He had scheduled the training camp for two weeks but ended it four days early. He feared that if he continued, A & M wouldn't have enough players to open their season.

In 1961, an unnamed Southeastern Conference coach was quoted in *Sports Illustrated* as saying of Bryant's practice sessions at Kentucky, Texas A & M, and Alabama: "It's obvious that the practices were made so brutal that untalented players were forced to quit. . . . He made it so tough on players with little ability that they quit, leaving him plenty of scholarships to recruit more talented boys."

Bryant himself said of his practices, "If a man is going to quit, I want him to quit in practice, not in a game."

In spite of their rigorous training, Bryant's 28 survivors won only one game out of ten, by far the poorest record of any team

he ever coached. In fact, it was the only team in his 38 years
as head coach to suffer a losing season.

In retrospect, the A & M Aggies' only victory was an ironic
one. They upset Wally Butts's favored Georgia Bulldogs, 6–0,
and they did so because of advance information. Here's how
Bryant described it:

> Georgia had us outmanned. We didn't have any play-
> ers. But we did have an exchange film of the Georgia
> team. Elmer Smith must have looked at it five thousand
> times.
>
> In the middle of one showing, Elmer snapped his fin-
> gers. "Hey, I got something."
>
> He said by watching the Georgia quarterback's feet,
> he could call every play except one, the draw play. If
> the quarterback's feet were parallel to the line, he was
> going to hand off. If one was behind the other, it was
> a pass, and the foot to the rear would be the direction
> he was going. We watched, and Elmer was right.
>
> I had Jack Pardee calling defensive signals. Jack watched
> the quarterback's feet and called out our defenses ac-
> cordingly. It worked almost every time. Georgia made
> a lot of yards, but they didn't score.

That same year A & M was put on two-year probation for paying
money to recruit players. As Kern Tip comments in his book,
Football Texas Style, "Bryant . . . with his unquenchable thirst
for victory in mind, grew overpersuasive in tempting promising
college prospects to think of a future in Aggieland. . . . He exceeded the speed limit with racy promises, and the NCAA turned
on the red light." Bryant denied that he personally engaged in
illegal recruiting, but admitted that alumni did so with his encouragement. He knew that recruiting prospects were being
offered money by other schools and told his alumni to "meet
the competition." He thought it was unfair that he had been
singled out when Rice and Texas had done worse. And he felt

he was the victim of a vendetta waged by the press and rival coaches, probably the first ever based on a 1–9 season.

In the two years following his disastrous debut at A & M, Bryant staged the most dramatic turnaround of a team in his career. In 1955, the Aggies went 7-2-1, with losses only to UCLA and Texas. The next year they won the Southwest Conference championship, with a spectacular 9-0-1 record. The taste of the championship was soured for Bryant, however; there was to be no Cotton Bowl for the Aggies because they were still on probation for the recruiting violations.

Though he drove himself as hard as his players at A & M, Bryant still found the time to engage in financial ventures. Opportunities abounded, given the number of Texas tycoons among the school's alumni. He bought stock in the A & M Bank of College Station, joined an alumnus in a successful oil-drilling venture (the government picked up the tab), was on the payroll of another alumnus's company, built some apartment houses that lost money, invested in real estate with Rice University coach Jess Neely, and made two or three poor stock deals. With the exception of the oil wells, all of these investments were losers.

After he won the Southwest Conference championship in 1956, the university offered him a bonus. He asked that they buy his house instead, which they did, at a $10,000 profit to him. He also received a percentage of the gate receipts, a fringe benefit unique among college coaches.

Bryant's next Aggie team appeared to be headed for another championship. They had won eight games straight and were first in the polls by a wide margin, when word leaked out that Bryant was moving to Alabama. Their morale crushed, A & M lost the final three games.

Since eight years remained on Bryant's contract with Texas A & M, the news of his leaving understandably caused considerable bitterness and puzzlement. And though he found it wrenching to face the Aggie players those last three games, he insisted that there were no possible terms under which he would stay. The lure of his alma mater proved irresistible to him.

Alabama, which had won only four games in three years, had mounted an all-out campaign to entice Bryant back to Tuscaloosa. Hundreds of grade-school children wrote him letters telling him how much they wanted to play for him. Countless friends and alumni reminded him that Alabama had taken him out of Moro Bottom and given him an education and his first coaching job. They told him he was the only one who could bring Alabama football back. Bryant did not believe this, but he was convinced they believed it. He remarked, "It was like when you were out in the field and you heard your mama calling you to dinner. Mama called."

One factor that influenced Bryant was that he could look forward to a much more favorable press situation in Alabama. At Texas A & M he had received plenty of attention from sportswriters, but not all of it was the kind he craved. The Fort Worth press had been particularly hostile in Bryant's early years. He felt isolated without a supportive big-city newspaper. At Alabama he knew the press would be for him because it was for the university.

Bryant used his bargaining power to get the best contract he possibly could for the Alabama football program. He was assured of an indulgent administration and was given carte blanche to enrich the program. He soon cashed in these commitments on first-class meals and travel accommodations for the team, a new stereo-equipped dressing room and swimming pool, a hospitality house for entertaining rookie prospects and their parents, an enlarged stadium, and university airplanes for recruiting travel.

For himself, Bryant negotiated a dean's salary, the income from a television show, and a $57,000 house on which he only had to pay the taxes. He was given the dual position of head coach and athletic director and stubbornly clung to both jobs long after most major universities split them up. Why did he reject the accumulated wisdom of other institutions and insist on holding two jobs, when efficiency of management and his personal health would have been served by stepping down as AD? Considering his makeup, three reasons may have been responsible. First, he wanted the two salaries, which eventually combined to reach $120,000 a year. (For a time there was a policy of keeping Bryant's salary under the university president's. One year the president's was $100,000 and Bryant's $99,999.) Second, he did not want an athletic director overseeing him to any extent. There was to be no one between Bear Bryant and the president of the university. Finally, there was an ego factor in holding both jobs, especially when fewer and fewer coaches did.

On paper, Bryant faced the most difficult challenge of his career at Alabama in 1958. Following decades of greatness under coaches Wallace Wade, Frank Thomas, and Red Drew, under J. B. (Ears) Whitworth, it had become the doormat of the Southeastern Conference. The 1955 Tide team, including future Green Bay Packer great Bart Starr, had lost all ten games. In three seasons, from 1955 to 1957, Alabama won three Southeastern Conference games by a total of eight points and lost eighteen by a total of 355 points. Bama did not defeat Vanderbilt once in that period and did not even score against Tennessee. In-state rival Auburn—seldom a problem in the past—had gained dominance with a vengeance. The War Eagles had drubbed the Tide four straight, culminating in a 40–0 humiliation in 1957. Bama scored 7 points to Auburn's 128 in this string.

With Bryant's triumphant return, however, Alabama's losing seasons were over. In 1958, he led them to a 5-4-1 season with no embarrassing one-sided defeats. With only a dozen conference-caliber players, he emphasized strong defense and mistake-free play. No opponent scored more than two touchdowns. The next year Alabama regained supremacy over hated Auburn and moved up to a 7-2-2 record. The Tide went to its first bowl game in six years, losing to Penn State, 7–0, in the Liberty Bowl. This began a string of 24 consecutive bowl games. Further improvement came in 1960—an 8-1-2 season and a 3–3 tie with Texas in the Bluebonnet Bowl.

1961 finally brought Bryant the national championship he had pursued for 16 years. Because of the Holt-Graning incident, however, it also inflamed criticism of the methods he used to gain victory. Implicit condemnation of his coaching came from the Georgia Tech coach, Bobby Dodd (who is known as one of the finest gentlemen ever to coach a college team), when he carried through on his threat to drop Alabama from Tech's schedule. And well before the 1962 season began, the issue of excessive roughness was taken up by the National Collegiate Athletic Association, which distributed a memorandum in July to its members entitled "Unwarranted Viciousness and Brutality in Our College Game." It read in part:

> In recent years there has been a growing concern about the malicious brutality which appears to be on the increase in our great game of intercollegiate football. At its January meeting the Rules Committee received with alarm reports from many districts of uncalled for viciousness, particularly in the area of striking or delivering a blow with the hand or forearm and "piling on" after the ball has been declared dead.
>
> The officers and trustees of the Football Coaches Association shared the concern of the Rules Committee as indicated in the draft of the following statement last June:
>
>> It is reported that in some isolated instances brutal play is being tolerated. It is the unanimous expression of our officers and trustees that the coach is responsible for eliminating brutality in football. Training methods that are aimed at injuring the opponent should be done away with.
>
> After long deliberations and a searching review of the rules it was concluded that the language in Rule 9 quite clearly defined the line between legal action and illegal practices with willful viciousness to inflict bodily harm to an opponent.
>
> The difficulty did not seem to be in rule construction but rather, first, in a laxness of officials to vigorously enforce the existing rules, and second, the unwillingness

of a few coaches to be worthy of their noble profession by properly instructing and disciplining their boys with regard to brutal play.

Who were these "few coaches" whose improper instruction was responsible for brutal play? Bryant later confirmed in writing that he was one of them. His friend Wally Butts, University of Georgia athletic director, had attended the July NCAA meeting as the Southeastern Conference's representative on the Rules Committee. When Butts returned, he called Bryant, who later described the call in a memo to SEC commissioner Bernie Moore:

> Sometime in July, Coach Butts telephoned me that while attending a coaches' meeting at Buffalo, late tackling, piling on, and butt blocking were discussed at length and that the officials over the country were going to be instructed to enforce this rule and to disqualify people who bordered on the edge of violating it. From what he heard there, it was his opinion that the University of Alabama was one of the teams that they felt like infringed on the borderline on this rule and that he thought it was his duty to tell me.

In time Bryant was to prove that he did not need unfair advantages and improper methods to win. He won by outcoaching rival coaches and outplaying opposing teams. His talent for coaching was helped by a number of qualities. In addition to a phenomenal capacity for hard work, he was exceptionally efficient in his use of time. For example, he was known for avoiding long telephone conversations, particularly long-distance calls charged to his budget. Between September 10 and November 30, 1962, Bryant made 86 long-distance calls on his Athletic Association credit card, 79 of which were ten minutes or less and 44 of which were three minutes or less. Only two lasted more than 14 minutes. The longest was a 67-minute call to Wally Butts. Another trait that contributed to Bryant's success was an extraordinary memory. All who knew him were impressed by his power of virtually total recall, perhaps none more so than his admiring coauthor John Underwood. In the preface to *Bear*, Underwood wrote:

> His ability to recall conversations, incidents, names, places, dates, yard lines, etc., was—and is—uncanny. I have on record the same stories told six years apart. Not only are his words the same but so are his voice inflections.
>
> But what really got me was that three months or six months or a year later he would throw something back at me that *I* had said, something in passing during a gin game on a private airplane, or at a poolside on the Florida Keys when he was relaxing. He would say, "Wait a minute. Didn't you tell me last June that so and so and so and so?"
>
> "Yes," I would be forced to admit, "but I thought I was interviewing you." I got by with no imprecisions.

He was a risk-taker, gambling even when it was far from a sure thing, as his business ventures at Texas A & M attest. He played poker and loved to visit Las Vegas and the racetrack.

Above all, Bryant was a worrier, always preoccupied with the next game and the things that might go wrong. He took all opponents seriously. As the 1962 season approached, Bryant had quite a lot at stake. He had a national championship to defend and was under pressure to live down the bad publicity over the Holt-Graning incident and his growing reputation as a "driver." He must have been apprehensive about facing the Georgia Bulldogs, a team that had surprised the Tide in the opening game of Bryant's second season at Alabama (1959) by inflicting one of his two defeats of the year with a decisive 17–3 win.

Opening games have a special potential for surprises. They are by far the most difficult for a coach to plan for. Scouting reports never show changes in an opponent's strategy, formations, or plays, since major changes are always made in closed, secret practices over the summer. Any coach would like to learn what an opponent does in these sessions. Each goes to great lengths to preserve their secrecy.

Although several members of his 1961 championship team were returning, for his opening game Bryant would be relying heavily on a promising but untested 19-year-old sophomore quarterback named Joe Namath. (Freshmen were not yet eligible to play on varsity squads.) He had other reasons for concern. Sportswriters were predicting that Georgia would field a much improved team. Alabama assistant coach Charlie Bradshaw's scouting report had described the Bulldogs as a fine football team that would be bigger, stronger, and faster than last year.

Georgia would be starting an unusually large number of sophomores of relatively unknown quality. Alabama's scouting report on Georgia was encyclopedic in detail, but it was necessarily of limited value for planning an opening game because it was based on the preceding year's performances and the spring intrasquad game. Such games are always made as simple as possible offensively in order to reveal a minimum of the team's potential to visiting scouts. During its spring game, Georgia had run from only two formations: the basic tight T and a simple variation, the slot formation, using it for 109 of 113 plays. Bryant could be certain that Georgia would show more than this on offense. Teams sometimes used eight or ten formations in an opening game.

Bryant's career would go through several phases, his image as a "driver" giving way in time to that of a mellow hero figure. He would change his coaching methods, too, adapting them to changes in his players. Two sportswriters aptly described Bryant's 1962 coaching philosophy in *Sports Illustrated* as "harsh and simple." More specifically, he preached—and practiced:

> . . . get tough, aggressive players, impress upon them that the only thing that matters is victory, no matter what it costs; train them and train them and train them to

an absolute peak of condition; teach them to hit—hit the opponent hard and keep on hitting until inevitably he falters and makes a mistake; capitalize on that mistake.

This philosophy had extricated Bear Bryant from the poor truck farm in Moro Bottom and, by 1962, had finally catapulted him to the top—where he meant to stay.

2

· · · · · · · · · · · · · · · · · · ·

The Fall of the Little Round Man

IT WOULD BE DIFFICULT to imagine two football coaches whose careers were in sharper contrast than Bear Bryant's and Wally Butts's in the fall of 1962. One was at the peak of his profession; the other had been forced from it.

Christmas of 1960 must have been a sour holiday for Wally Butts. For the first time in his life, he faced a major professional setback—the loss of his coaching job. That fall, high school recruiting for the next year's freshmen had not been going well for the University of Georgia, especially in the talent-laden Atlanta market. Some blamed Butts—who was spending much of his time in Atlanta, 70 miles from the Athens campus—for impeding the recruiting efforts of Georgia alumni.

In late November a group of four young Georgia alumni met in Atlanta with Bill Hartman, an Athens businessman. Formerly a Georgia player and assistant coach, Hartman was prominent in Georgia athletic and alumni affairs and was Butts's closest personal friend. He was highly respected by both pro- and anti-Butts factions of the alumni and was a logical person to undertake a difficult middleman role. In Hartman's words, the alumni were "extremely upset" over recruiting difficulties in Atlanta and felt that they could not recruit effectively as long as Butts was head coach. Hartman was urged to persuade Butts to resign and was told that the matter would be taken to the Georgia Athletic Board (the body of university administrators, faculty, and alumni at whose pleasure Butts served) if Butts did not step down voluntarily.

The cause of Atlanta's alumni discontent was Butts's involvement in the Georgia capital's so-called "Night League." As Hartman put it, the alumni disapproved of Butts's "appearances in public places over there, such as nightspots and so forth, with groups, girls, and so forth." Hartman could not defend his friend against the charges. The deterioration of Butts's personal life, which involved excessive drinking in public and frequent out-of-town trips and nightclub appearances in the company of his young mistress, had become common knowledge in Georgia athletic circles. His indiscretions were so open and notorious, in fact, that even Atlanta high school seniors knew of them. Hartman readily acceded to the alumni request and undertook the unpleasant task of urging his friend to resign as coach.

Hartman's task was soon accomplished. On Christmas Eve, 1960, Atlanta newspapers carried headlines announcing that Butts had resigned as coach, effective December 31; he was to continue as athletic director. The truth was well concealed behind University of Georgia president O. C. Aderhold's expressions of regret and Butts's false front: "I've thought it over. I've had every honor a coach can get. This'll probably add ten years to my life."

The press accounts declared that influential friends in alumni ranks had attempted to dissuade Butts from resigning and that opposition to him was limited to a vocal minority of alumni. The reasons for the minority's discontent were not given. Butts himself promoted a self-serving theory, claiming that some unidentified persons thought he was "too rough and mean" and held it against him. He had indeed been a stern taskmaster and disciplinarian throughout his 22 years as head coach but could not really have believed that his coaching methods, which had produced a record of 140-86-8, had contributed to his ouster.

Furman Bisher of the Atlanta *Constitution* wrote that Butts's decision "to remand himself" to an administrative office was accepted with regret by all who knew him. After noting the existence of an unidentified "anti-Butts" faction, he added the faint praise that if a vote were taken among Georgia alumni, the "probability" was that Butts would be restored as coach. The subtlety of this assessment of alumni sentiment was probably lost on most of Bisher's readers.

The Georgia Athletic Board probably had serious reservations about letting Butts stay on as athletic director. Butts's personal indiscretions would continue to be an embarrassment to the university. Furthermore, he had never shown the managerial and financial skills that were essential to a successful athletic directorship. In short, had Butts been an outsider applying for the job, employing him as athletic director in 1961 would have been out of the question. Nonetheless, as Butts correctly assumed, he was allowed to continue as athletic director; he still had too strong a following among alumni and sportswriters to be completely severed from the university against his will.

From the beginning, however, it was apparent that Butts's athletic directorship would be a severely crippled position. He was not even invited to the meeting of the athletic board at which the search for his successor was begun.

The salary he was offered as athletic director was less than his total salary as athletic director and head coach had been. This may sound logical, but as Butts later complained in correspondence with the university treasurer, J. D. Bolton, coaches at other universities who also held athletic directorships did not receive pay cuts when they stopped coaching; he cited Crisler of Michigan, Neyland of Tennessee, and Enright of South Carolina. Other administrative rebuffs were soon to follow.

That unhappy winter of 1960–61, Butts must have looked back on his achievements and wondered how he had managed to let them slip into such a sorry state. At the age of 55, a glowing career was rapidly tarnishing, his personal life was a shambles, and he was in financial trouble and professional disrepute.

The coach's love of football and drive for success dated from his early boyhood in Milledgeville, Georgia, where he was born on February 7, 1905. His father was in the business of felling trees, moving heavy loads, and performing difficult handyman jobs. As Jess Moore, editor of the local paper, recalled, from the time "Wally was knee-high to a cat . . . he was so busy helping his father that he never had time to get into any mischief or hang around any of the town's joints." But whatever free time he did have, Moore added, he would spend playing football by himself. He drove himself at a killing pace even then, for his one desire was to be a football star. Eventually he interested other kids in playing with him, and although he was one of the smaller boys, he controlled the games. "If a big boy picked on a smaller lad, he had to whip Wally. Very few ever achieved that."

Butts's father was able to send his scrappy son to the local Georgia Military College grammar school, where he threw himself into organized sports, guided by his lifelong slogan, "You can win if you pay the price." Despite his squat stature, he starred in football, basketball, and baseball, earning scholarships in all three sports to nearby Mercer University in Macon.

At Mercer his coach was Bernie Moore, who later became commissioner of the Southeastern Conference. As a 155-pound end, Butts gained All-Southern honors. Moore always remembered Butts as the hardest-blocking end he ever saw. The determination and perfectionism that marked Butts's coaching career began to show at Mercer. He was always the first player on the practice field and the last to leave.

He began coaching in 1928 at Madison A & M, a small Georgia prep school. After producing a Southern prep championship team there, he returned to his alma mater, Georgia Military College, where in four years he won thirty-seven games and lost three. In 1935 he moved to Male High in Louisville, Kentucky, where he not only coached but taught history. In ten years in the prep ranks, he lost only ten games. The University of Georgia was Butts's next and final stop.

By most fair tests, Harry Mehre had been a successful coach at Georgia. He had defeated Yale, then a major power, five times, including an upset win at the dedication of Georgia's Sanford Stadium in 1929. In ten seasons Mehre's Bulldogs defeated archrival Georgia Tech eight times, and his 1936 team knocked undefeated and unscored-on Fordham out of a Rose Bowl bid.

Yet Mehre was seldom able to fill the stadium, and his program consistently ran in the red. He also fell short of producing a bowl team or a conference champion. In 1938, the Georgia administration yielded to alumni pressure and terminated Mehre's "lifetime" contract. With his solid record and fine personal qualities, however, Mehre was still an attractive prospect for a major coaching job, and he soon landed the head position at the University of Mississippi.

Butts applied for the Georgia vacancy but lost out to Joel Hunt, an assistant at L.S.U., who persuaded Butts to take a job as his assistant. Hunt lasted only one year, proving to be weak in alumni relations. The affable Butts was promoted to the head coaching job and in 1939 launched Georgia football into its first "Golden Age." (The second was not to come until the Herschel Walker–Vince Dooley era.)

The Georgia players Butts inherited in 1939 were short on both talent and conditioning. He corrected the latter by installing a spring practice grind that lasted from January to June, with only Sundays and a few other days off. Fully half the original squad dropped out; those who survived were ready to pay the price with Wally Butts.

The 1939 team won five games and lost six, but the freshman squad went undefeated, playing point-a-minute football. Butts initiated successful recruiting efforts in Ohio and Pennsylvania, setting a pattern of recruitment in the North that was to pay off for years to come.

In 1940, sophomore Frankie Sinkwich of Youngstown, Ohio, was the nucleus of the first of nine consecutive winning teams. That year they won five games, including a 19–18 victory over Georgia Tech; lost four; and tied one. The next year the "Little Round Man," as Butts affectionately came to be called, beat Tech, 21–0, had an overall record of 8-1-1, and took the Bulldogs to their first bowl game. On January 1, 1942, less than a month after Pearl Harbor, Georgia trounced Davey O'Brien and the Horned Frogs of Texas Christian in the Orange Bowl in Miami. The score was 40–26, the highest point total in bowl game history to that date. The nation took notice; the craftsmanship of one of the greatest offensive coaches in American football had begun to produce exciting winners at Athens.

Under Butts, Georgia was to return to the Orange Bowl twice and would make trips to the Presidential, Oil, Gator, Sugar, and Rose bowls as well. His teams won four conference championships. Noting the "beautiful but deadly flow of pass patterns, sound execution of fundamentals, and . . . hard-nosed style of play" that characterized Butts's teams, Frank Leahy of Notre Dame called him "one of the greatest coaches of all time."

Butts's honors included the presidency of the Football Coaches of America and three coaching assignments in the college all-star game, then played annually against the professional championship team. He produced 12 All-Americans, including Frankie Sinkwich, the South's first Heisman Trophy winner; Charlie Trippi; Zeke Bratkowski; and Fran Tarkenton. Ironically, Butts was elected to the Helms Football Hall of Fame on the day he resigned as coach.

In spite of all this recognition, as the years passed, Butts increasingly felt that his effectiveness as a coach was being undermined by the university's reluctance to meet the escalating costs of big-time football. He quarreled constantly over finances with treasurer J. D. Bolton and faculty members on the athletic board, who struggled continuously to keep Butts within his budget and to resist his pleas for more money. Bill Hartman observed Butts's "running battle" with the board, a conflict caused by the simple fact that "he wanted to win football games and they wanted to stay in the budget." The problem also had human dimensions, as Hartman recalled:

> The University of Georgia is not a rich school from
> the standpoint of gate receipts, and we have had a prob-

lem getting enough dollars for the number of scholarships permitted by the Southeastern Conference. The Southeastern Conference permits 140 scholarships in basketball, football. At Georgia I was chairman of the Scholarship Committee from '53 through '56, and in many instances we knew when we started the season that we could sign 140 boys, but we also had to take into consideration our dollar problem. We would set up definite schedules that if we signed up 140 and entered them in the fall quarter, we'd have to lose ten of them by January, the winter quarter, because we would not have the dollars to pay for 140 scholarships at the winter quarter registration, and we'd have to lose another ten by the spring quarter and get down to 120, so that we had the constant problem of trying to recruit and fit our personnel inside the dollar budget, whereas many schools in the Southeastern Conference had no dollar problem and simply got the 140 boys, and that was it.

Hartman shared Butts's deep-seated feeling that he was up against financial handicaps not found at most Southeastern Conference schools. Georgia, after all, had fired Harry Mehre in 1938 because his program ran in the red. Yet Butts managed both to stay within his budget and produce winners consistently until 1949, when he slipped to a 4-6-1 record. Though he did not have another losing season until 1953, the Bulldogs' 3–8 record that year was Butts's worst at Georgia. His team suffered decisive losses to rivals Alabama, Georgia Tech, and Auburn, and an embarrassing 14–0 upset by Mississippi Southern, despite superb passing by senior Zeke Bratkowski.

After climbing back to a respectable 6-3-1 record in 1954, the Bulldogs then endured a string of losing seasons, winning only four games in 1955, three each in 1956 and 1957, and four in 1958. In 1959 a surprising Cinderella team won the conference championship with a 9–1 record and went on to defeat Big Eight champion Missouri in the Orange Bowl. A disappointing 6–4 sequel in 1960 left Butts with a record of 29-34-1 for his final six years of coaching.

If Butts blamed his faltering success entirely on the university's insufficient financial support, even those who sympathized with his position saw other reasons for his decline. Some attributed it to his conservative resistance to the new wide-open football of the 1950s. He clung stubbornly, for instance, to the old tight T formation long after most major schools' coaches had abandoned it. Others maintained that the distractions of his personal financial problems and sexual indiscretions contributed to his decline.

Butts's successor as head coach was his youngest assistant, John Griffith. Shortly before Griffith's selection, Butts told Furman Bisher, "I'm going to do everything in my power to help the next coach at Georgia succeed. He's going to need my help. I don't care who he is. He's going to need all the help he can get." Butts had every reason to expect that any new coach would consult him, but he had special reasons to expect Griffith to seek his advice. Griffith had played for Butts at Georgia. Butts had hired him as an assistant in 1954, after he coached South Georgia Junior College to three consecutive state championships, and had invited him back to Georgia in 1956 after he left for a one-year stint as an assistant at Furman University. Butts even loaned his young protégé money to help finance his move back to Athens. Butts could have rightfully claimed that he was personally responsible for putting Griffith in a position to land the Georgia head coaching job at the relatively young age of 32.

It must have come as quite a blow, then, when Griffith made it clear from the outset that Butts was to have nothing to do with his football program. The new head coach wanted to steer the Bulldogs as far from Butts's tainted image as possible. University president Aderhold concurred, and personally told Butts, in effect, that the football program was off limits to him. During the entire 1961 season, Butts was conspicuously excluded from strategy sessions; he did not even see a single game plan.

Deeply embittered by Griffith's actions, Butts was torn in two.

The part of him that was loyal to Georgia must have wanted to see Griffith succeed, while the rest of him must have wanted his successor to fail. And though he may not have deliberately set out to sabotage Griffith, he did begin to criticize the new head coach openly. Some even believe that Butts hoped to win his old job back. He apparently convinced himself that Georgia's long-range interests would not be served if Griffith were to have an extended career as head coach. In any event, Butts launched a course of conduct that could only have helped to hasten Griffith's demise.

One issue that fueled Butts's resentment of Griffith was the fact that the latter's football program enjoyed greater financial support from the university than his own had, and he revealed his feelings on the subject early in his tour as athletic director. In a letter of May 1961, thanking Harold Heckman, a long-time faculty member on the athletic board, for supporting him in a successful internal battle over his travel allowances, Butts voiced his disappointment that Georgia had lost assistant coach Sterling Dupree to Florida. He added that Florida had "recognized Dupree by giving him a better job than any assistant at Georgia." He then compared his financial support with that of his successor:

> I am happy because Johnny Griffith is getting the necessary financial support—at the same time, I will never believe an all-out effort was made to help me when the going was tough. I think all concerned were conscientious in their decision—but ill-advised.
>
> Years ago I advised that the policy on athletics at Georgia would send us to the bottom. I am glad I had enough guts to take the punishment and get Georgia back on top.

During his tenure as athletic director, fund raising was one of the few functions Butts was expected to carry out. Surprisingly to many, he handicapped himself unnecessarily in this difficult task by telling audiences of prospective donors about Griffith's new-found riches. The contradiction may have escaped Butts, defensive as he was about his own record. Time and again Griffith was astounded to learn that Butts was hurting fund raising by declaring in public that the new head coach now had the necessary financial support to return Georgia to its winning ways. The clear inference was that if Griffith failed, the cause had to be inferior coaching.

Reports also came back to Griffith that Butts claimed he had had poorer material to work with than the recruits now playing for Griffith. (In one of Butts's public statements when he resigned, he had told Furman Bisher that "there was a time when we couldn't get football players to come to Georgia. We've done better lately. We're getting good players from small towns, and our coaching staff has done as good a job as anybody making college players out of them.") And Butts criticized Griffith for not getting the most out of the players he had inherited.

Most objective observers of the Georgia scene sympathized with the young coach's efforts to cope with an athletic director who, wittingly or not, seemed to be undermining him in every possible way. Yet there were anti-Griffith factions as well—those who thought Butts had been treated unfairly and others who felt assistant coach Charlie Trippi should have succeeded Butts. Griffith was hampered by a relationship between coach and athletic director that is probably unique in American football history.

Butts began quarreling again with Georgia administrators over finances. Despite his earlier indication that his travel allowances were adequate, he was soon complaining about details. On June 2, 1961, he wrote to Treasurer Bolton:

Dear Mr. Bolton:

Your idea concerning my travel and expense allowance is amazing to me. Why should I travel any less as director?

I expect to follow all regulations in requesting and using expense money. At the same time, I want my expenses paid by the Athletic Association.

I am trying to do a better job in raising gift money. Public relations and contacts are important factors in this work.

I have never discussed salary with anyone at Georgia. I have too much pride. I think my salary is alright but I should have been given a liberal subsistence allowance.

I am not complaining by reference to my situation. I realize that I will have to take anything "dished out" or else.

Bolton is now dead, and little documentation of his budget battles with Butts is available. But there is another letter, a poignant, pointed note from Butts to Bolton, written after Butts attended the funeral of Tennessee great Bob Neyland:

Dear J. D.:

I think it an unfair deal for you to turn down my expense account to General Neyland's funeral.

He is one of the outstanding men developed in the Southeastern Conference. If I had not gone to the funeral, Johnny had planned to send two members of the coaching staff and their expenses would have been paid by the University of Georgia.

Sincerely,
Wallace Butts
Athletic Director

This well-warranted complaint was undoubtedly indicative of friction on a wide front between Butts and university administrators. Butts was apparently destined from the beginning to a brief tenure as athletic director; to that end he was probably subjected to indignities that he endured only because of his lack of alternatives.

Banishment from coaching was not without its rewards, however. It enabled Butts to devote more time to two things in the next two years: his business activities and his attractive young mistress. The two were not unrelated.

During his last year at Mercer College, Butts married his boyhood sweetheart, Miss Winifred Taylor of Milledgeville, a gentle lady known as "Winnie" to her friends. The marriage was blessed by three lovely daughters. Having no inherited wealth, Butts could do little more than care for his family on his coach's salary. To gain greater financial security, he turned to a succession of business ventures and speculative investments, but proved to be a very poor businessman.

One of his efforts was a restaurant in Athens. Athletic figures have often sought success in the restaurant business. Two well-known examples are Jack Dempsey's in New York and Gino's, the fast-food chain, named for pro football star Gino Marchetti. But "The Huddle," as Butts aptly named his place, failed in 1951, a poor year for his football team, too—the Bulldogs went 5–5, with sophomore Zeke Bratkowski as quarterback.

By 1960, Butts had built a financial house of cards. Successful college coaches have little difficulty finding wealthy sports fans who want to cultivate their friendship and assist them financially by letting them in on lucrative investment opportunities. One was a wealthy Georgia alumnus and benefactor, Louis Wolfson, who was to gain fame in several ways, including his ownership of the racehorse Affirmed, a Triple Crown winner in 1978; a relationship with Supreme Court Justice Abe Fortas which was publicized in connection with Fortas's resignation from the bench in 1969; and stock dealings that led to Wolfson's conviction and imprisonment under federal securities laws. The stock involved was that of a company named Continental Enterprises.

Butts and Bear Bryant both invested heavily in Continental Enterprises. At one point Bryant had $60,000 in the stock. Butts glumly watched his 7,000 shares decline in value from $6.00 a share to less than $1.00. Both coaches said Continental Enterprises was discussed in some of their 1962 telephone calls.

Louis Wolfson was one of a number of businessmen around the country who endorsed Butts's notes so that he could obtain loans. Another was a trucker, Lewis Tose of Philadelphia, who endorsed a loan for Butts and let him in on a Coca Cola operation in Bridgeport, Pennsylvania. (Tose's brother, Leonard, later owner of the Philadelphia Eagles football team, once admitted losing nearly $2 million in Atlantic City casinos. According to Howard Cosell's book, *I Never Played the Game*, Leonard Tose's total gambling losses came to many millions more.)

Still another benefactor and friend was Frank Scoby, a Chicago beer dealer who gambled on college football games. He sometimes bet as much as $2,000 on a game and $50,000 during a season. On Scoby's endorsement his Chicago bank loaned Butts $6,000 in 1962. Scoby had even included Butts in plans to introduce a new Scotch whiskey in the United States, plans that were never realized. Butts sometimes called Scoby for advice on investments. In September of 1962, his calls to Scoby were unusually numerous—14 in all.

Costly speculation in Florida orange groves and other real estate also added to Butts's financial woes.

In addition, Butts was a founder of Instant Loan Company, a chain of loan offices whose activities resulted in official investigations, license revocations, and adverse publicity. He was also a director of at least three corporations, including Foundation Life Insurance, whose employees included a transplanted Texan named George Burnett. In July 1961, Butts filed a personal financial statement with Instant Loan's application to the Georgia comptroller general. It showed assets of $349,287 and liabilities of $143,299, for a net worth of $205,988. The statement vastly inflated asset values and omitted major personal debts. He later admitted that he was actually on the verge of insolvency at the time.

Despite his financial problems, Butts continued seeing his mistress. Her full name is widely known in Georgia, but here she will simply be called Evelyn. It is not known when the illicit relationship with Evelyn began, but it was flourishing during the 1960 football season. One of Butts's friends believes he was faithful to his wife until his final few years as coach.

Butts's affair with Evelyn must have been an expensive habit. His financial troubles drove him to charge much of the cost to the university. Although Evelyn was employed as a salesperson in a fashionable women's store, he paid for her lodging, travel, entertainment, and more. Records of the Phoenix Hotel in Lexington, Kentucky, show that Butts charged the university $155.70 for alcoholic and other beverages during the weekend of October 22, 1960, when Georgia played Kentucky there. This may have been official entertainment, but the same cannot be said of a hotel room registration for Evelyn, which was also charged to the university.

In 1961, he gave her a new Pontiac convertible. The car was registered in her name, but a title retention contract recorded in Athens showed Butts as the purchaser. The matter became public in some way and came to the attention of J. D. Bolton, who considered it an embarrassment to the university and said as much to Butts. Butts told Bolton that he had bought the car for Evelyn's brother.

Records of Delta Air Lines show trips by Butts and Evelyn to Miami in January, May, and July 1962, to Birmingham for the Alabama game in September, and to Jacksonville in November for the Florida game. All of Evelyn's tickets were charged to the Georgia Athletic Association.

Butts was said to have shown Evelyn off to Georgia players on these occasions and at times to have been seen drunk in public with her. Early in their affair, Evelyn sometimes even traveled on the team plane, but this stopped after some of the players objected.

There is also evidence of a trip by Butts and Evelyn to the Bahamas and numerous liaisons in Atlanta hotels, including the Atlanta Biltmore, Air Host Inn, Dinkler Plaza, Henry Grady, and Piedmont.

Butts's misuse of university credit cards for travel was matched by his misuse of his athletic department telephone credit card. Telephone company records indicate that between October 1961 and February 1963 he charged $2,818.10 in personal long-distance calls to his official account; more than 300 of these calls were to Evelyn.

What caused Butts to become so reckless about his personal and professional life? One friend thinks he was temporarily insane. A more likely explanation is that, sensing he was over the hill professionally, he underwent a classic, if late, midlife crisis.

One of Butts's daughters wrote a sympathetic letter about her father's troubles to his lawyer, William Schroder. In part, she said:

> . . . If Dad has a fault, it is an obsession about growing old. This of course is because of the profession he was in with its great emphasis on youth. But Dad let it get out of proportion to reality in my opinion. I truly believe this had much to do with his early relationship with Evelyn. He actually thought people would *admire* him if he was seen with a young girl. . . . Of course, I am not so naive as to think sex didn't play a hand in it; but if you will check with Dr. Williams in Augusta and possibly Dr. Hubert, you will find that his prostate gland was in such bad shape that sex relations for him was at best very painful.*

By the fall of 1962, Butts was on a collision course with disaster. Personally, professionally, and financially his life was a shambles. He was reckless and vulnerable. His actions were totally out of character for the devoted family man and disciplined, dedicated professional who had ground out so many winners for Georgia between 1938 and 1959.

This was Butts's situation when he picked up a telephone in Atlanta and called Bear Bryant on September 13, 1962, nine days before the Georgia Bulldogs and the Alabama Crimson Tide were to open the coming season.

---

* This quotation is taken from the master's degree thesis of Jonathan Schroder, a son of Butts's lawyer. It is in the University of Georgia library.

3

$\bullet \quad \bullet \quad \bullet \quad \bullet \quad \bullet \quad \bullet \quad \bullet \quad \bullet \quad \bullet \quad \bullet \quad \bullet \quad \bullet \quad \bullet \quad \bullet \quad \bullet$

The George Burnett Connection

ON THE MORNING OF THURSDAY, September 13, 1962, Wally Butts was in Atlanta, where he frequently went for personal business and social purposes—too frequently, many thought. To make phone calls, Butts used a rear office at Communications International, Inc., a public relations firm in downtown Atlanta operated by friends. At 10 A.M. Butts made a long-distance call to Frank Scoby, his business associate in Chicago who gambled on college football games. This call was followed immediately by one to Bear Bryant. Both were made on his university credit card.

While Butts was talking to Scoby, a man named George Burnett arrived late at the offices of his new business venture, Steryl-Ray, near downtown Atlanta. No one was there, not even Steryl-Ray's one secretary. Burnett needed to talk to his two partners, Milton Flack and John Carmichael. He called each at home, but neither answered. Then he tried the office of Communications International, where Flack could often be reached.

Burnett kept getting a busy signal. He dialed repeatedly, knowing that Communications International had two lines. After the fourth or fifth try, Burnett heard some electronic noises and then an operator say, "Coach Bryant is out on the field, Coach Butts, but he is on his way to the phone. Do you want to hold, or do you want him to return the call?" Butts said he would hold, and after a slight delay Bryant came on the line. Butts said, "Hello,

Bear," and Bryant said, "Hi, Wally, do you have anything for me?"

Nothing in Burnett's background made him a likely candidate for the role about to be thrust upon him, a role pitting him against two of college football's giants. His most notable achievement on the gridiron was earning all-city recognition as a guard on his high school team in his native San Antonio, Texas.

George Price Burnett, a descendant of General Sterling Price of Civil War fame in Missouri, was born in 1921 and was one of five children. His father went broke in the Depression as a paper box manufacturer, then switched to the insurance business and built his own general agency.

As a boy Burnett was active in the Boy Scouts, earning Eagle Scout honors, and later served as an assistant scoutmaster. In January 1942, during his second year at Texas A & M, he volunteered for the Air Force. After graduating from navigation school as a second lieutenant, he was assigned to England. On his sixty-third mission he was shot down over Belgium and spent the balance of the war in a German POW camp. One of the American soldiers who released him was a Georgian named Milton Flack.

Except for a brief stint in civilian life right after the war, he continued to serve in the Air Force until 1950. Then, after working for three publishing companies, he decided to follow in his father's footsteps and entered the insurance business. By 1960, he had found his way to Atlanta with his wife and seven children, two by her former marriage and five of their own.

In 1962, Burnett joined Flack, now a public relations man, and John Carmichael, a businessman with a wide range of experience, to form Steryl-Ray, Inc. They had high hopes for their new company, which would market a line of products for sterilizing toothbrushes and making bathrooms odor-free. Each of the men was in his early forties. Both Carmichael and Burnett were with Foundation Life Insurance Company, one of the directors of which was Wally Butts. Though Burnett had seen Butts in the offices of Foundation Life, he did not know him personally.

As soon as Butts and Bryant began their telephone conversation, Burnett's curiosity was aroused. He knew that these two rivals' teams were to play the next week, and Bryant's opening remark, "Do you have anything for me?" seemed to indicate not only that the Alabama coach had been expecting the call, but that it was for his benefit. Suspecting that something unusual might be happening, Burnett stayed on the line. He next heard Butts describe a particular Georgia lineman as "the greatest in history." Then, according to Burnett, Butts proceeded to discuss Georgia's players, coaches, formations, and plays for nearly 15 minutes. At times Bryant would ask a question, and Butts would answer, "I don't know." Bryant would respond, "Can you find out?" and Butts would say, "I'll try." Nothing in the conversation concerned the Alabama team.

In their final exchange Bryant asked Butts if he would be at home on Sunday. Butts said he would, and Bryant said he would call him then.

Just before or shortly after Butts and Bryant ended their conversation, Carmichael arrived at Steryl-Ray. Flack appeared a bit later. Both would later confirm that Burnett had notes in hand that he claimed he took during a phone call between Wally Butts and Bear Bryant. The three began discussing what Burnett should do with his information. Carmichael and Flack both urged Burnett, in the strongest terms, to do nothing. Flack recalls, "I didn't ask him. I told him. He should have hung up."

Carmichael would later admit that he was motivated in part by friendship for Butts. Both he and Flack may also have feared adverse consequences to their new business if one of the partners were to stir up controversy over a public figure like Butts.

The question of betting arose. Insisting that Burnett had only overheard "general football talk," Carmichael asked, "George, which team would you bet on?" Burnett admitted he wouldn't know how to bet.

Burnett did not argue. He deferred to his partners' wishes, carried the notes home, and put them in a drawer. Ten days later the headline "Tide Mauls Bulldogs" leaped from the sports page of Burnett's Atlanta paper, and he wondered if he had done the right thing by keeping silent.

The game was played on Saturday night, September 22, in Birmingham's Legion Field. Although Georgia was rumored to have a greatly improved team, Alabama, the defending national champion, was a 14–17 point favorite. Returnees from the 1961 Tide team included Charlie Pell, Bill Battle, and All-American linebacker LeRoy Jordan. One of the newcomers was sophomore quarterback Joe Namath, who had come south from Pennsylvania after being rejected by his first choice, the University of Maryland, because of grades.

The game turned out to be a colossal mismatch, even more of a rout than the 35–0 score indicated. It was Alabama's worst defeat of a Georgia team since 1923.

On Georgia's first possession, quarterback Larry Rakestraw threw an interception. Then Joe Namath, handling the fourth snap from center of his college career, threw a 52-yard scoring pass. An attempted Georgia punt produced a safety, and Namath threw a second touchdown pass, giving Alabama a 15–0 halftime lead.

Namath passed for a third touchdown early in the third quarter. He probably cost the Tide another when he fumbled at the Georgia 7-yard line. At that point, Bryant mercifully pulled Namath. A reserve quarterback engineered the next touchdown, and Alabama led, 28–0, with 11 minutes remaining. As the clock ran out, Bryant put in more reserves, but the weary Bulldogs could not hold them, and the Tide scored a fifth touchdown.

The best evidence of the game's one-sidedness was the fact that Georgia's deepest penetration was the Alabama 45-yard line; this occurred on the last play of the game, one of the two times the Bulldogs crossed midfield. Georgia made only seven first downs, netting 37 yards running and 79 yards passing.

In his account of the game, Atlanta sportswriter Jesse Outlar wrote that Georgia quarterback Larry Rakestraw "never had an opportunity to muster a scoring drive. Every time Rakestraw got the ball, he was surrounded by center LeRoy Jordan and his ever eager playmates." The combined effect of Alabama's offensive and defensive units was termed "devastating" by the *Birmingham News'* Benny Marshall.

Cletus Atkinson of the *Birmingham Post Herald* interviewed losing coach John Griffith after the game. He reported in part:

> Johnny Griffith is a tall, wavy-haired, handsome man in his mid-30s. But Saturday night he looked older.
>
> His Georgia Bulldogs had just been humiliated by Alabama's defending national champions 35–0.
>
> Coach Griffith, dressed neatly in a black blazer and a tie striped with Georgia's red and black colors, shepherded his players into the dressing room, closed the door and slumped against the wall outside.
>
> With hands that shook he sipped a Coke and lit a cigarette. He was a picture of complete dejection.
>
> "What is there to say?" he asked softly, almost to himself. . . . The disconsolate coach kept his eyes on the ground and virtually whispered his answers.

Griffith went on to tell Atkinson how difficult it is to open against a national champion, how poorly his team had played, of his need to reexamine every position, and of the good football lesson that had been administered.

Athletic director Wally Butts gave the press a somewhat ambiguous description of Georgia's performance: "Potential is the word for what I saw, unlimited potential." Did he mean that he saw nothing *but* potential—no accomplishments?

The account of the game did not move George Burnett to break his silence, and he kept the information to himself as John Griffith's young team struggled through a 3-4-3 season, a slight improvement on 1961's 3-7-0 performance in the coach's rookie year. They scored impressive victories over Clemson, 24–16, Auburn, 30–21, and Vanderbilt, 10–0. Their ties came in games with respectable opponents—Kentucky, South Carolina, and North Carolina State. Besides the Alabama fiasco, they were beaten by Florida State, 18–0, Florida, 23–15, and Georgia Tech, 37–6. The Tide meanwhile went 10–1, losing only to Georgia Tech, 7–6, and whipping Oklahoma, 17–0, in the Orange Bowl. They allowed only 39 points all season.

Early in January 1963, however, George Burnett had a change of heart. He was attending a meeting of regional managers of Foundation Life Insurance Company at its Atlanta headquarters. At the end of a meeting, Burnett tarried for a friendly drink with Bob Edwards of distant St. Simon, Georgia. Burnett knew that Edwards and Georgia coach John Griffith were friends and that Edwards was a close follower and strong supporter of Georgia football.

At some point in their conversation, the subject turned to football. Burnett said, "Bob, I want to get something off my chest. Does Georgia have a player named Wood-something, maybe 'Woodruff'?"

"Sure," said Edwards. "We have Brig Woodward; he plays safety."

Burnett proceeded to tell Edwards of the phone call he had overheard and of Butts's comment that Woodward committed fast as safety man.

"That's right," Edwards said. "Woodward did commit fast. He was very poor on pass defense."

Burnett then related the rest of the conversation as best he could without the benefit of his notes.

What prompted Burnett to tell Edwards about the Butts-Bryant call at that moment? It was, apparently, a spontaneous decision; he had seen Edwards several times since the incident without mentioning it. Whatever the reason, knowing Edwards's involvement with Georgia football, Burnett had to be sure that the information he had been withholding would be of great interest to Edwards.

Edwards was more than interested; he was outraged. He condemned Butts in the strongest possible terms and urged Burnett to allow him to arrange a meeting with John Griffith. Burnett agreed.

The earliest convenient time for Griffith and Burnett to meet was January 24, when Griffith came to Atlanta for a Southeastern Conference meeting. Edwards accompanied Burnett to Griffith's hotel room. Burnett recalled Griffith's comment after seeing the notes: "This looks like our game plan. I figured someone had given information to Alabama. This game was like a couple of others; we were just stymied—couldn't get anything going." Griffith asked Burnett to let him keep the notes. Burnett readily agreed and gave up his only copy.

The seven pages of notes John Griffith received from George Burnett are reproduced on the following pages.

Even before Burnett's notes began circulating among University of Georgia officials, Wally Butts's future as athletic director was in serious jeopardy. In early January 1963, just two years after he had been forced to step down as head coach, the executive committee of the Georgia Athletic Board met to consider whether he should stay on as athletic director. Citing his indiscreet personal life and declining professional reputation, his outside business activities and open criticism of John Griffith, the committee members came to a unanimous decision: Butts should be urged to resign.

A two-man delegation, board members Cook Barwick and William T. Bradshaw, was assigned the task of informing Butts and persuading him to step down voluntarily. Barwick, a prominent Atlanta attorney, had served as Butts's lawyer. Bradshaw, a successful young businessman from Canton, Georgia, had played for Butts in the golden days, graduating in 1951.

On Saturday, January 18, when Butts was in Atlanta for the annual Touchdown Club banquet, the three met in Barwick's office. Bill Bradshaw informed Butts that the executive committee had decided he should step down. Barwick explained that if the matter were taken to the full board, Butts would get only one favorable vote—Barwick's own. Out of kindness to his old coach,

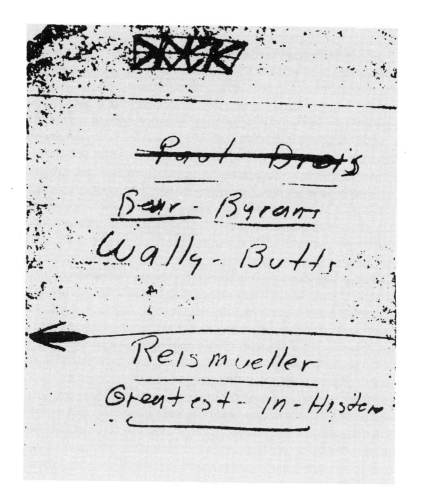

Rakestraw to R.t.

Optional LeFT Pass
IF can Block man on
corner keeps Running.

well Disiplined Ball
Club —
Added Two Coaches

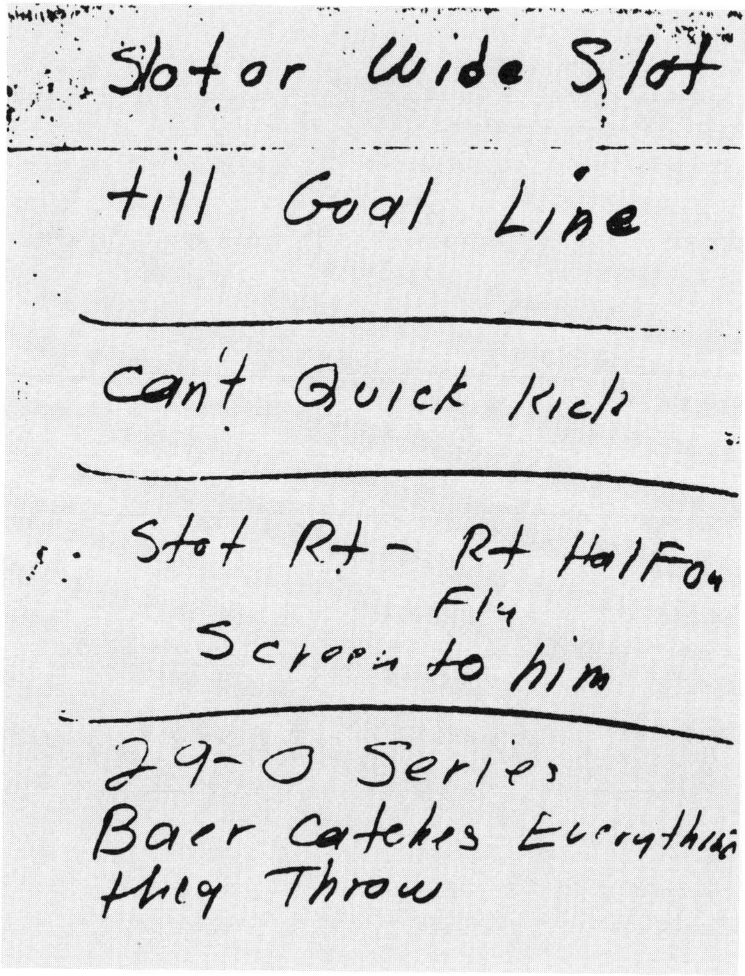

Slot or Wide Slot

till Goal Line

Can't Quick Kick

Stot Rt — Rt HalfOn
Flu
Screen to him

29-0 Series
Baer Catches Everything
they Throw

Baer /slot.Rt

Split Rt End out

Long Count

Left Half in

motion

Best since Trippi

Porter Field

on Side guard pulls
on Sweep —

Don't over shift.

Woodard commits
Fast — Safety Man

weak
DeFense
any body except
Blackburn

Baer on a Hook
on Goal Line

Slot to Rt

Ends Normal (3yd

Rt half Back on Fly –
Lt. Half Back
Q.B. Gives to L.H.
L.G. Pulling Blocks on
Corner –

Slot R.t

LT End out 15 yrds

Drop End off
Ga > contain with Tackl
(Defense)

▬▬▬ —Wally—
Give Ring Sunday
∧
—641— Athletic
Office
10-40 AM — Sept. 13-1962
Ja·5-3 536 Compliments H. R. KNIGHT

Bradshaw did not enumerate all the board's charges against him, omitting the matter of the indiscretions in his personal life. He said the board felt that Butts's business interests were interfering with his duties as athletic director and that the adverse publicity his loan companies had received had harmed the image of the university.

Butts listened without arguing and then said simply, "I'll talk to President Aderhold and do whatever he advises."

Butts returned to Athens on Sunday. After thinking it over for a few hours, he called Aderhold and asked if he could come to his home to discuss a personal problem. Aderhold had dinner guests and suggested they meet the next morning. Butts agreed and was at Aderhold's office at 9:30 A.M. on Monday.

Aderhold had been with the university, his alma mater, since 1926 and had been its president since 1950. He and Butts had once enjoyed a solid personal relationship. It saddened him to see Butts reduced to such a low and vulnerable condition. The president was a gentle person; he listened with compassion and talked patiently with Butts for 2½ hours.

Butts focused on his financial difficulties—the Florida orange groves and real estate and the foundering loan company. In a final desperate appeal to his old friend to help him keep his job, he told Aderhold that his financial situation would collapse if he lost the income from his athletic directorship.

Finally, Butts said simply, "Dr. Aderhold, what advice would you give me? I came for advice, and what would you advise?"

Aderhold answered, "Well, Coach, this is completely beyond me; I don't know. So much is involved."

They then added up Butts's liabilities and calculated a deficit of $75,000 to $100,000.

Aderhold closed the discussion of finances by suggesting someone who might be able to help Butts. "Coach," he said, "I don't know of anybody that is better to advise you about these matters than Bill Hartman," remembering, no doubt, the part Hartman had played two years earlier in persuading Butts to resign as coach. "Bill is a man that you have confidence in," he added, "and he's a businessman who knows something about these figures."

Aderhold then turned the conversation to Butts's other difficulties. He said that members of the board were concerned about Butts's open criticism of Griffith and the university. Butts replied that the reports were exaggerated; he had never meant to undermine Griffith, the athletic program, or the university.

Aderhold also brought up Butts's "relationship with persons in Atlanta." He then ended the conversation by saying, "Well, Coach, I think that the board is going to take positive action about this thing, one way or the other. There is so much feeling that our athletic program isn't going, and it is because we do not have cooperation and leadership at the head. Whether this is true or not, I don't know, but this is what's being said, and that, as I see it, there are two things that you might do. One is that you might request that the board give consideration to resigning and retiring at the end of this fiscal year, June 30, but I think the board is going to take some kind of action, and I don't know what the board will do with the request."

A week later, at the January 28 meeting of the athletic board, Butts announced his intention to retire as of June 30, giving the pressure of his business activities as the reason. For pension purposes, it was important that he serve out the fiscal year.

Two days after that, on the night of January 30, Butts learned of the Burnett connection. He was in Philadelphia for the funeral of business associate Lewis Tose, when he got a call from John Carmichael. Carmichael told him that George Burnett had gone to Coach Griffith with his notes and the story of an improper call from Butts to Bryant. Butts listened to Carmichael, thanked him for his trouble, and said that if he had talked to Bryant, it was just general football talk. He insisted that he would "never do anything to hurt Georgia."

The exact route of Burnett's notes through the Georgia hierarchy is not entirely clear. It is known, however, that treasurer J. D. Bolton was at the SEC meeting and was the next person to see them after Griffith. They agreed that the matter should be brought to the attention of President Aderhold immediately. As soon as Griffith returned to Athens, he delivered the notes to Aderhold, along with his opinion that the information they contained would have helped Bear Bryant.

Aderhold was ex-officio chairman of the Georgia Athletic Board, the executive committee of which was the proper group for initial consideration of George Burnett's accusations. The committee was soon convened. Its first action was to ask one of its members, Cook Barwick, attorney and former FBI agent, to investigate the matter and act as its counsel.

Barwick took custody of the notes and went to work. Considering the possibility that Butts might have charged the call to his university credit card, Barwick asked Georgia officials to have Southern Bell check its records. Sure enough, on September 13, 1962 at 10:29 A.M. Butts had placed a person-to-person call from Atlanta to Bryant in Tuscaloosa. The call lasted 15 minutes and 2 seconds. Telephone company officials also confirmed that it was technically possible for a third person accidentally to overhear such a call. Such a malfunction was unusual but it occurred often enough that the industry had a special term for it, a "cross-connect."

Barwick then held a lengthy meeting with George Burnett, who allowed a 35-minute statement to be recorded and gave a sworn affidavit that it was true. He also passed a lie detector test administered by an Atlanta private detective selected by Barwick.

Barwick was convinced that Burnett was telling the truth. Despite his long-standing friendship with Butts and despite the fact that Butts was already on his way out as athletic director, he felt the matter had to be pursued. President Aderhold agreed and took over the investigation personally.

On Tuesday, February 19, Aderhold called Bernie Moore, commissioner of the Southeastern Conference, at his Birmingham office. Aderhold told Moore that he had information of the utmost importance to the conference and asked him to meet with the athletic board's executive committee in Atlanta on Thurday, February 21.

Since the conference is governed by the presidents of its member universities, Moore agreed to the meeting with no questions asked. During the session, which lasted five or six hours, he listened to the tape of Burnett's statement and was told of the affidavit and lie detector test. At the end of the meeting, Moore suggested that the group invite Wally Butts to meet with them and give them his explanation.

When President Aderhold returned to Athens that night, he called Butts and asked him to attend a meeting in Barwick's Atlanta office the next day. He did not tell Butts the purpose of the meeting; the executive committee had agreed that no one would discuss the subject with Butts in advance, as they wanted to surprise him. Butts, in turn, did not ask Aderhold what the meeting would be about. He said later that he assumed the committee wanted to discuss his pension.

J. D. Bolton drove Aderhold and Butts to Atlanta. Not once during the hour-and-a-half trip did any of them mention the upcoming meeting. With little to do but study the wintry, monotonous countryside, it must have been an awkward journey.

When the meeting opened, Barwick moved quickly to capitalize on the element of surprise. He informed Butts of Burnett's disclosures and told him that Burnett had sworn to an affidavit and passed a lie detector test. He then identified Burnett's notes and handed them to Butts.

How did Butts react to the notes? First, he felt for his reading glasses and, realizing he had left them at home, borrowed Bolton's. He then looked at the notes. Witnesses differed sharply as to whether Butts read the notes. They also disagreed on exactly what he said about them. SEC commissioner Bernie Moore took his own notes during the meeting and on his return to his Birmingham office dictated a file memorandum. On this subject, it read:

A meeting with Coach Butts and this group was arranged on Friday, February 22. It was agreed by the group that

Cook Barwick was to inform Coach Butts of the alleged telephone conversation, which he did. He asked Butts if such a conversation took place and also asked him about the content of the conversation. Coach Butts did not show any surprise or emotion when informed about the matter. He did not deny the conversation. His first statement was that "Mr. Burnett and you gentlemen have placed the wrong interpretation on this conversation and on the notes that Mr. Burnett was supposed to have taken."

All present did agree that Butts did not *deny* that he and Bryant had had the conversation described by Burnett. They also concurred that he quickly changed the subject from the Burnett notes and spoke instead about the common practice among coaches to talk to one another. He said several times that he would never do anything to hurt Georgia, but he never returned to the Burnett notes, and no one questioned him about them. It was an incredible two hours of tiptoeing around the issue at hand. Butts made a remarkable recovery from any initial surprise and got by with a bare minimum of attention to Burnett's specific accusations.

The meeting fell short of producing a "smoking gun" or an undisputed confession of guilt from Butts, but it did have one major result: in the face of Burnett's charges, Butts resigned the next day. Though he had announced a month earlier that he would retire effective June 30, his pension rights were still unresolved. His resignation, which was to become effective February 28, clouded his hopes for a favorable settlement of the pension issue.

At the end of the meeting with Butts, Commissioner Moore said he wanted George Burnett to meet with the group. Burnett was able to join them that same afternoon. The idea that Burnett's notes might reflect an innocent conversation surfaced at this meeting. Burnett was first questioned by Bill Hartman, who said, "Mr. Burnett, don't you think you overheard two coaches talking about general football?" Burnett disputed this interpretation on the grounds that the conversation had been so one-sided; Bryant, after all, had given Butts no information on Alabama. But Hartman pressed the point, saying, "Aren't you aware that coaches talk all during the year?"

Burnett was surprised and alarmed by the tone of the meeting. He had been told that Bernie Moore had requested that he be called in, yet the commissioner asked him no questions and conspicuously avoided looking him in the eye the entire time.

Even more ominous treatment of Burnett came from Jimmy Dunlap, chairman of the board of regents of the University of Georgia and a staunch Butts supporter. Early in the meeting he pulled out a piece of paper and said, "Mr. Burnett, we have a complete record of your financial situation and your bad checks."

Burnett was stunned. His relationship with university officials had been cooperative and courteous up to that point. Now he felt as though he were a defendant against whom a case was being made.

Commissioner Moore later said that Burnett misread his attitude in Barwick's office, but Jimmy Dunlap's approach could not be misunderstood; it was calculated to frighten him into some sort of retreat.

After Dunlap launched into a detailed account of Burnett's bad checks and the suits against him for debts in Georgia and Texas, Aderhold intervened. "After all, Jimmy," he pointed out, "the man has seven children. He is bound to have financial troubles once in a while."

But Dunlap persisted, warning Burnett of the risks of being sued for libel and asking provocatively, "What else are you trying to hide in your past life?"

Burnett left the meeting shocked and fearful. He was worried that the whole affair might become public in a way that would whitewash Butts and damage him. In his words: "I was worried about all of this if it came out in bad publicity about me being a hot check artist . . . of what it would do to my children in school because kids can be pretty cruel to other kids."

He went straight to the offices of Pierre Howard, his lawyer and close personal friend. Unbeknownst to Burnett, Frank Graham, Jr., a free-lance sportswriter, had flown to Atlanta from New York the day before and had met with Howard and Milton Flack. Graham's purpose was to confirm the rumor that Burnett had overheard an incriminating phone call from Wally Butts to Bear Bryant and to purchase the story for publication in *The Saturday Evening Post*.

Burnett told Howard how he had been treated by Dunlap and asked his friend's advice. Howard, acting both as Burnett's lawyer and as his potential agent, said, "The best advice I can give you is to tell the story the right way before it gets distorted and told the wrong way."

The "right way" in Howard's opinion, apparently, was to tell the story to Bryant's old nemesis, *The Saturday Evening Post*, whose writer was standing by.

Until then, Burnett had rejected the idea of selling his story for publication. After giving up his notes, he had told John Griffith that he preferred to have no further involvement. But Burnett met with Graham, and the *Post* soon had its scoop.

4

· · · · · · · · · · · · ·

Sophisticated Muckraking

IN 1962 AND 1963, while Wally Butts was fighting a losing battle for his professional life, another struggle for survival was being waged at the Curtis Publishing Company. At the center of this conflict was its flagship, *The Saturday Evening Post*—America's magazine.

Dramatic changes in the leadership of Curtis began in March 1962, after president Robert A. MacNeal announced that the company had lost nearly $4.2 million in 1961, its first annual loss since its incorporation in 1891. In early summer MacNeal was abruptly fired by the Curtis board of directors while he was away in Europe. Refusing to face up to the internal waste and mismanagement that were at the core of the company's problems, the board set out to cure Curtis's ills by replacing MacNeal with a Madison Avenue marketing genius, Matthew Joseph Culligan.

A second-generation Irishman in his early forties, Culligan's hero was Joseph Kennedy. He sported a black eye patch, earned at the Battle of the Bulge. He had been spectacularly successful with NBC Radio and the McCann-Erickson advertising agency.

One of Culligan's first moves was to set off on a six-month trip, during which he personally called on the top 200 corporate advertisers in the country. When worried bankers threatened to call in loans, Culligan engineered a totally new line of credit of $26 million. He also hired a tough, cost-cutting executive who eliminated over 2,000 out of 10,000 jobs. Culligan rescued the

55

company from bankruptcy and appeared, temporarily, to be its savior.

But the decay at Curtis was too deep and widespread for Culligan's remedies to salvage it. Losses persisted, skyrocketing to $19 million in 1962 and continuing at $3.5 million in 1963.

The runner-up candidate for the Curtis presidency had been Clay Blair, Jr., managing editor of *The Saturday Evening Post*. Culligan discovered that Blair knew more about the internal affairs of Curtis than anyone else in the company; he had developed an elaborate plan for its reorganization when he sought the presidency. In October of 1962, Blair was appointed editor-in-chief of the *Post*.

The *Post* had fallen on hard times, and its troubles were the single major cause of Curtis's financial woes. Although both the *Post* and *Ladies' Home Journal* had circulations of 6.5 million, the *Post* published 45 issues a year, the *Journal* only ten. Of Curtis's other three magazines, *American Home* also appeared only ten times a year. And *Holiday* and *Jack and Jill* had circulations of less than one million. The *Post* accounted for $3 million of the $4 million Curtis lost in 1961.

The eventual demise of *The Saturday Evening Post* in 1969 ended the reign of the most distinguished and enduring magazine in American history, one that traced its lineage to Benjamin Franklin. The *Post* first appeared in 1821 as the successor to a line of publications that originated in 1728 with Franklin's *Pennsylvania Gazette*. Edgar Allan Poe published "The Black Cat" in the *Post*. Other early contributors included Harriet Beecher Stowe and James Fenimore Cooper. Its transformation from a minor local newspaper into a national magazine began in 1899, when it was purchased for $1,000 by Cyrus H. K. Curtis, founder of Curtis Publishing Company and owner of the prestigious *Ladies' Home Journal*.

Curtis hired George Lorimer as editor and launched the *Post*'s incredible ascent. Circulation soared from 33,000 in 1898 to 182,000 in 1900, rose to one million by 1909 and to two million by 1913. With the advent of the automobile and other nationally marketed products, advertising revenues followed suit, climbing from $8,000 in 1898 to more than $1 million in 1905, reaching $3 million in 1909, and $5 million in 1910. By the end of the twenties, revenues from advertising were over $50 million. Thirty cents of every American advertising dollar spent on magazines went to the *Post*. In 1929, it produced an issue 272 pages long. The magazine's prosperity continued with little abatement into World War II. Then a 1942 article entitled "The Case against the Jew" brought subscription and advertising cancellations, boycott threats, and an editorial shakeup.

The new editor was Ben Hibbs of Pretty Prairie, Kansas. He believed in stability, patriotism, free enterprise, and traditional American small-town values. The *Post*'s Norman Rockwell covers and Hibbs-commissioned articles made Americans feel good about themselves.

The Hibbs era is called the *Post*'s "Silver Age" by Otto Friedrich in *Decline and Fall*, the definitive work on the *Post*'s collapse. Hibbs upped circulation from 3.3 million in 1942 to 6.5 million in 1962. Advertising revenues rose from $23 million to $104 million a year. Yet Friedrich found something hollow about Ben Hibbs's "rural, familial, conservative *Post*."

Hibbs retired in 1961 at the age of 60. Friedrich believes that he took an early retirement because "the *Post* was widely considered to be old and stodgy, edited by the old and stodgy to be read by the old and stodgy and Ben Hibbs couldn't accept it."

The *Post*'s woes in the early sixties were the result of a complex set of factors: corporate waste and mismanagement, lackluster composition, competition from TV for advertising revenues and from *Life* and *Look* for the declining general magazine market. When the mercurial Clay Blair took over the editorial reins in 1962, *The Saturday Evening Post* was in an unprecedented twelfth consecutive year of decline in advertising pages. This, despite the seemingly inconsistent fact that circulation had increased from some 4 million to more than 6.6 million. The increased circulation figures were deceptive, however. The *Post*'s newsstand sales had dropped markedly, from two-thirds of its total circulation to less than 10 percent. The gain in circulation was due to the successful but uneconomical promotion of subscription sales, a major cause of the $3 million loss in 1961. Even so, the *Post*'s circulation fell behind that of competitors *Look* and *Life* for the first time.

Blair's tumultuous editorship has been chronicled in detail by Friedrich in *Decline and Fall*. After losing out to Culligan, Blair apparently never ceased his drive for the presidency. Friedrich, himself a *Post* editor at that time, became a co-conspirator in a campaign by Blair to overthrow Culligan and take control of Curtis. Blair knew that the editorship of the *Post* was the only weapon available to him, and he set out to use it in ways that would serve his quest for power most effectively. First, he realized he would have to succeed in rescuing the *Post* from its financial doldrums. Second, he would have to turn the magazine itself into an instrument of far greater influence than it had ever been before.

One part of the reorganization plan Blair had proposed when he was vying for the presidency of Curtis a few months earlier was to transform the *Post* into a "high quality reading magazine for influential people" that would be in a class of its own, like *The New Yorker*. As soon as he was named editor-in-chief, he seized the opportunity to carry out his proposal.

At his first meeting with the *Post* editors, Blair took the latest issue and tore it apart—literally. He then tacked up the pages, one by one, on the walls of the conference room and, using a pointer, scathingly ridiculed virtually every item. His treatment of the cover was typical. A Thanksgiving cartoon, it showed a dismayed truck driver staring at a flat tire that had left him stranded with a truckload of gibbering turkeys. Blair said, "The gag cover is an anachronism. We've got to go beyond that. We've got to have covers that have something timely to say."

Blair summed up his critical dissection of the issue by saying that the *Post* was "aimless and bland." He challenged his editors to make the magazine "compelling" and to aim "not only to inform but crusade" with "hard-hitting articles that are timely and mean something."

An earlier experience with crusading journalism had helped to give Blair his heady vision of a magazine's potential. When he was working for *Time* in Washington, he had spearheaded the magazine's exposé of the U.S. Navy's suppression of Captain Hyman Rickover's nuclear submarine and Polaris missile proposals. Blair told the *Post* editors, "I dug out the facts, and I made them public. And we took on the whole Navy Department—started a Congressional investigation—and we won!"

In January 1963, in a written memo that was leaked to *Newsweek* and reprinted there without comment, Blair complimented the *Post*'s staff on the progress they were making. He used the term "sophisticated muckraking" to describe his editorial policies and boasted that six pending lawsuits were proof that "we are hitting them where it hurts."

The climate was ripe for George Burnett's story. Word of the story reached the *Post*, oddly enough, through its lawyers. Some of the *Post*'s editors suspected that the lawyers promoted the story and may even have influenced the decision to pursue it in order to hurt Bear Bryant's suit against Curtis over Furman Bisher's "brutality" article. One of the company's Birmingham lawyers, Roderick Beddow, was the first to find out about the story; he happened to be working on an unrelated matter with Pierre Howard, the Atlanta lawyer who represented George Burnett. Knowing of Beddow's interest in Bear Bryant's case against the *Post*, Howard told him of Burnett's experience and the scandal brewing behind the scenes at the University of Georgia. Whether Howard was just making casual conversation or sensed an opportunity for personal gain may never be known; he is now dead.

Beddow immediately called Philip Strubing, the Philadelphia lawyer who was handling the Bryant case for Curtis. Strubing in turn relayed the information to Davis Thomas, managing editor of the *Post*, who promptly huddled with sports editor Roger Kahn and executive editor Don Schanche.

Kahn said later that he had counseled caution on the basis of his previous experience at *Newsweek*, where "solid rumors" of fixes in big-time sports were not pursued for fear of problems of proof in the event of litigation. Schanche and Thomas both thought the story should at least be investigated. Schanche was particularly excited. A native Georgian and a fan of southern football, he had attended the University of Georgia with one of Wally Butts's daughters.

It was agreed that Frank Graham, Jr., a free-lance writer, would be commissioned to investigate the matter and write the story if it proved publishable. Graham had written for the *Post* before and was a known quantity. One of his greatest assets was his name, which could not have been more prestigious in athletic circles; his father was one of the giants among sportswriters, in a league with Grantland Rice, Ring Lardner, and Red Smith.

The younger Graham had been writing about sports since his graduation from Columbia University as an English major in 1950. His first job was publicity director for the Brooklyn Dodgers. His association with the team led to an unauthorized biography of Casey Stengel that severely tested the crusty manager's 40-year friendship with Frank Graham, Sr.

After five years with the Dodgers, Graham accepted an editorial position at *Sport* magazine, where he wrote primarily about baseball and boxing. Two years later he left *Sport* to become a free-lance sportswriter, and by 1963 would describe himself as a specialist in "general sports." But he had written little on football before taking on the Butts-Bryant story. His leisure interests included baroque music and lyric poetry.

The *Post* editors saw Graham as conservative and thoroughly professional, and they presumed he had no axes to grind regarding his new assignment. He later admitted, however, that he did hold a bias against big-time college athletics. In his book, *Farewell to Heroes*, he wrote:

> I had been disenchanted with collegiate athletics. (Of course, in view of the results, what Columbia man hadn't?)

The revelations about dumping and rigging basketball games at the City College of New York, Kentucky, and other schools in the 1950's snuffed out whatever interest I had in that pastime. Even the strong basketball team that Columbia put together during my time there left a bad taste in my mouth, as two of its starting five players later ran afoul of the law, one of them for rigging games. Meanwhile, friends in various college athletic departments had told me horror stories about the recruiting violations and the exploitation of scholar-athletes that had become almost a necessity as football coaches scrambled to keep their jobs. Coaches themselves violated their contracts and jumped to more lucrative posts. The old college game, I reasoned, needed a good shaking up.

As it turned out, Graham's predisposition against big-time football was perfectly suited to the crusading journalism Clay Blair preached. Viewing Blair as the leader of an assault on the "citadels of iniquity," the young sportswriter became a fellow crusader and, charged with "moralistic fervor," wrote a story he would come to regret.

Graham was instructed to go to Atlanta and contact Burnett through Pierre Howard. He was authorized to buy Burnett's story if he found it to be reliable, though its publication would be subject to approval by legal counsel. On the morning of February 21, Graham met with Howard and Milton Flack, Burnett's friend and advisor, and that afternoon he interviewed Burnett himself. The next day, on the basis of his interview with Burnett, an affidavit Burnett gave him (couched mostly in general terms), and his conversations with Flack and Howard, Graham bought Burnett's story. Burnett was paid $2,000 at the time and was to receive $3,000 more upon publication. Howard and Flack each received $500. The requisition for Flack's check stipulated that it was in payment for a "research fee & guarantee of exclusivity on SECRET SPORTS STORY–Article."

Graham did not see the notes Burnett had made on the Butts-

Bryant call. He was told they were in the hands of University of Georgia authorities and was promised they would be mailed to him in New York for use in his writing.

Graham learned that in addition to Flack, a man named John Carmichael had seen the notes and had talked to Burnett shortly after he overheard the phone call. When Graham asked to meet with Carmichael, Flack and Howard told him that Carmichael did not want to get involved because he was a friend of Butts and strongly disapproved of what Burnett had done.

Back in his Brooklyn apartment on February 24, Frank Graham, Jr., immediately went to work on his article. Within 24 hours he had completed a first draft. Inexplicably, Burnett's notes never arrived in New York, nor did a promised transcript of a secret tape recording Graham had made of part of his interview with Burnett.

Atlanta Journal sports editor Furman Bisher happened to be in New York at this point. He had learned of Burnett's revelations from a university source but was unaware of the fact that the *Post* had bought the story until he called Roger Kahn. Kahn had already decided that additional investigation was needed in Georgia for corroboration of the story from sources other than Burnett. Kahn asked Bisher to handle it, despite his adversary relation to Bryant in the *Post*'s Birmingham litigation.

Bisher spent a day in Athens interviewing participants in the Alabama-Georgia game. He then telephoned Graham with quotes that were incorporated into the article and attributed to Georgia player Mickey Babb, trainer Sam Richwine, and coach John Griffith. After Graham's article was in final form, a copy was mailed to Bisher for his corrections. He had none. The copy was also intended as a reference for him in writing his own article for the *Journal*, which was expected to break the story simultaneously with the *Post*.

The *Post* editors then rushed Graham's piece to publication with little editing and no further verification. Graphic evidence of their haste is the fact that the story was carried toward the end of the issue, on page 80, and went to press so late that there was not even enough time to advertise it on the cover. It was a "crash" closing, in editors' terms.

Several factors contributed to the *Post*'s rush to publish the article. For one, normal objectivity was greatly impaired by Bryant's involvement. Anything that discredited him would not only aid Curtis in defending Bisher's article in Birmingham, but add fuel to Blair's fiery crusade against wrongdoers in high places. The first anti-Bryant article thus spurred the *Post*'s editors onward with the second. The chance to deal Bryant a second blow must stand as one of the most unfortunate coincidences in journalistic history.

Besides the *Post*'s special animosity toward Bear Bryant, another factor operated against the usual journalistic safeguards: it was simply an unbelievably sensational story. As *Post* sports editor Roger Kahn said, "I never saw another story like it." Many publications might have compromised their standards for the opportunity to stage such a historic coup. If true, Burnett's allegations revealed a blatant act of corruption in high athletic circles that had enormous implications for the future of college football. If true, the story's value to any publication was incalculable.

In *Farewell to Heroes* Graham summarized the *Post*'s mistakes as "excessive haste and secrecy." He attributed both to "a compulsion to excel professionally, to pull off a stunning scoop." The compulsion to pull off a scoop was real. To excel professionally? Hardly. There appears to have been a greater excess of secrecy than of haste. Surely there had been time for much more factual verification than was done. After Graham returned to New York, he found the atmosphere at the *Post* tightlipped, "as if another whispered question, another phone call to Atlanta, would shatter the secrecy and with it the *Post*'s investment in this exclusive story."

Otto Friedrich puts the blame on Clay Blair and attributes the flaws in the story's preparation to an in-house secrecy that was characteristic of Blair's brief regime—a policy that failed to appreciate the value of checks and balances. In particular,

Friedrich points to the exclusion of articles editor Bill Emerson and his assistant, Don McKinney, from the editorial process. This irregularity was probably caused by internal bickering at the time, but there was no shortage of editorial talent on the story. Those who passed on the article included at least four relatively young but highly competent journalists: Clay Blair, who later coauthored General Omar Bradley's autobiography; sports editor Roger Kahn, who would write the classic *Boys of Summer* about the Brooklyn Dodgers and *Good Enough to Dream*; managing editor Davis Thomas, later editor of *Ladies' Home Journal*; and executive editor Don Schanche, later editor of *Holiday*.

Frank Graham's view that normal verification of facts was inhibited by the *Post*'s zeal for ensuring external secrecy is more persuasive. In this regard, the editors took several badly calculated risks:

1) The Burnett notes were never obtained. In *Farewell to Heroes*, Graham states that he thought the notes had been impounded by the attorney general of Georgia. Although the attorney general did indeed obtain a copy later, at the time the article was written the originals were in the possession of Atlanta attorney Cook Barwick, the Georgia Athletic Board member who was leading its investigation. He said later that he was never contacted and would have returned the notes to Burnett if he had been asked to. Since the affidavit Burnett had given Graham was very sparse on details—it mentioned only two specific facts about the Georgia football team*—the *Post* gambled that the

---

* The description of Butts's discussion of the Georgia football team accounted for less than a half-page of Burnett's affidavit. It reads: "Coach Bryant asked, 'Do you have anything for me?' whereupon Wally Butts proceeded to give detailed information pertaining to the University of Georgia's offense and defense to be used in the Alabama-Georgia game the following week. At regular intervals Bear Bryant would ask Wally Butts certain questions pertaining to defensive and offensive maneuvers. Wally Butts would either answer him in detail or would say, 'I don't know about that, I will have to find out.' A question in particular that Bear Bryant asked was, 'How about quick-kicks?' and then Wally Butts answered by saying, 'Don't worry about quick-kicks, they haven't got anyone who can do it.' He also told him that Woodward committed himself fast on pass defense."

details of the notes would support the article's allegation of a fix if the question arose in court.

2) Graham did not interview John Carmichael, one of the two men who talked to Burnett and who saw the notes immediately after the overheard conversation. The *Post* took the risk that Carmichael would not contradict Burnett.

3) The *Post* published hearsay without verifying the accuracy of quoted statements with the purported speakers. Graham knew that this was a violation of basic standards of responsible journalism and came to feel that he should have removed his name from the article when the *Post* editors insisted on having Bisher complete the investigation in Georgia instead of sending him back.

The *Post* editors closed the story and went to press despite a strongly worded warning telegram from Butts's lawyer and an emotional phone call from Butts's daughter Jean to Clay Blair. Through her tears she tried to plead with him not to publish the article, but to no avail.

Did the *Post* editors honestly believe the story was true? The chances they took in their procedures may be the best evidence that they did. In their defense, they were lulled into a false sense of confidence by a number of facts, including Burnett's lie detector tests (he ultimately took two), the widespread belief among Georgia officials that Burnett was telling the truth, and Butts's resignation. They also felt certain that *The Atlanta Journal* would break the story simultaneously, which would have added to its credibility and provided a strong local ally. In Graham's words, the *Journal* was expected to "carry the public relations burden." That the *Journal* backed off from a story on which its sports editor was a paid contributor came as a considerable shock to the *Post* editors.

On March 2, the *Post*'s Philadelphia legal counsel cleared the article for publication. (At that time lawyers probed less into writers' investigations than they do today. The lawyers assumed that the *Post* could prove its facts.) And on March 18, 1963, when the March 23 issue of *The Saturday Evening Post* hit the newsstands, the nation was scandalized by an article entitled "Story of a College Football Fix."* One week later, Wally Butts and Bear Bryant sued Curtis Publishing Company for libel.

---

* For the full text of the article, see Appendix, pp. 231–42.

. . . .

A Spectrum of Reactions

BEFORE THE MARCH 23 ISSUE of the *Post* was published, Butts and Bryant had already obtained advance copies and had gone on television to issue heated denials. Rumors of the story had been circulating in journalistic circles for weeks, in part because Furman Bisher had shown the article to other sportswriters covering spring baseball training in Florida, where the proofs had been sent to him for his corrections.

Press reaction was immediate and highly critical of the *Post*. On April 1, *Newsweek* opened its account by questioning the *Post*'s judgment in accepting the story:

> The story was for sale during the past few months. *Newsweek, Sports Illustrated,* and several other magazines turned it down. It verged on libel; there were holes in it.

Newsweek also faulted the *Post* for not revealing that it had paid a reported $6,000 for the piece and for saying instead that Burnett decided to tell his story because he was "living in his private misery." (*Newsweek* ignored the fact that Burnett had gratuitously revealed his story to the University of Georgia long before he sold it to the *Post*.)

Time (March 29, 1963) was puzzled that the "well-publicized" story was "tucked away strangely on the back pages" but described it as every bit as sensational as its advance billing. *Time*'s coverage emphasized the financial problems of Curtis Publishing Company and Clay Blair's new editorial policies. Quoting the staff memo in which he boasted of six pending lawsuits, *Time* commented, "By Blair's bizarre measure the *Post* last week succeeded beyond its wildest dreams." Blair's goal, in *Time*'s view, was to hit the *Post*'s readers with a "blockbuster" a week, and "as long as the blockbusters make a lot of noise, the *Post* does not seem much concerned with the fallout."

"A Debatable Football Scandal" was *Sports Illustrated*'s March 25 headline. It found the *Post*'s story to be "full of puzzles." Among them were the questions of why George Burnett didn't alert Coach John Griffith to Butts's betrayal before the game and whether Burnett was certain he heard discussions of defenses, which aren't normally set up until the week before the game. Another question raised by *Sports Illustrated* was what "improbable relationship" between Butts and Flack would permit Butts to use Flack's telephone for long-distance calls. The possibility that Butts had used a credit card was not considered.

The most intriguing item in *Sports Illustrated*'s story was the revelation that Burnett decided to reveal his secret on the same day Bear Bryant filed suit in Birmingham against Furman Bisher and the *Post* for the October 1962 story about brutality and the Holt-Graning incident. The relevance of this coincidence was not explained. It was also misleading. Bryant's suit was filed January 4, 1963. Burnett did not reveal his secret to the *Post* until February 21.

The *Birmingham News* reported from Washington, D.C. on March 20 that the most common view among journalists in the nation's capital was that the *Post* had "climbed way out on a limb and oversold a libelous story." The lack of evidence that either Butts or Bryant had made money on the game or that Bryant had passed any Georgia secrets along to his players was cited as a major hole in the story. Legally minded observers were said to have been surprised that a major national magazine would print obviously libelous charges on the basis of a phone conversation overheard by one person who made no recording and took no stenographic notes.

The venerable Red Smith of the New York *Herald Tribune* was quoted in the *Birmingham News* piece as observing that the article did not live up to its billing as a "second Black Sox scandal" and explained why:

> In this case there is no suggestion of misbehavior by players. If it were established that one embittered man had done the old school dirty, this would hardly constitute evidence of widespread corruption in a conference. . . . Nothing more has been charged than unseemly conduct between two men.

Smith wondered what kind of information Butts could have given to "a coach who already has all his rival's plays charted and tabulated, with films to complement the scouting reports." He also questioned whether Bryant could have made use of any "deep secrets" without letting his assistants and players know he had "guilty knowledge."

The *Post* article's statements that college football would be permanently damaged and its implications that misconduct like Butts's and Bryant's might be widespread brought a publicized denial from the president of the National Football Foundation and Hall of Fame, Chester J. LaRoche. He said that even if this "alleged act of infamy without parallel in intercollegiate football history" were proven, there would be no justification for the *Post*'s generalizations. The statements were described by LaRoche as "gross magnifications" that unjustly stigmatized "a game that has won the devotion and trust of millions through almost 100 years of honorable history." He pointed to rising ethical standards in football and attributed this trend to "the moral character of the vast majority of the 5,000 college coaches and 20,000 high school coaches."

Sports Illustrated belittled the *Post*'s story in more detail on April 8, two weeks after its initial coverage. By this time the magazine was armed with the text of George Burnett's notes, which it had distributed to Wally Butts and to "a number of football authorities, including coaches, for evaluation."

In its article, entitled "The Scandalous Notes," *Sports Illustrated* broke down the notes into 19 items and printed each item separately, followed by Butts's and the experts' evaluations. It is not clear whether the unnamed experts evaluated the notes individually or as a group.

Butts and the experts did not concur in their evaluation of every note, but they did agree that as a whole the notes contained little or no information that would have been helpful to Bryant. Twelve of the notes were dismissed by the experts as containing nothing that could be construed as secret or that any well-coached team wouldn't be prepared for. Three were adjudged harmless "opinion." Three others were meaningless to the experts, and one was described as "foolish."

A few examples illustrate the experts' certain, if cryptic, judgments. Burnett's note precedes each evaluation:

Reismueller (Rissmiller) greatest in history . . .
EXPERTS: Meaningless opinion.

Optional left pass / if can block man on corner / keeps running . . .
EXPERTS: Probably description of the sprint-out pass, a basic weapon used by most all college teams and hardly a secret.

On side guard pulls on sweep . . .
EXPERTS: Most sweeps are designed for the onside guard (who moves with the flow of play) to pull and block against normal defenses, and it is no secret.

Weak defense anybody except Blackburn . . .
EXPERTS: Opinion again, and coaches do not prepare for games on opinion.

Slot to Rt / Ends normal (3 yards)
EXPERTS: Vague, but apparently a basic formation and predictable.

This last note described Georgia's slot formation, including the three-yard width of the slot between the end and the tackle. Another note described the pro-set formation, the other of the two formations used by Georgia against Alabama. These two notes had been considered the most incriminating by John Griffith and others who had examined them earlier.

Of the note describing the pro-set formation, Butts told *Sports Illustrated*, "A standard formation from which you can run any number of plays." The experts said, "Agreed. But useless information, like much of the rest, unless a defense knows exactly when certain plays will occur."

This comment should have been puzzling to any reader who knew football. Could knowledge of an opponent's offensive formations possibly be "useless" information? Surely not. Although many plays can be run from a given formation, the number and variety of plays are limited by the number of formations. The number of defenses needed by a team is also determined by its opponent's offensive sets. Multiple formations mean multiple offenses and plays, and they force opponents into multiple defenses, with their great potential for confusion and mistakes. The experts were really straining to call this information "useless." It is a key element of every scouting report.

In two instances the experts conceded that the information in Burnett's notes was "perhaps indiscreet"—the basic offensive formation described in the note, "Baer [Babb] slot rt / split rt end out / Long count / left half in motion," and a defensive formation, "Drop end off / Ga—contain with tackle"—but in both cases concluded that these were maneuvers an opponent should have expected.

Despite the experts' general downgrading of the Burnett notes, *Sports Illustrated* hedged its bets in the article's conclusions. It said that if Burnett was telling the truth, Butts was guilty at most of "a profound indiscretion," but one that raised the question of the ethics of the entire football coaching fraternity. Coaches were said to have become fond of pregame conversation with each other. One prominent coach, apparently one of the "experts," was quoted as saying:

> Maybe we talk too much to each other. I know we all try to con one another a little bit. But if I had to be one of the two men in that conversation, I would rather be the listener than the speaker.

Official reaction to the *Post* article in Alabama and Georgia varied much more widely than the reaction of the press did. It contrasted as sharply as the professional status of Butts and Bryant in their respective communities.

In Alabama the official establishment quickly closed ranks in support of the state's number-one hero. Governor George C. Wallace said, "I don't know anything about it, but I'll tell you this—*The Saturday Evening Post* is the sorriest authority on the truth." The board of trustees of the University of Alabama unanimously adopted a resolution expressing its support for Bryant and condemning the *Post*'s "scurrilous attacks" on the university, the state, and the people of Alabama. Resolutions were introduced in the Alabama legislature denouncing the *Post* for its "misstatements, slurs, distortions, and untruths" about the state, the university, and Alabama football players. A United States district attorney in Birmingham called for a federal grand jury investigation of the *Post*. The article, he said, was a clear violation of federal wiretap laws, a "confession of crime" on its face.

The response was vastly different in Georgia. Not a single public figure came to Butts's defense. Newspaper accounts were temperate and factual. If it was a time to choose between loyalty to Wally Butts or to the University of Georgia, Butts was the clear loser.

One of Butts's major public mistakes had been his open opposition to Georgia governor Carl Sanders in his 1960 race against a former governor and Butts's drinking buddy, the segregationist Marvin Griffin. (Griffin had pushed for funds to build a wall around the Bulldog practice field so Butts could guard his team's secrets from possible spies.) Rumor had it that Governor Sanders was understandably irritated by Butts's campaigning against him and had never welcomed the idea of Butts's staying on as athletic director at Sanders's alma mater.

When Sanders first heard about Burnett's story, he moved quickly to use the power of his office against Butts. Two days before the *Post* article came out, he took a rare action for a governor, although one expressly authorized by Georgia law. He formally and publicly directed state attorney general Eugene Cook to investigate reports of an improper phone call between Wally Butts and Bear Bryant and to determine if criminal prosecutions for violations of Georgia law were in order.

The Georgia attorney general gave the matter top priority and reported to the governor two weeks later, on April 1, 1963. Cook's highly publicized report is one of the most remarkable official documents ever to pass between two elected officials concerning a constituent. It concluded that there was no evidence that Butts had violated any Georgia criminal law, but it did not end there. Rather, Attorney General Cook went beyond Sanders's charge and gratuitously found that Butts had in fact telephoned Bryant on September 13, 1962, and also that:

> . . . the information given by Butts to Bryant in advance of the September 22, 1962 Alabama-Georgia game was unethical and improper, and unsportsmanlike and that the furnishing of such information might well have vitally affected the outcome of the game in points and margin of victory.

Cook based his finding that the September 13 call had taken place on George Burnett's statement and on telephone company records, which confirmed that a call from Butts to Bryant had indeed occurred on that date at the time and for the duration reported by Burnett. As for his finding about the content of that conversation, Cook credited a statement he had taken from Burnett as well as the results of a second lie detector test.

The first lie detector test Burnett took—and passed—had been administered by an Atlanta private detective selected by Cook Barwick. This test had satisfied ex-FBI agent Barwick, but for some reason—perhaps a preference for an official test—Attorney General Cook thought it was unsatisfactory. He asked Major G. B. Ragsdale, director of the Georgia Bureau of Investigation, to administer a second test. Ragsdale had 15 years of experience as a polygraph operator and was president of the American Academy of Polygraph Examiners. Burnett passed Ragsdale's test as well.

Cook's report to Sanders also included Major Ragsdale's evaluations of lie detector tests reportedly taken and passed by Butts and Bryant. Though Butts had refused to take a lie detector test before he resigned as athletic director, after his resignation he journeyed to Jacksonville, Florida, which his lawyer called "neutral ground," and passed a test administered by Edward L. Quinn, a private detective. Major Ragsdale talked to Quinn and made lengthy, scathing comments in his report to Cook on the efficacy of Quinn's training and equipment. Quinn had merely used a galvanometer, called a "B & W machine," which Ragsdale said was not recognized as "a valid instrument for giving a deception test" by either the American Academy of Polygraph Examiners or the Academy of Scientific Interrogators, the two leading organizations of polygraph experts. Ragsdale went into great detail on the virtual worthlessness of a galvanometer test, particularly as compared to a polygraph, and concluded that it "should never be used as a single unit to give a deception test."

Like Burnett, Bryant was reported to have passed a polygraph test. It was administered by Fred Nichol, a public prosecutor in Tuscaloosa. Ragsdale reported that he had been told that Nichol had a "Keeler Polygraph (old model)" and "ran a test now and then." He had no information on Nichol's qualifications;

apparently he was not a member of the American Academy of Polygraph Examiners.

Interpretations of Burnett's notes by experts were the basis for Cook's conclusion that the Butts-Bryant conversation was improper and might have affected the game. Coach John Griffith gave the attorney general a lengthy explanation of how the notes related to the Georgia team, and nine Georgia assistant coaches signed this statement:

> After viewing the alleged notations made by George Burnett while listening to an alleged telephone conversation between Wallace Butts and "Bear" Bryant on September 13, 1962, it is my opinion, as one of the coaches of the University of Georgia football team, that if such information was given to Coach Bryant before the opening game of the season, it conveyed vital and important information with respect to the offensive and defensive plays, patterns and formations that could have been of value to the University of Alabama football team, and could have affected the outcome of the game on September 22, 1962.

One person whose opinion Cook cited came as a great surprise. It was Southeastern Conference commissioner Bernie Moore, who had spent many hours studying the notes, including a three-hour session with John Griffith. Moore told Cook that the only two offensive formations used by Georgia in the game with Alabama were described in the notes and that it would help an opposing coach to be able to limit his defensive preparation to two particular formations. Moore also stated in general terms that there were circumstances when it would be "unethical and unsportsmanlike" for a coach of one team to give information to an opposing coach.

The most fascinating item in the Cook report was the revelation of the account Bear Bryant gave to University of Alabama president Frank Rose about the incriminating phone call. On Sunday, February 24, Rose had met in Birmingham with Cook Barwick, President Aderhold, and Commissioner Moore, who informed him of Burnett's disclosures. He agreed to investigate the matter thoroughly, returned to Tuscaloosa, and ten days later wrote to Aderhold to report his findings. His remarkable one-page letter is worth reproducing in its entirety:

March 6, 1963
Confidential

Dr. O. C. Aderhold, President
The University of Georgia
Athens, Georgia

Dear Dr. Aderhold:

I have spent a great deal of time investigating thoroughly the questions that were raised during our meeting in Birmingham and have talked with Coach Bryant at least on two occasions. As best as I can ascertain, this is the information that I have received.

Coach Butts has been serving on the football rules committee, and at a meeting held last summer of the Rules Committee the defenses used by Coach Bryant, L.S.U. and Tennessee were discussed at length and new rules were drawn up that would severely penalize these three teams unless the defenses were changed, particularly on certain plays.

Coach Butts had discussed this with Coach Bryant and the two were together at some meeting where Coach Butts told Coach Bryant that the University of Georgia had plays that would severely penalize the Alabama team and not only would cause LeRoy Jordan, an Alabama player, to be expelled from the game, but could severely injure one of the offensive players on the Georgia team.

Coach Bryant asked Coach Butts to let him know what

the plays were, and on September 14 he called Coach Bryant and told him. There was a question about another one of the offensive plays of the Georgia team that could seriously penalize the Alabama team and bring on additional injury to a player. Coach Bryant asked Coach Butts to check on that play, which he did, and called him back on September 16.

It was then that Coach Bryant changed his defenses and invited Mr. George Gardner, Head of the Officials of the Southeastern Conference, to come to Tuscaloosa and interpret for him the legality of the defenses. This Mr. Gardner did the following week. The defenses were changed and Coach Bryant was grateful to Coach Butts for calling this to his attention.

Coach Bryant informs me that calling this to his attention may have favored the University of Alabama football team, but that he doubts it seriously. He did say that it prevented him from using illegal plays after the new change of rules.

I have checked into other matters that were discussed and can find no grounds for Mr. Bisher's accusations, and as I understand it he has now decided for lack of information to drop the matter.

Dr. Aderhold, this continues to be a serious matter with me, and if you have any additional information I would appreciate your furnishing me with it as I am not only anxious to work with you but to satisfy my own mind.

Thank you for coming to Birmingham to meet with me and for sharing this information, I am

Most cordially yours,
Frank A. Rose

Cook saw Rose's letter as proof that "offensive and defensive plays of the Georgia team" were discussed by Butts and Bryant, but the letter fell far short of confirming that their conversation included the information recorded in George Burnett's notes. Some thought the main thing the letter proved was that Bryant had not told his president the truth.

Rose's reference to SEC head of officials George Gardner's visit to Alabama as a result of the call was disproved by Gardner's own statement to Cook. He had visited Tuscaloosa the week before the call. Butts and Bryant might still have been talking about roughness rules after his visit, but it is highly unlikely.

As reported in Rose's letter, Bryant's explanation of the call was extremely implausible. There was no way that particular Georgia "plays" could have penalized Alabama or caused LeRoy Jordan to be expelled from the game. And if there were, why would Butts be telling Bryant how to keep his All-American in the game? It is simply impossible to believe that Bryant would have told Rose these things in a candid explanation of the phone call. The most logical inference from the letter is that Butts and Bryant had a conversation that Bryant recalled, but whose true content he preferred not to disclose. While this inference does not prove they had the talk indicated by Burnett's notes, it is fully consistent with Burnett's story and raises suspicions that something irregular had occurred.

Other portions of Cook's voluminous report hinted at possible motives for Butts's betrayal of Georgia, including references to Butts's financial situation and to his involvement with gamblers. A financial statement prepared by a certified public accountant in July 1961, when Butts's annual salary was $16,000, showed total assets of $349,287 and liabilities of $143,299, for a net worth of $205,988. (Cook erroneously assumed that the statement was accurate.)

In the course of Cook's investigation, Butts appeared with his lawyers before the attorney general for the limited purpose of answering questions about his alleged involvement in gambling. He denied that he gambled personally, and Cook found no evidence to the contrary. The attorney general did find, however, that Butts made personal long-distance phone calls to persons who were "known to be interested in gambling." Butts insisted that he did not know that these people, unnamed in the report, were involved with gambling and claimed that the calls were made for business and social purposes.

The Cook report essentially confirmed the truth of much of the *Post* article and added meat to its insinuations linking the phone call to Butts's finances and to gambling. In the name of ethics and sportsmanship, the state of Georgia's highest law enforcement officer had joined the *Post* as an ally.

Emboldened by the Cook report's findings, the *Post* ran an editorial on April 27 in which it reaffirmed the "fix" story's truth. It also accused its critics in the national press of being sore losers about not getting the scoop themselves. The *Post* editors now claimed they knew that Butts had made phone calls to known gamblers during the football season and that he had amassed gross assets of $349,287 on a salary of $16,000—facts reported by Georgia Attorney General Cook. The editorial concluded:

> As we said before, our philosophy is radical. We believe that any coach who rigs a football game should be exposed. We will continue to cling to this radical belief despite what our detractors in and out of the publishing business may say about us.
>
> If another story of similar nature should come our way in the future we will not hesitate to pursue the same course we took with this one, track it down, satisfy ourselves that we have the truth and then publish it.

If the meager file Frank Graham, Jr., had brought back from Atlanta, supplemented by Bisher's findings, had left any doubts, the *Post* editors were certain now. The Georgia attorney general had nailed it down. Breathing had to be easier both in the ivory towers of the University of Georgia and in the board room of the Curtis Publishing Company.

6

. . . .

What Were the Stakes?

THE AUGUST TRIAL DATE of Butts's case against Curtis Publishing Company was fast approaching. "A trial that has the South seething," said *Sports Illustrated*. No lawsuit had generated such heated emotions since the 1925 Scopes "Monkey Trial" in Tennessee. The *Post*'s assault on two southern football heroes was compared to Clarence Darrow's assault on the Genesis account of creation.

There did seem to be more at stake than merely whether Wally Butts would tap the treasury of Curtis Publishing Company. The *Post* article had predicted not only that individual careers would be ruined—Butts's and Bryant's, at least—but that "A great sport will be permanently damaged. For many people the bloom must pass forever from college football." Was this doomsaying only wishful rhetoric on Frank Graham's part? Or did the issues transcend Butts and Bryant and threaten the entire sport?

To the Southeastern Conference, the case was bigger than the litigants. SEC commissioner Bernie Moore viewed the matter as the most serious of his 15-year tenure in office. From the beginning, he investigated it as vigorously as the resources of his office permitted.

The lawsuit dragged the conference and Bear Bryant deeper into the wave of bad publicity that had begun with the Holt-Graning incident and Furman Bisher's brutality article. Bryant was widely perceived as ruthless and hell-bent to win. The conference was seen as tolerating misdeeds in winners who brought in revenues from television and bowl bids, partly because all members of the conference shared these revenues.

Some members of the northern press viewed the South's indulgences of football heroes as symptomatic of a regional amorality. In April, *The Nation* magazine published a brief, unsigned piece entitled "Gridiron on the Grid." It cited the salient facts of Graham's article and Attorney General Cook's findings and concluded:

> In New York, the district attorney's office is busy with several cases involving the fixing of basketball games. In Detroit, Chicago and other points on the professional football circuit, there are ugly rumors concerning associations between players and gamblers. But in the Southland, the magnolias are blooming (or have bloomed) and spring should not be defiled by sordid thoughts. Sports lovers will continue to believe that all is best for the best of all possible worlds, especially in Georgia and Alabama.

The Nation's charge that southerners would rather smell the magnolias than face facts about their sports heroes was certainly unfair to the University of Georgia. Its officials had done all they could: Butts was out as athletic director. The governor of Georgia had taken the unusual step of ordering a criminal investigation, and the attorney general had found Butts guilty of uncriminal misconduct.

Alabamians took Graham's article as more than a smear of Butts and Bryant; it struck at the soul and character of their entire state. Bryant had become the dominant figure in the state; he could have had any award its people wished to bestow. In Alabama an "atheist" was defined as "a person who doesn't believe in Bear Bryant."

When the *Post* predicted that the "fix" story would damage college football permanently, it could safely assume that it would at least damage Alabama football permanently if the coaching career of Bear Bryant was brought to an end. But Frank Graham and the *Post* editors had much more in mind; they felt that the Butts-Bryant incident was symptomatic of deeper, more widespread corruption in college football. Their target was probably what is loosely called "big-time football," a term frequently used but seldom defined.

Would big-time football be on trial in Atlanta? If Butts and Bryant were proven guilty, would the decision have implications beyond the careers of these two men? Friends and foes alike felt that it would, that big-time college football *was* going to trial. Its life was not at stake, but something else was—an intangible something that struck at the very heart of the game.

"Big-time football" may be defined as the football that is played at major universities by scholarship athletes who are recruited for that express purpose. Much more than just a recreational activity, it is a means for a school to gain recognition and revenues. Sacrificing academic standards in admission and retaining students for it is not uncommon. It is a significant part of the national entertainment market.

More empirically, big-time football comprises the member teams of six major athletic conferences and a few independent schools. With the exception of the Northeast, it is a national phenomenon, ranging from the Atlantic Coast Conference in the East to the Pacific Ten in the West, with the interior bridged by the Big Ten, the SEC, the Big Eight, and the Southwest. Less than twenty independents throughout the country are accorded "big-time" status.

Big-time football is largely the province of state-supported universities. The Big Ten and the SEC have but one private member each. The Big Eight has none. The few private universities in the conferences generally produce less successful teams: Duke, Vanderbilt, Northwestern, and Rice are examples. Big-time football's identification with state universities outside the Northeast has given it an image problem. As we have seen, the *Post* article resulted in part from a bias against big-time football. This bias is shared by many writers and opinion makers in eastern literary circles. When the *Post* moved its editorial offices from Philadelphia to New York in 1962, it plunged deeper into a bastion of college football skeptics that runs from Washington to Boston. In their scorn for the sport, many of these skeptics assume that it cannot coexist with high-quality academic programs. They are mistaken.

Big-time football is not only compatible with academic excellence, it helps to support university academic programs. In 1969, James Reston of *The New York Times* wrote of the positive effect sports have on state university education. Thinking perhaps of his alma mater, The University of Illinois, Reston observed that football teams had become symbols of state pride; the games kept alumni in touch with the university and helped generate educational appropriations on a scale that would never have been possible without "the attraction and pride engendered by these sporting events at the universities on autumn Saturday afternoons."

In *The Big Game* Professor Edwin H. Cady of Duke University develops Reston's idea at great length. He argues convincingly that universities with strong athletic programs are healthier academic institutions as a result. He attributes the relative weakness of higher public education in the Northeast in part to weak athletic programs. To illustrate his thesis, Cady cites the University of Tennessee:

> One of my favorite places to go to a football game is the University of Tennessee at Knoxville, especially at night when you can watch the dozens of lighted launches dropping down Lake Loudoun, partying, and tie up at the piers to deliver their passengers for the game. What a party! The stadium is a sea of orange—eighty thousand maniacs [now ninety-five thousand]. You see why the bumper stickers stream by on the highway all day long, announcing: "This is Big Orange Country." Now, Tennessee is a state relatively small in population and thin

in resources. It is not many years since major national investments were made to rescue Tennessee. Yet UT is supported academically at levels of influence, affluence, and significance which the ancient Universities of Paris or Bologna or Göttingen would turn green with envy to contemplate. Why?

In answer to his own question, Cady suggests, although he admittedly cannot prove, that UT's relatively generous legislative support is due in part to its superb athletics program:

> Do away with the games, the teams, the mythology, the glamor, the exposure, and the contacts. Take down those proud, affectionate signs. Deprive those people of their parties and cut the chains of connection between the citizenry of the state in all directions and the university, and what would happen? Where would all those zealous, wild, and loving constituencies go? Right or wrong, many universities have decided that they would rather not break those golden but magnetic chains.

Cady is more certain that big-time athletics increase endowments to private universities. He cites fund raisers at Yale who believe that disillusionment with its deemphasized athletic program cost the Ivy League school millions of dollars in gifts. Both private and state university fund raisers told him that giving often begins with relatively small sums for athletics and flowers into substantial support of academic programs.

Universities may be able to promote corporate support as much by inviting executives to sit in presidents' football boxes as by winning contracts for scientific research. As a dean at Ohio State, this writer witnessed firsthand the great fund-raising value of invitations to the president's massive pregame luncheons.

It is certainly no coincidence that state universities with big-time athletic programs are also larger and more prestigious academically than those without such programs. Perhaps for this same reason, calls to deemphasize athletics have been disappearing everywhere, both within and outside academia.

This is not to say that there is no academic gap between athletes and other students. On the contrary, the scholarship athlete often does not end up with the same education as his classmates. Bear Bryant was one of the first leading coaches to speak out candidly on this subject:

> I used to go along with the idea that football players on scholarship were "student-athletes," which is what the NCAA calls them. Meaning a student first, an athlete second. We were kidding ourselves, trying to make it more palatable to the academicians. We don't have to say that and we shouldn't. At the level we play, the boy is really an athlete first and a student second.

If the student-athlete were truly both, Bryant's view that he is an athlete first might not be troubling. Unfortunately, the pressure to excel in athletics too often exceeds the pressure to do even passing academic work. Bryant once indicated in an interview that poor academic performance by an athlete may be no great loss:

> Asked why his University of Alabama football players were housed in a luxury dorm, fed a diet twice as expensive as that provided other students, and given private tutors, the legendary coach Paul "Bear" Bryant replied: "Our first concern is to teach these kids to play hard-nosed football. If they do, we'll keep filling that stadium and we'll be able to keep on giving scholarships to athletes who might never have gone to college otherwise. Sure, Joe Willie (Namath) never graduated. We got eleven players in the pros (professional football) right now and only two of them graduated. But Joe Willie, he signed with the Jets for more than $400,000 and the rest of them, they average about $30,000 a year. You know your

typical college graduate, even if he's magna cum laude
he's going to be damn lucky to start at $10,000 a year."

The player who gets a pro contract but no degree may indeed
earn more than the graduate with a B.A. *magna cum laude*, but
too few make the pro ranks to justify abandoning the student-
athlete concept. Because of it, many athletes receive college
degrees who would not have otherwise.

In addition to the athletes and schools themselves, many others
reap the benefits of big-time football, including students, faculty,
alumni, local businesses, athletic equipment companies, television and radio stations, sportswriters, and all manner of fans,
from corporate executives to the man in the street. A move to
deemphasize a football program would meet with widespread
opposition far beyond the university's walls.

The sociology of big-time football is complex and has received
little systematic study. Every major program operates under the
aegis of a loose, shifting "establishment," an informal body ex-
tending beyond the formal structure of the university. This establishment becomes most visible when a coach has a string
of losing seasons and a cry goes up for his removal; his supporters
will know where to turn to enlist allies. The establishment usually
consists of a select few members of the board of trustees, professors who have made the grade after years of service on the
athletic committee, and—perhaps most typical of all—former star
players who have become successful businessmen and major
contributors to the university.

In *The Big Game* Cady identifies two subcultures that share
power over athletic programs. One is the "Irregulars," who have
the same relationship to a coach as the Baker Street Irregulars
had to Sherlock Holmes. They may not be welcomed by the coach
but are "rich, powerful, or persistent enough to buy, bludgeon,
or worm their way in." Their involvement in recruiting is Cady's
greatest concern. They are the "representatives of the athletic
interests" for NCAA rules purposes and often harm the school
with recruiting excesses. (When the definitive work on alumni-

recruiters—or boosters, as they are commonly called—and their place in the establishment is written, the role that four Atlanta boosters played in Wally Butts's downfall should form a small chapter.)

The second group, which Cady calls a "Fifth Column of trustees, high administrators, leading citizens (doctors, bankers,) and professors," works at a higher level. An astute university president must have close links to the Fifth Column if he is to have any hope of maintaining real control over the athletic program.

To say that big-time football serves an establishment bigger than the institution is not a condemnation. Those formally in power at a university at a given time do not own it. Most members of a university's establishment have reason to believe they have earned a piece of the the action.

The chief characteristic of big-time football is an emphasis on winning. Losing programs may be endured, but losing coaches are not. The pressure to win is the cause of most of the wrongs associated with the sport, ranging from recruiting violations to spying. But the pressure differs in degree from school to school; some schools simply take their team's record more seriously than others. At some a coach can survive with a record that would be fatal at others. Ray Perkins, for instance, went 8–4 in his first year as Bear Bryant's successor and entered his second year under a cloud.

Why is football so much more important in some places than in others? James Michener, in *Sports in America*, advanced some possible answers in his search for our "football capital," the school with the "craziest" fans. After visiting nine colleges, he narrowed his choice to Nebraska, Alabama, and Oklahoma.

The chancellor of the University of Nebraska told Michener that one reason for the state's "total mania" over his school's football team is the lack of competing teams:

> Nebraska is almost unique in that we have no second university to divert attention. Even Oklahoma has Oklahoma State, a very strong school. Colorado, Alabama,

Kansas. You name them. Their loyalties are divided, but not us. If you live within the confines of this state, you're a Nebraska fan. And thirdly, we have no competition from any professional teams. We are football.

Another Nebraskan overheard the chancellor's explanation and took it a giant step further:

> He leaves out the fact that the State of Nebraska has no opera, no drama, no symphony, no exalted social life and not much intellectual life. In this state if you don't go for football, you're a pariah. And it's the same throughout the Big Eight. Our football is good because we haven't anything else. And if you look at it honestly, that holds true for Ohio State and Arkansas and Penn State and Texas and Auburn and all the powers. They support football because their towns don't offer anything else.

At Alabama Michener was astounded by Bear Bryant's stature as a living legend. On his second trip to Tuscaloosa, he was able to place this hero worship in a larger context. While attending inductions into the Alabama Sports Hall of Fame, he was struck by the passion with which the state praised its heroes of yore:

> As they came to the podium, these great baseball players, and golfers, and racetrack drivers evoked empathies I had never witnessed before. They were the grain and fiber of Alabama, more important than politicians and bankers, and finally the old-time football players came forward, the deeply revered predecessors to the Namaths and Stablers, and these men were living gods.

The three explanations that Michener discovered for college football mania—the Nebraska chancellor's "only-one-in-the-state" theory, the "nothing-else-to-do" explanation of the Nebraska cynic, and his own "no-other-heroes" theory—all derive from the same underlying principle: football fills a vacuum and serves a collective need. Whatever this need may be, it produces a mania at some schools that is satisfied only by a winning football team and not one that merely racks up more wins than losses; championships and bowl bids are expected on a regular basis.

Bear Bryant was a master at satisfying his fans' need. But how far was he capable of going in order to keep his fans happy? The *Post*'s charges that Bryant was not above converting an opposing athletic director into a spy to insure a Crimson Tide victory and that Butts knowingly betrayed his team to an archrival opened the question of the integrity of the game. How much other cheating went on? In how many other ways was the game not what it pretended to be? Was it worthy of the emphasis it received? If two greats like Butts and Bryant would stoop to this, what would lesser figures do on their way to the top?

The implications for the Southeastern Conference were particularly ominous. Commissioner Moore had spent many hours investigating the matter, listening to Butts and Burnett and talking to Griffith, Attorney General Cook, and representatives of both universities. The NCAA stayed its hand pending the SEC investigation but made it clear that some action should be taken if the *Post*'s charges were true. As Butts's trial neared, the commissioner still felt he did not know the full truth and was apprehensive about what the trial would reveal and what the verdict might be.

In the worst-case scenario, if Butts were to lose his case against the *Post*, there would surely be a call for Bryant's ouster at Alabama. Crimson Tide supporters might not give up their championship coach so easily, though, especially since Bryant's own case would still be pending; he could conceivably win in Birmingham even if Butts lost. Some Alabamians thought that if Burnett was telling the truth, it was Butts, not Bryant, who was the villain. Bryant had only listened—to help his team, not hurt it. If Alabama refused to move against Bryant, Alabama's expulsion from the conference would have to be considered. If the conference did nothing, expulsion of Alabama from the NCAA and sanctions against the conference might be next. If Butts lost, Moore must have realized, there was no way the conference could win.

Commissioner Moore decided that the conference needed an observer at the trial who could advise the executive committee on the proceedings. A law professor from a conference school seemed the logical choice, and on the recommendation of his son-in-law, a Nashville attorney, Moore asked this author, then a professor at Vanderbilt Law School, to attend the trial. The commissioner and I agreed on my employment as a "special observer" on a Sunday afternoon in July, sitting on the porch of his farmhouse near Winchester, Tennessee. After outlining all that he knew, he said, "Jim, if those two men did something wrong, they ought to take the consequences. Don't hold back."

The taciturn commissioner was a straight arrow of the old school. Before he became commissioner in 1947, he was the highly respected head football coach at Louisiana State University. A devoted farmer all his life, he was a man of uncommon openness, honesty, and simplicity. This incident had thrown him into a world he could barely fathom. He was baffled by the realization that the truth could be so elusive. It was particularly puzzling to him that witnesses who contradicted each other could pass lie detector tests. He expected the trial to bring out the truth and was braced for the worst.

7

. . . .

Football in the Courtroom

ON MARCH 25, 1963, only one week after the *Post*'s "fix" story appeared on the newsstands, Butts's seven-page complaint against Curtis Publishing Company was filed. The unusual speed with which Butts's lawyers initiated the lawsuit was meant to indicate his sense of outrage and desire for early vindication. Alleging the article to be false in its accusations of a fix and to have been published recklessly and maliciously, the complaint demanded $5 million in punitive damages and $5 million in general, or compensatory, damages.

The defendant moved rapidly, too. On April 10, Curtis Publishing Company filed a brief answer, the essence of which was: "the statements complained of . . . are true."

Butts could have sued in a Georgia state court but chose instead to bring suit in the United States District Court for the Northern District of Georgia, seated in Atlanta. His lawyers were well aware of the fact that as an out-of-state corporation, Curtis could have removed any state court action to federal court and undoubtedly would have. But they may have preferred federal court in any event because of its superior procedures for discovering evidence, both favorable and unfavorable, in advance of trial.

The case was assigned to District Judge Lewis R. (Pete) Morgan, a graduate of the University of Georgia School of Law. As it turned out, he had reason to excuse himself from the case; after the trial was over, he told newsmen that he had attended the football game on which the *Post* article was based. It never became apparent during the trial, however, that he had any personal knowledge about the game.

Judge Morgan, 49, had been appointed to the federal bench in 1961 from private practice in LaGrange, Georgia, by President Kennedy. His experience included a term in the Georgia general assembly and a stint as executive secretary to Congressman A. Sidney Camp. (He would later be elevated to the U.S. Court of Appeals for the Fifth Circuit by President Lyndon B. Johnson.) Morgan ran a tight ship, but he did not let the judicial robe turn him into a tyrant. He was firm yet courteous to all who appeared before him.

The pretrial proceedings in the case were unusually complex and time-consuming. Among other things, from April through July Judge Morgan presided over a series of disputes among lawyers concerning discovery proceedings—that is, procedures a litigant may use to obtain evidence in the possession of an opponent or a third person, or sworn testimony from a prospective witness in advance of trial. When such testimony is given orally, it is reduced to a written deposition.

Discovery depositions were taken in New York, Chicago, Tallahassee, Birmingham, Jacksonville, Athens, Lexington, and Atlanta. They were all attended by one or more lawyers for each side, a costly expenditure of time and energy. The *Post*'s lawyers were still taking depositions in Tallahassee as late as July 25, less than two weeks before the August 5 trial date.

Judge Morgan had set the trial for early August—a time when many courts do no business at all—because he wanted a decision before the 1963 college football season opened. His desire to "clear the air" over college football meant that Butts's case came to trial only 4½ months after it was filed, unusually little time for a case involving such complex litigation and high stakes.

The lawyers who tried the case were among the best Atlanta had to offer. Curtis also employed the services of Philip Strubing, one of its Philadelphia lawyers who had approved publication of the article. Strubing, General Counsel to Curtis, was a senior partner in the prestigious firm of Pepper, Hamilton, and Scheetz, a founder of which was George Wharton Pepper, author of the classic *Philadelphia Lawyer* and the lawyer most often associated with that term. Strubing had helped to mount many successful libel defenses for Curtis; between 1935 and 1962, the *Post* lost only one libel verdict. He also handled libel matters for *Time* and *Life*. In his mid-fifties, he was conservatively dressed and trim. A former athlete—he had played three major sports at Princeton—in time he was to become president of the United States Golf Association and chairman of the board of the Ladies Professional Golf Association. In the courtroom, the serious, square-jawed Strubing reminded one of the high-powered, imported prosecutor played by George C. Scott in *Anatomy of a Murder*.

Atlanta lawyer Welborn Cody, number-two partner in the prominent firm of Kilpatrick, Cody, Rogers, McClatcher, and Regenstein, was in charge of trial strategy and tactics for the *Post*. Balding and solemn, the bespectacled Cody's appearance at age 64 belied the fact that he had starred as a varsity baseball player at the University of Georgia. A seasoned trial lawyer, Cody specialized in insurance defense work. Strubing had hired him on Cook Barwick's recommendation, which was based in part on Cody's recent successful defense of ABC in a libel suit. A reporter described Cody in court as "plain, mild mannered, quite confident."

Butts's principal lawyer was 48-year-old William Schroder of the equally prominent Atlanta firm of Troutman, Sams, Schroder, and Lockerman. He had played football at Notre Dame and coached the freshman team while studying law at the University of Georgia. He graduated from both schools with high academic honors. His firm's decision to represent Butts was attributed by some to the influence of the firm's senior partner, Henry Troutman. At 77, Troutman was a lifelong follower of Georgia football and a loyal friend of Wally Butts.

Like Cody, Schroder was an experienced and successful trial lawyer, but not as mild-mannered or low-keyed. He was silver-haired and lean, without a line on his face, and his courtroom style was to pounce with the quickness of a puma and to press tenaciously for every possible advantage.

Cody and Schroder were the principal protagonists in the trial, although both had the assistance of numerous younger associates who moved in and out. At one point twelve lawyers were counted at the counsel tables, seven at one and five at the other. Schroder's principal assistant was an older partner, Allen Lockerman, a tough, grizzled former FBI agent who had helped gun down John Dillinger.

On the eve of the trial, Butts was clearly the underdog. Not only was his personal and professional deterioration widely known, but he faced a wealthy corporation and a respected national magazine of established integrity, long symbolized by the portrait of Benjamin Franklin on its masthead. Among themselves, Atlanta lawyers were saying that Butts's reputation had sunk so low that no jury in the state of Georgia would return a verdict for him. A supporter of Butts, sportswriter Benny Marshall of the *Birmingham News*, said of the pretrial atmosphere:

> Because Georgia's president had lent his office to the kangaroo court that Cook conducted, and Johnny Griffith, the coach, had gone along, Butts would have to bring suit in a city in a state which had heard nothing except ill of him for months.

This was a rare twist on the typical scenario of a local citizen suing an out-of-state corporation. Usually the "foreign" corporation is the likely victim of local prejudice. It is for this reason that federal courts have jurisdiction over cases between citizens of different states.

The trial began at 10 A.M. on Monday, August 5. The setting was the Old Post Office and Court House Building, a solemn granite edifice typical of the federal buildings constructed in the thirties. Its dignified presence, silhouetted against booming Atlanta's new skyscrapers, gave those approaching it a feeling that it might truly house a temple of justice.

Judge Morgan's courtroom was on the third floor and could be reached by marble staircases or charming old, manually operated elevators. Like most federal courtrooms of the period, it had a high ceiling and walls paneled in dark mahogany. For spectators in the rear of the 200-seat room, the acoustics left much to be desired. A modern working clock hung on the rear wall. Beside it was an antique clock, stopped forever at 9:40, a silent monument to the federal bureaucracy.

The courtroom was filled well before the trial began. Wally Butts's wife and three attractive grown daughters had reserved seats in the front row behind him and his counsel. Cook Barwick and I were seated inside the rail, between Butts and his family. Barwick was not to be a witness, despite his involvement; he was present as a representative of the University of Georgia. Like the SEC, the university was an interested third party whose officials wanted a legal observer. Judge Morgan had accommodated us with seats almost as good as those of counsel.

Promptly at ten o'clock, a U.S. marshal shouted, "Everyone rise." As we stood, Judge Morgan emerged from his chambers, black robe swirling, and strode briskly to his high-backed swivel chair behind the bench. His first order of business was to read an order banning all photo, tape, and broadcasting equipment from the entire building. He then quoted a recent statement of the U.S. Judicial Conference condemning the use of cameras in court proceedings. Though he did not say why he had imposed stricter regulations than the Judicial Conference advised, this was our first hint of his determination to maintain maximum calm and dignity throughout the trial.

Jury selection went rapidly. The usual questions about relationships with parties, witnesses, and counsel produced only one excuse for cause: one man's wife worked for Curtis Publishing Company. Another prospective juror was excused when he admitted that he had formed an opinion on the basis of pretrial publicity. Of three who had played football, only one was selected, and he as an alternate.

When asked if any of them subscribed to *The Saturday Eve-*

ning Post, six prospective jurors raised their hands. None subscribed to any other of four named Curtis publications: *Holiday,*
Ladies' Home Journal, American Home, and *Jack and Jill.* On
further questioning, one of the six said he had been subscribing
to the *Post* for 25 to 30 years. Another said, "many years." Both
were accepted for the jury. But a matronly woman who had
subscribed to the magazine "off and on for 30 years" was removed
by Butts's lawyers when each side was allowed its three strikes.
The strategy behind this decision might have been that an all-
male jury would operate to Butts's advantage, particularly if evidence about Evelyn were admitted.

The 12 finally chosen were an all-male, all-white cross-section
of middle-class citizens from Atlanta and northern Georgia, including a feed mill operator, an architect, a mechanic, a su-
permarket clerk, a landlord, a finance company clerk, a former
deputy sheriff, and a lumberjack. They ranged in age from 40
to 60. The jurymen seemed to relish their selection.

Over the next eleven days, these men would hear the testimony
of 35 sworn witnesses; the transcript of the trial would exceed
1,400 pages. Yet much of what the jury saw was not incorporated
into the official record, including a film of the game, which was
not entered as an exhibit. Football coaches who testified made
liberal use of chalk and a blackboard to diagram plays and formations. These were quickly erased and lost to the record and
to history.

In an attempt to recapture the emotionally charged atmosphere
in the courtroom, the following account of the trial draws on
both the official transcript and personal observations noted down
at the time. The testimony of every witness is reflected, though
greater emphasis is given to the handful of witnesses who were
key to the principal issues: (1) Did the phone call occur? (2)
What was said? (3) How did it affect the game?

The opening statements to the jury by opposing counsel brought
no surprises. Cody and Schroder outlined the proof they planned
to put before the jury. Cody said the *Post* stood behind the truth
of its claim in the "fix" article that Butts had passed information

to Bryant that was calculated to influence the results of the Alabama-Georgia game of September 22. Schroder pointed out that although Curtis had the burden of proof in the case, Butts's counsel would not have to rely on that "technicality." Rather, he stressed, "We are going to show Wally Butts did not and could not have done these things."

Normally the plaintiff (Butts in this instance) has the burden of proof and presents his evidence first. If he does not make out a *prima facie* case—that is, offer enough proof so that a jury can reasonably find for him—then the defendant wins without offering any evidence; the judge simply directs a verdict for the defendant. In a few exceptional cases, however, the defendant has the burden of proof. As the law stood in 1963, a defendant such as Curtis, who relied on truth as a defense in a libel action, had the burden of proving the truth of its defamatory publication.

In an emotional case like this one, it really mattered little where the burden of proof lay. Both parties were claiming that truth was on their side, and neither would make technical arguments based on burdens of proof. The case was sure to go to the jury.

Having the burden of proof meant that the *Post* went first in presenting its evidence. At this initial stage, Curtis only needed to offer enough proof to escape a directed verdict, and Burnett's testimony alone was sufficient.

As the trial began, the *Post*'s lawyers conspicuously violated a cardinal rule of corporate representation in court: besides them, no one from Curtis Publishing Company was there. It is an elementary strategy to have at least one representative of a corporation—the higher placed, the better—present in the courtroom to remind the jury that human beings are involved on both sides, not just an impersonal legal entity against an individual.

Cody's opening piece of evidence was the article itself, which he read aloud. Schroder objected to the references to Burnett's passing a lie detector test. Judge Morgan allowed the jury to hear this but instructed them that lie detector results were not admissible as evidence for judging George Burnett's truthfulness but only for mitigating any damages that might be awarded the plaintiff because of "the credence which the defendant might have lent to the test."

The toll ticket of the phone call from Butts to Bryant on Thursday, September 13, 1963, was then placed in evidence. Its date revealed the first inaccuracy in the *Post* article: Graham had written that Burnett overheard the call on Friday, September 14. This may have been a minor, immaterial discrepancy, but it was ironic that the very first sentence contained so basic an error.*

Both sides of this ticket are reproduced on page 99. The time and date appear on one side, the parties to the call on the other. The operator apparently misunderstood Butts and recorded Bryant as "Coach Paul Brince," foreshadowing George Burnett's own mistakes in spelling players' names after hearing Butts pronounce them.

The defendant's next exhibit was the record of a 67-minute call to Butts at home on September 16. It was placed from Tuscaloosa and was later conceded to have been made by Bryant. This corroborated Burnett's statement in the article that Bryant would call Butts at home the next Sunday.

The first witness Cody called to the stand was George Burnett. The stocky, balding 40-year-old took the oath calmly and responded to Welborn Cody's questions in a detached and unemotional manner. After briefly confirming the *Post*'s account of how he happened to get plugged into Butts's call, Burnett testified that Bryant's first words were "Hello, Wally," followed by Butts saying, "Hello, Bear," to which Bryant responded, "Do you have anything for me?" whereupon Butts began talking about the Georgia football team.

Burnett was allowed to rely on his original notes to refresh his memory about further details. The seven pages of gray 4 × 6-inch scratch-pad notes (reproduced on pages 41–47) were

---

* Burnett's affidavit said the call occurred on Friday, September 13. This was impossible; the thirteenth fell on Thursday. Graham caught Burnett's mistake but made an unlucky guess in choosing between Thursday and Friday.

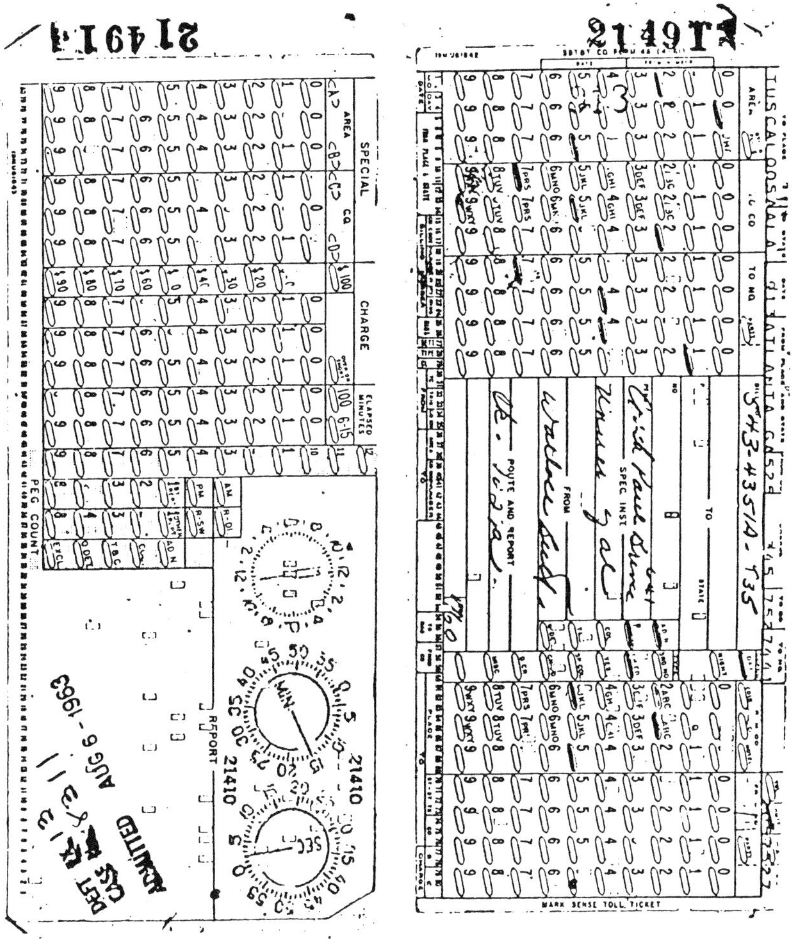
21491T
MARK SENSE TOLL TICKET
TUSCALOOSA ALA
ATLANTA GA
SPECIAL
CHARGE
PEG COUNT
REPORT
21410
AUG 9 - 1963

stipulated to have been in the possession of Cook Barwick since January 29, 1963. From this point on, the central focus of the trial would be the conversation allegedly reflected in the Burnett notes. The notes were the defendant's detailed proof of the article's general accusation that Butts "outlined Georgia's offensive plays for Bryant and told him how Georgia planned to defend against Alabama's attack."

Contrary to the article's statement that he "recorded all that he heard," Burnett testified that he did not start taking notes for a minute and a half, and that even then he did not record everything. Later, on cross-examination, when asked if he took notes on all that he considered to be "significant," he responded:

> No, sir; not exactly. I was taking notes, Mr. Schroder, as they were talking. What was significant and what was insignificant at the time I had no way of knowing. I was writing the notes as fast as I could, but not taking shorthand, abbreviating when I could. There were things that were said as I was writing that I didn't catch all of it and didn't write down.

Burnett's description of the conversation added little to the notes. Most of the entries meant nothing more to him than what he had written. One note he did enlarge upon was "well disciplined ball club—added two coaches." Burnett recalled that Butts had also said that the team's discipline was "no thanks to John Griffith," implying that the two new assistant coaches were responsible for it. On cross-examination, Schroder questioned Burnett at length about his use of the term "well-disciplined" in the notes. Schroder's purpose was unclear. Was he implying that the term "discipline" was not meaningful in football and would not have been used by Butts? He established only that to Burnett it had the same meaning as it would have in a military sense.

Burnett said his note "29–0 series" was based on a statement by Butts to Bryant to the effect: "You remember my 29–0 series. They're using that."

And the note "can't quick kick" referred to an exchange in which Bryant asked, "What about quick kicks?" and Butts answered, "Don't worry, they haven't got anyone who can do it."

Burnett could not clarify the note "don't overshift," and on cross-examination Schroder's sharp questioning revealed that Burnett didn't know what the term meant in regard to football:

Q. The next note reading "don't overshift." I recall you saying that that had to do with some defensive maneuver.

A. No, sir; I didn't say that.

Q. Well, I'm sorry; I didn't mean to misquote you. What was it you said?

A. I said I wrote this down by itself. I don't recall whether it had anything to do with the play above or not. The statement was made by Coach Butts to Coach Bryant, "Don't overshift," telling him not to overshift.

Q. Not to overshift what, offensively or defensively?

A. His defense.

Q. His defense?

A. His defense.

Q. Of course, you don't know that overshifting is a principal part of every defense of every team?

A. I don't know what?

Q. Overshifting is a principal part of every defense of every team that plays football?

A. Overshifting?

Q. Yes.

A. No; I don't know that overshifting—

Q. You don't—

A. —is a principal part of defense. I'm sorry.

Q. And you are a football fan?

A. Yes; I am a football fan. If you overshift, you are in trouble, Mr. Schroder.

Q. Explain that to me, please, sir.

A. You shift yourself out of position, I imagine.

Q. Well, not what you imagine; I mean, you must tell me about this overshifting and how it gets you into trouble.

A. Well, you can overshift on a spread formation, and they will go the other way on you, and you are in trouble.

Q. What is a spread formation?

A. When the teams are all spread out, the offense is all spread out.

Q. You mean great distances are between the offensive players?

A. That's right.

Q. And your description of overshifting is that if you over-shifted in that sort of a situation and they went the other way, you would be in trouble?

A. Yes, sir.

Q. You don't know that the basic defense of Georgia is over-shifting, an overshift, as is Alabama's?

A. No; I don't.

Q. You don't?

A. I don't know that.

(Experts later confirmed that Schroder was right and Burnett wrong about the meaning of "overshift." Butts would probably not have said simply, "don't overshift." It was never suggested that he might have used the term in some larger context.)

The exchange on overshifting did establish one important fact: Burnett's knowledge of football terminology and the technical aspects of the game was limited.

None of the players named in the notes were familiar to Bur-nett. He was not allowed to testify that he learned later that he had misspelled some of their names. He had never attended a Georgia football game and did not follow the team closely.

On cross-examination, Burnett was asked if he had heard Butts tell Bryant that Georgia quarterback Larry Rakestraw tipped his plays by the position of his feet—one of the chief allegations in the article. Burnett answered that he did not hear this and that he had made no such statement to Frank Graham, Jr.* He did not speak to Graham after the sportswriter left Atlanta and did not receive a copy of the article for proofreading.

Burnett admitted to Schroder that when Cook Barwick asked him if he had a record, he falsely answered that he did not. But he added that he authorized Barwick to investigate his background. He also admitted that he promised Barwick that he would not sell his story for publication.

Schroder drew another admission from Burnett; in his discussion of the phone call with business associates Milton Flack and John Carmichael, he agreed with Carmichael that on the basis of what he had overheard, he wouldn't have known how to bet on the game.

Burnett's testimony began on Monday, the first day of the trial, and was completed late Tuesday morning. On the whole, his demeanor on the stand was impressive, and his testimony stood up well. Nothing was made of the bad checks in his background. He was weakened on cross-examination only on minor matters, not on anything that challenged the truth of his basic story. Unlike subsequent witnesses, he was not excused when he left the stand. Bill Schroder asked that he be held for further questioning. But his hopes to weaken Burnett's testimony on further cross-examination never materialized. Burnett spent the balance of the trial waiting in the witness room; he was never recalled to the stand.

With the Burnett notes admitted as evidence, Cody's next move was an attempt to link Butts to the conversation shown in the notes. The instrument of this linkage was to be Butts's old nemesis, University of Georgia treasurer J. D. Bolton. Bolton testified that he had first seen the notes on Thursday, January 24, at a Southeastern Conference meeting at the Biltmore Hotel in Atlanta, in the room of Georgia head football coach Johnny Grif-

---

* Graham said Flack and Howard supplied this. Flack had seen the notes on the day of the call and may have mistakenly enlarged on the "Rakestraw to the right" entry.

fith. He said Griffith delivered the notes on Saturday morning to University of Georgia president O. C. Aderhold, who turned them over that very night to Cook Barwick, attorney and member of the Georgia Athletic Board. Bolton and Aderhold drove to Atlanta to deliver the notes to Barwick at his home.

On February 22, Bolton attended a meeting in Cook Barwick's Atlanta office at which Butts, President Aderhold, James Dunlap, chairman of the Georgia board of regents, and Bernie Moore, commissioner of the Southeastern Conference, among others, were present. Bolton was asked what comments Butts made when he first saw Burnett's notes. The treasurer replied that Butts looked at the notes and said:

> "No doubt the guy heard what he said he heard. I don't blame him for placing the interpretation that he did on the conversation. If I had been in his place, I probably would have thought the same thing, but he is mistaken. It's just conversation, ordinary football talk among coaches, and you know I would not give old Bryant anything to help him and hurt Georgia. If I did give any information to hurt Georgia, it was not intentional."

Bolton's testimony that Butts had admitted that Burnett had "heard what he said he heard" corroborated the authenticity of Burnett's notes, but it told the jury nothing about the meaning or value of the information contained in them. Could it have been just "ordinary football" talk as Butts claimed? The defendant's key witness on this issue was John Griffith, head coach of the football team Bryant and Butts had discussed.

Slight, low-key, and soft-spoken, Griffith hardly looked the part. He took the oath with obvious discomfort. It soon became apparent that he was a reluctant witness and that he never dreamed that his lending credence to George Burnett's story would have led to this. Griffith's original sense of betrayal and indignation seemed to have fallen by the wayside.

Cody first asked him about Georgia's general plan for the 1962

Alabama game. Griffith responded that although a team normally used seven to nine offensive formations in the course of a season, he had decided to limit his offense to two standard formations for the opening game. The number of sophomores he was playing with dictated simplicity. Griffith found that both formations were described in Burnett's notes: "Slot to right / ends normal 3 yds" was the slot formation; "Slot right / left end out 15 yards" was the pro-set formation. On cross-examination Griffith admitted that both formations had been used by Georgia the year before and that both were probably used by every team in the conference.

Griffith explained that the note "Optional left pass" was Butts's name for a pass play. He was sure the term was no longer used in 1962, though he was not sure about 1961, his first year as head coach. On cross-examination he admitted that the term had been used in one game plan early in 1961.

Of the note "On side guard pulls on sweep," Griffith said Georgia pulled its onside (strong side) guards on sweeps in the second half against Alabama.

He confirmed Burnett's note that safetyman Brigham Woodward ("Woodard" in the notes) committed himself fast on defense. (This meant that he had a tendency to come up to the line of scrimmage before knowing whether the opponent's offense would run or pass, thereby taking the chance that a pass might be completed behind him in the safetyman's zone.) When Schroder cross-examined Griffith on this note, however, he gained an admission that it was information Bryant should already have known:

Q. Woodward was not a sophomore, was he?
A. No, sir; he was not.
Q. Woodward had played an entire season as safetyman for Georgia in 1961, hadn't he?
A. Yes, sir.
Q. Georgia was scouted by Alabama in 1961, weren't they?
A. Yes, sir.

Q. Alabama had films of the Georgia games in 1961, didn't they?

A. Yes, sir.

Q. Well, it would be no news to anybody coaching Alabama that Woodward committed fast, would it?

A. No, sir.

Indeed, Schroder's whole cross-examination of Griffith was calculated to prove that the notes were merely a collection of innocent, meaningless, or inaccurate pieces of information. Item by item, he had a plausible basis for challenging the accusation that Butts had passed on secret information to Bryant. His approach succeeded in eliciting admissions from Griffith that minimized the significance of most of the notes. Here are a few examples:

• "Slot right—right half on fly / screen to him" did describe a Georgia screen pass play, but the pass was thrown to the left half on the fly, not the right half.

• "Long count / left half in motion" is a common offensive technique used by Georgia and many other teams. Taken alone it is only an action of the halfback, not a play.

• Georgia had no "29–0 series," although it had a "0–29" series.

• "Can't quick kick" was challenged by Schroder as inaccurate. Griffith admitted that his second-string quarterback, Saye, could quick-kick, but only from a double-wing formation. He had done this once in 1961.

• "Ga.—drop end off / contain with tackle" is a defensive stunt used by many teams, including Georgia. Schroder described it as a common defense against a pro-set passing situation. (No one ever mentioned the fact that this note followed the one describing the pro-set formation.)

• The note "Slot or wide slot till goal line" should not have been news to Bryant. It is common for teams to tighten up offensive formations in goal-line situations.

• The cryptic note "Rt. halfback on fly—lt. halfback / Q.B.

gives to L.H. / L.G. pulling blocks on corner," made no sense to Griffith.

Under Schroder's scrutiny the notes on players fared no better than those on plays and formations did. There were three references to a player named "Baer," who was presumed to be Georgia's star end, Mickey Babb. (Butts had a soft southern drawl and could easily have pronounced the ending of "Babb" so indistinctly that it escaped Burnett's ear.) He was the key to the Bulldog passing game, but Griffith admitted that the notes about him would have added nothing to what Bryant already knew.

"Best since Trippi / Porterfield" referred to the player Griffith regarded as Georgia's best running back, Don Porterfield, but the Georgia head coach conceded that he was not comparable to All-American Charlie Trippi, who ran, passed, kicked, and played defense when he played for Butts in the forties.

The name of Georgia's best defensive back appeared in the note "weak defense anybody except Blackburn," but Griffith again conceded that this would have told Bryant nothing new.

Sophomore tackle Ray Rissmiller was assumed to be the subject of "Reismueller Greatest-in-History." Although he was an outstanding prospect, he was still untested in conference play. In the game itself Alabama ran at him freely, and he was knocked out once.

Schroder concluded this part of his cross-examination of Griffith with two questions about the ultimate value of the notes:

Q. You testified that a good number of those notes were inaccurate and didn't even apply to anything that the University of Georgia had; is that correct?
A. Yes, sir.
Q. The only two things that you saw in those notes that, in your opinion, might be of any benefit to an opposing coach are the two formations. Correct?
A. Yes, sir.

Griffith had conceded that both formations had been used in 1961 and that Bryant should have known about them. It would have been of value to Bryant to know in advance that his opponent intended to use *only* these two formations, which was indeed what happened in the game, but this information did not appear either in the notes or in Burnett's testimony. At this point there was a vast gap between George Burnett's notes and Frank Graham's story of a "fix."

Schroder next questioned Griffith on the references to him in the *Post* article. To a greater or lesser extent, Griffith contradicted all the statements made about him: He had never threatened to resign if Butts were not fired. He never said, "We knew somebody had given our plays to Alabama," although he had said that he figured somebody had given "information" to Alabama. Nor did he say that his players came to the sidelines saying, "Coach, we have been sold out. Their linebackers are hollering out our plays while we're still calling signals." What he had said was that some players came out of the game saying, "They knew what we were going to do," or words to that effect. Finally, Griffith denied that he had ever said, "I never had a chance, did I?" as quoted in the closing lines of the article.

Griffith also testified to the inaccuracy of one statement not attributed to him in the article. When asked about the statement, disclaimed earlier by Burnett, that Butts told Bryant that Georgia quarterback Rakestraw tipped plays by the way he held his feet, Griffith said it simply was not true.

Schroder's cross-examination of Griffith on the notes was superb. Patiently, steadily, he pressed the witness into a succession of qualifications and concessions. He was perfectly prepared.

On redirect examination, Welborn Cody did virtually nothing to rehabilitate Griffith's testimony about the notes. He failed to ask such obvious questions as whether some of the entries could have been fragments of useful information or whether changing a word or two might have made an entry meaningful.

The main thing Cody revealed was his own ignorance of football in general and of this game in particular. Griffith even appeared to be embarrassed for Cody during one near-comical exchange:

Q. Now, to reduce football really to its most common denominator, what you try to do when you get the ball—see if this is correct—you have four downs to make ten yards; is that right?

A. Yes, sir.

Q. If you don't make the ten yards in four downs, what happens?

A. Well, you don't get to that fourth down as far as running the game goes. You kick the ball normally on the fourth down.

Q. And then the opponent has the ball?

A. That's correct; yes, sir.

Q. Is that when the opponent has a better opportunity to make a touchdown, when they have the ball?

A. Yes, sir.

Cody's final effort in his brief redirect examination of Griffith was to point to the one-sidedness of the game. But the only statistic he had in support of his argument was the final score. He asked Griffith about yards gained and passing completions. Griffith did not recall, and Cody did not have the facts at hand—an astonishing lapse in preparation. The huge discrepancy between Cody's and Schroder's factual preparation for the trial was frequently obvious but never more glaring than at the close of John Griffith's testimony.

Georgia assistant coaches Frank Inman and Leroy Pearce followed Griffith to the stand and repeated the general opinions they had given Attorney General Cook on the value of Burnett's notes. They both felt that knowledge of the two formations would have been particularly helpful to Bryant.

Both assistant coaches were impressive witnesses. Coach Pearce in particular came across as a thoughtful, scholarly student of the game. Unlike Griffith, he took issue with the aggressive Schroder several times during cross-examination. At one point he accused Schroder of being "technical" as they argued over the difference between a guard "pulling" and a "swing block." Inman was examined by Welborn Cody, whose direct examination filled only 7 pages in the trial transcript. Pearce was examined by Thomas Joiner, a young associate in Cody's firm. Joiner had done a much more thorough job in preparing himself for the witness and filled 36 pages with direct examination, provoking 31 pages of contentious cross-examination by Schroder.

Pearce offered further insights into the special problems of preparing a team's defenses for an opening game. From one year to the next, coaches commonly change their entire offense. If a major change is to be made, it will appear in the opening game— such changes are impossible thereafter. For planning defense the opening game differs from all later games in that a coach's information is limited to films and scouting reports of the preceding year and the spring intrasquad game, much of which might well be obsolete.

Commenting on specific items in the notes, Pearce said that safetyman Woodward made several tackles at the line of scrimmage in the Alabama game as a result of committing himself early. A long count with a halfback in motion was practiced for the Alabama game and used in it. The coaches worked hard at getting an exact three-yard slot in the slot formation, as described in the notes. Advance knowledge of the width of the slot in the slot formation would be very helpful to an opponent in coaching defensive ends. In sum, the Burnett notes appeared to Pearce to be directly concerned with the offense Georgia planned to use in the Alabama game.

Portions of Georgia's film of the game were shown during Pearce's testimony. He pointed out the slot and pro-set formations, a halfback in motion, a guard pulling on a sweep, and safety Woodward committing fast—all of which were mentioned in Burnett's notes.

The subject of secrecy in football came up in both assistant coaches' testimony. Pearce was asked by Tom Joiner to state what measures his team took to prevent other teams from obtaining information. In response he described Georgia's "closed practices," which were conducted behind a wall, with a manager posted at the entrance to keep out unauthorized persons. Joiner then asked him about Georgia's use of "play groups." He explained that Georgia broke its players into groups of backs, ends, and linemen, and each player was given his assignment at a meeting of his group. The result was that none of the groups knew the assignments of the other groups and no opponent could obtain Georgia's complete plays without getting information from players in all three groups.

On cross-examination of Inman, Schroder sought to challenge the effectiveness of Georgia's secret practices by asking if someone could spy on Georgia's practices from the upstairs windows of the Georgia Center for Continuing Education. Inman replied that he had wondered about this himself because it was a tall building with a view of the practice field. On redirect examination Cody asked the distance from this building to the field, and Inman estimated it at 200 yards. Inman also established that Athletic Director Butts sometimes attended the closed practices Pearce had described.

The *Post* then rested its case. Spectators were surprised. So were Butts's lawyers. They had fully expected the writer and editors of the article to be put on the stand by the *Post* to defend their handiwork and, at least, to testify to their belief in its truth when they published it.

The *Post*'s case was deficient in other respects, too. At most it had established that Butts and Bryant had had the phone conversation reflected in Burnett's notes, but Schroder's cross-examination had raised doubts about whether the information conveyed by Butts was helpful to Bryant or had any effect on the play of the game. The game film had shown no instance of Alabama taking advantage of the information. Also, no motive on Butts's part to betray Georgia had emerged from the *Post*'s evidence. Observers felt that Cody must be saving something for rebuttal.

It was early on Wednesday afternoon when the *Post* rested. Schroder had planned to lead off his case with his star witness, Bear Bryant, but Bryant was not due to arrive from Tuscaloosa until that night. Bryant had been expected to testify on Thursday morning at the earliest. With time on his hands and his primary witness unavailable, Bill Schroder chose to open by filling in a major gap in the *Post*'s case. He introduced the jury to the author of the *Post*'s article by reading the deposition of Frank Graham, Jr., a seemingly key witness who had been conspicuously avoided by the *Post*.

Graham's deposition had been taken in New York in May and was now presented from the witness stand by Schroder and Allen Lockerman, with one reading the questions and the other the answers. Graham's replies were read very matter-of-factly and without feeling, making him sound as if he cared little for the human consequences of his work. It was bad enough that Graham did not testify in person; having his adversaries perform his role for him compounded the error.

In the deposition Graham first recounted the events that took him to Atlanta and led to the purchase of Burnett's story on terms negotiated with Milton Flack and Pierre Howard. He admitted that he had been told that John Carmichael was with Flack and Burnett after the call was overheard. He had also been told that Carmichael was a friend of Butts and did not want to get involved. Graham went on to claim that the reference to Rakestraw tipping his plays with his feet had come from Flack and Howard and was supposed to be checked against Burnett's notes. He said that other sources for the article included newspaper accounts of the game and Furman Bisher, who had contacted the *Post* and had been employed to complete the investigation of the story after Graham had returned to New York. The words *rig* and *fix*, he testified, were added to the story by the *Post* editors, as were the references to the Black Sox scandal and corruption. Nor was the depiction of southern coaches as "minor deities" Graham's. In fact, the editors composed the entire paragraph in which this appeared. Finally, Graham admitted that he had had Butts and Bryant in mind when he closed the story by saying that careers would be ruined.

The entire deposition consisted of Schroder's questions and Graham's answers. Although Welborn Cody had been present when the deposition was taken, he apparently had no questions for the author of the article whose truth he was defending. (He must have assumed that Graham would testify in person at the trial.)

The next day, the performance of Butts's star witness made national news. Walter Cronkite opened the CBS Evening News on Thursday, August 8, 1963, by saying, "Bear Bryant walked into an Atlanta courtroom today and laid it on the line." Cronkite's account of Bryant's testimony left no doubt that it had been forceful.

I was introduced to the tall 49-year-old coach as he arrived at the steps of the courthouse with a mutual friend, Fred Russell, sports editor of the *Nashville Banner*. He was dressed for the steamy August heat in a fashionable southerner's summer attire— seersucker jacket, dark pants, and brown alligator shoes. Bryant was polite enough as he firmly shook my hand, but his rugged countenance was unsmiling, and his words were few. He seemed grim and preoccupied. After Russell identified me as the Southeastern Conference's official observer, Bryant quickly moved by me and up the courthouse steps. (I sensed at the time that Bryant resented my presence. He confirmed my suspicions 13 years later in his autobiography. I must have symbolized the conference's treatment of him, which he viewed as one-sided and unfair because it "investigated Wally and me, but never investigated the people who were to blame for all of it—the *Post*, and the eavesdropper, and the writers.")

When Bryant first took the witness stand, his voice was surprisingly low. Schroder even had to ask him to speak up so the jury could hear him. This was never necessary again. He may have momentarily felt out of his element, but any uneasiness quickly vanished. He rose to the occasion and was soon relishing his role.

Early in his testimony Bryant was asked about his defensive planning for the game. He went to the blackboard and launched into a lengthy, complex explanation, complete with numerous diagrams. Significant parts of his testimony were not preserved; they were lost when the blackboard was erased.

Bryant's masterful fogging of the issues began with a description of his defensive strategy for the Georgia game, as the following exchange illustrates. After acknowledging his great respect for Georgia quarterback Larry Rakestraw and the need for an opponent to force him to pass instead of run, he said:

> So what we decided to do, something we didn't do very often—let's put the three-deep back here—we decided to play a five-man line, a five-three, or what amounts to a five-three. We usually play a rover, a wide tackle six, a wide tackle—I will show that. We, normally speaking, play defense like this, and put an extra man to the formation.
>
> Q. To strengthen the formation?
> A. To strengthen the formation, or to the field position. In other words, if that was on the hashmark—
> Q. Tell us what a hashmark is.
> A. A hashmark is the mark there where they put the ball down. Sixty-seven percent—normally speaking, sixty-seven percent of your football is played on one of the two hash-markings. You are only in the middle thirty-three percent of the time, normally speaking.
> Q. That is with reference to side-to-side?
> A. Yes, sir.
> Q. All right.
> A. We either put it to the formation of the extra man, or

if it is along the side of the field, we put the extra man
or double-wobble, meaning by double-wobble—let's take
the halfback, move a little wider out, move this safety
over a little bit more, and this man here plays a little
deeper because he has an extra man up there to take
care of that area. But we were afraid on that defense
that their fine quarterback would hurt us coming out
there on the option, either way, running or passing. We
decided—wait a minute; before I leave that, if we call
our north category and move the guards. In other words,
with our ends there, our tackles here, our linebackers
here and have the guards either move like that or play
balanced, and that becomes a stack, you can see where
one is stacked behind the other.

Few persons in the room understood this, especially the great
majority who could not see the blackboard, but all were impressed. Bryant played strictly to the jury, as if by a game plan,
but jurors and spectators alike—even the judge—were held spell-
bound.

When Burnett's notes were handed to Bryant, he said, "I don't
have my specs. I left them on the plane." He tried Bill Schroder's
glasses, but they didn't fit, so he used Wally Butts's instead.
(Butts himself had also had to borrow glasses to examine the
same notes in February; it was an ironic coincidence.) Bryant's
reaction to the notes was casual, almost flippant. It was as if
he were seeing them for the first time and did not consider them
important. Taking them one by one, he flatly denied that he
and Butts had ever discussed during any telephone conversation
any of the information in them except for player Ray Rissmiller,
whom Bryant had tried to recruit. He insisted that most of the
notes would have been of no help to him.

About one of the notes he quipped, "If I didn't know that,
I oughta be bored for a hollow head." In ridiculing another, Bryant
said, "If my little boy didn't do that, I would want to spank him."

In two instances Bryant denied knowledge of information that Schroder had pressed John Griffith into admitting was common knowledge. One was that safetyman Brigham Woodward committed fast; Bryant said he did not know this and that if he had known it, he would have taken advantage of Woodward by passing into his zone, which he did not do. The other was the pro-set formation. Bryant claimed that it took him by surprise; as a result his defense was in an unsound formation against it, which allowed Georgia to gain from it until the Tide made a defensive adjustment.

At times Bryant's customary self-deprecation surfaced, but always in a way that served his purposes. When Schroder read him the erroneous passage in the *Post* article about Georgia quarterback Rakestraw tipping plays by the position of his feet, Bryant responded by relating a lesson he had learned while coaching at Kentucky:

Q. Would that have been of interest to an opposing coach or opposing players, to know that a quarterback on the offensive team did have that tendency?

A. Well, sir, it might have been to some, but due to an experience I had once, it wouldn't have been to us.

Q. How is that?

A. We wouldn't have been interested at all.

Q. It is of no interest to know whether or not the quarterback is going to pass or run?

A. Well, if he knew that, but we knew that about a quarterback once, and we played him. We had gotten it out of a film, and we double-checked it the week before, and I thought we were going to win the game, and the press and experts and so forth thought we were favored, and we played the quarterback, and were beaten thirty-four to seven or thirty-four to nothing, and I haven't been interested in what quarterbacks do anymore.

Q. What team was it?

A. It was L.S.U., that means Louisiana State University, L.S.U., when I was with Kentucky.*

Thus, Bryant swore that what had appeared to be the most incriminating accusation against Butts and him in the *Post* article involved information he would not have used even if Butts had told him and it had been true. Although the information did not appear in Burnett's notes, Bryant's testimony managed to undermine the very idea that material of the sort found in the notes or alleged in the article could ever have been useful to him.

Bryant claimed that coaches frequently talk to each other by phone. He could not remember anything specific about the calls of September 13 and 16, but supposed that he and Butts could have talked about such matters as tickets, finances, bands, scheduling, rules on roughness, and investments. He concluded his remarks about phone calls between coaches on a characteristically sarcastic note:

> I used to talk to Coach Woodruff down in Florida, and I probably shouldn't say this, but Coach Woodruff is longer-winded on the phone than Coach Butts is. You get him on there, and you are going to miss dinner.

At this point Schroder asked him directly whether he and Butts had had the telephone conversation reflected in Burnett's notes. Bryant categorically denied it. Pressing further, Schroder asked whether the information in the notes would have been of any assistance to him, and he replied:

> Sir, there may have been a couple of things in there I would have rather known than not known, but those

---

* As mentioned earlier (see p. 10), in his autobiography Bryant related an almost identical incident, but the point he made was just the opposite. In that case he boasted of using similar information about a quarterback to defeat the Georgia Bulldogs when he was at Texas A & M.

notes, as far as I am concerned, would not help me one
iota. As a matter of fact, all it would do is get me confused.
The kind of things I want to know weren't in the notes.

When queried about the sorts of things he would like to know,
he went to the blackboard again and gave another dazzling chalk
talk. He said that first of all he would like to know an opponent's
game plan, adding quickly that "the kind of stuff we have been
talking about is not the game plan." Using the blackboard, he
said that the next thing he would like to know was what an
opponent was going to do on the hashmarks and in midfield.
He would then like to know what his opponent would do on
first downs and on the five or seven big plays between the 20-
yard lines that determine the outcome of every game. Bryant
was particularly impressive in analyzing the value of knowing
an opponent's first-down tendencies:

> Now, the next thing I'd like to know is, you have eleven
> to fourteen or fifteen first downs in the ball game. You
> are going to get the ball, normally speaking, from eleven
> to fourteen or fifteen times. If you get it any more than
> that, you are getting beat and they are kicking off to
> you. What I want to know, both offensively and defen-
> sively, I want to know what they are going to do on first
> down, because it is a guessing game on first down. After
> the first down somebody has an advantage, see . . .

By this time Bryant had been talking at some length without
interruption. Suddenly he cut himself off, saying, "I know I am
talking too much," promised to sit down soon, and went right
on talking about the usefulness of knowing an opponent's big-
play tendencies. He then expressed a total lack of concern for
an opponent's tendencies or plans on the goal line, implying that
his team had the ability to make a goal-line stand regardless
of the plays used by a foe.

Finally, with the skill of a championship debater, still standing at the blackboard, Bryant summed up:

> So, if you will tell us what they are going to do field position-wise, and what they are going to do on first down, and what they are going to do on these big downs, five to seven of them, then we have a game plan, and if you can't win then, why, you are playing somebody that is an awfully lot better than you are. Does that answer your question?

Schroder had no further questions on this subject.

Though this part of Bryant's testimony was a powerful assault on the value of the Burnett notes, he did confirm that there are secrets in football and that some forms of advance information about an opponent would enable him to defeat any team except a vastly superior one. His main point was that the type of advance information that would be meaningful to him differed greatly from the information in the Burnett notes.

The emotional high point of Bryant's testimony was his last answer on direct examination. Schroder read the editorial introduction to the *Post* article, spitting out the words *fix, sell out,* and *corrupt,* and asked if he and Butts had thrown, fixed, or rigged the game. Bryant replied angrily, "Absolutely not, and if we did, we ought to go to jail, and anybody that had anything to do with this ought to go to jail, because we didn't. Taking their money is not good enough."

On cross-examination Welborn Cody did not score a single point. Bryant showed Cody the same contempt he had just shown toward those responsible for the *Post* article. At several points Cody was visibly taken aback by the ferocity of Bryant's answers.

The thrust of Cody's attack was on Bryant's claim that he did not remember specifically what he and Butts had talked about in any particular phone call and could only conjecture about what they might have discussed. When asked about the March 6 letter from Alabama President Rose to Georgia President Aderhold in which Rose related the account Bryant had given him of the call, Bryant vehemently denied every statement attributed to him by Rose. He closed the subject by saying, "You get him up here. He'll clear that up."

Bryant aggressively volunteered information beyond the scope of Cody's questions. In answer to a question about the September 13 phone call, he said, "I don't even know the call was made. I am not sure all these notes weren't made after the call was made." This brought a motion from Cody to strike the answer as unresponsive. Judge Morgan said simply, "Well, let's get the session down to what the facts are."

Cody questioned Bryant briefly about his and Butts's investment in the stock of Louis Wolfson's Continental Enterprises venture, a topic both he and Butts said they might have talked about by phone. Bryant placed his current loss at $30,000 but added that overall he was still a "pretty good" winner on the stock because he had bought and sold some of it earlier at a profit.

On this Cody ended his cross-examination; he gave up after only ten minutes. Schroder waived redirect examination; there was no damage to be repaired.

Bryant's performance did not stop when he was excused as a witness. The previous witnesses had left the courtroom immediately, most with obvious relief, but not the Bear. A few steps from the witness stand, he hesitated, looked around at no one in particular, and said, "Can't I wait for my boys?" A chair was found for him, and he sat through the testimony of Alabama players Jimmy Sharp and Charlie Pell, a move that seemed to score him an extra point.

It was a virtuoso performance, and its effect was enormous. Bryant's denials of guilt could not have been more forcefully delivered. His football genius and his powerful personal presence left one convinced that a team coached by Johnny Griffith would never come close to beating a team coached by Bear Bryant and that Bryant would never really need improper advance information for such a game. Bryant continues to be the single most

Paul (Bear) Bryant played end on the University of Alabama team that defeated Stanford in the 1935 Rose Bowl. The great Don Hutson was his opposite.

Bear Bryant celebrating in the University of Kentucky dressing room with Kentucky governor Happy Chandler, later Commissioner of Baseball, after Bryant's first major bowl contest, a 13–7 victory in the 1951 Sugar Bowl. His Kentucky Wildcats handed Bud Wilkenson's great Oklahoma team one of their rare defeats.

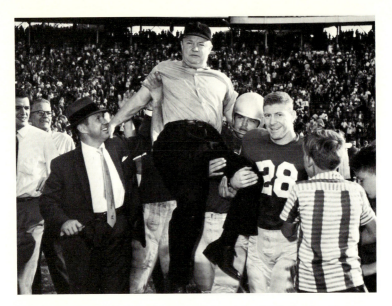

Players and fans carrying Wally Butts from the field after his Georgia
Bulldogs defeated Missouri, 14–0, in the 1960 Orange Bowl. This was
the last bowl game he ever coached.

Wally Butts (*left*) congratulating his successor as head football coach
at Georgia, John Griffith (*right*), 1961. University president O.C.
Aderhold looks on.

Frank Graham, Jr., free-lance author of The *Saturday Evening Post* article, "The Story of a College Football Fix."

BELOW, RIGHT: Key witness George Burnett, who overheard the controversial Butts-Bryant phone call, entering the federal court building in Atlanta on the first day of the trial.

Federal District Judge Lewis R. (Pete) Morgan was a model of judicial temperament in presiding over a difficult and nationally spotlighted case.

OPPOSITE PAGE: Bear Bryant (*center*) and Winston McCall, his personal Birmingham attorney (*left*), approaching the Atlanta federal courthouse on the morning of Bryant's testimony.

RIGHT: Welborn Cody, the *Post*'s leading trial counsel, appears to be puzzling over one of his many tough strategy decisions.

BELOW: William Schroder (*center*), Wally Butts's chief lawyer, arriving at the courthouse with star witness Charlie Trippi, former Georgia All-American and assistant coach (*right*).

John Carmichael, former business partner of George Burnett, arrives at the courthouse to testify that Burnett's controversial notes were a fabrication.

The *Saturday Evening Post* editor-in-chief, Clay Blair, Jr., arriving at the trial during its second week. Like author Frank Graham and other *Post* editors involved in the "fix" article, he was never placed on the witness stand to testify in person.

University of Alabama president Frank Rose, called as a witness against Butts by the *Post.*

Furman Bisher, sports editor of the *Atlanta Journal*, who wrote an earlier anti-Bryant article for the *Post* and contributed disputed quotes to the "fix" article.

Wally Butts gets a kiss of congratulations from his wife, Winnie, as their three daughters look on at a celebration and press conference just after his stunning jury verdict was announced.

awesome figure this writer has ever seen in a courtroom, including lawyers and judges.

Three Alabama players testified for Butts. They all commented on the effectiveness of the pro-set formation when it was used by Georgia in the first half. Jimmy Sharp, a guard, said Alabama was "totally unprepared" for it and was thrown into "mass confusion." Both Sharp and tackle Charlie Pell testified that they had expected the slot formation because it had been used for 109 of 113 plays in Georgia's spring game. The pro-set, however, which Georgia used five times in the first half, succeeded because Bama was in an unsound defense against it, and All-American linebacker LeRoy Jordan had to move out wide to cover Georgia's split end, when his defensive strength was needed in the middle.

LeRoy Jordan himself testified on a later day, flying in from the Dallas Cowboys' training camp. He said Alabama had been coached to expect four formations—slot, unbalanced, regular T, and slot with man in motion—and that they were surprised by the pro-set, "which took me out of the action on running plays—I had to move out on the split end."

Jordan looked at Burnett's notes and found nothing in them that Alabama had concentrated on in preparation for the Georgia game. He remembered that there were no changes in Alabama's plans during the week before the game and that no names of Georgia players were particularly emphasized.

Schroder asked each of the three Alabama players a question of very dubious admissibility: "In your opinion could two coaches rig or fix the outcome of a football game without the players' knowledge?" The *Post*'s lawyers did not object to the question. All three players answered in the negative. On cross-examination, Cody failed to ask the obvious question of how a player would know the sources of a coach's information about an opponent.

After letting Schroder get away with murder in this and so many other ways, Cody finally raised one of his few objections. It came on Schroder's last question to LeRoy Jordan. Schroder asked the All-American what his weight had been for the game. The objection to the irrelevant question was of course sustained.

(Jordan had probably weighed about 185 pounds, exceptionally light for a star linebacker.) It seemed at the time that Cody was straining at gnats and swallowing camels.

Cody did not cross-examine Sharp or Pell. When Jordan testified, however, Cody was armed with an Alabama football publication, from which he read the names of the current—1963—coaching staff. Among them were Jimmy Sharp and Charles Pell, a fact that had not been disclosed when they testified, even though the judge had asked one of them whether he was studying to be a coach. Cody also drew from Jordan the admission that Georgia had gained only 37 yards on the ground.

The three Alabama players were very impressive. Each came across as intelligent, clean-cut, and sincere. (Two went on to become head coaches—Pell at Florida and Sharp at Virginia Tech.) They were credits to Bryant, to the University of Alabama, and to college football. They seemed to belie the *Post* article's accusation that their sport was tainted by corruption.

On the fifth day of the trial, Friday, August 9, the courtroom filled up early, and there was a sense of great anticipation in the air; Wally Butts was about to testify. He was flushed and nervous as he took the oath, his face lined with fatigue. Outlining his background and accomplishments in football seemed to warm the Little Round Man to his task, however, and by the time he told of his 1960 resignation from the Georgia coaching job, which he attributed to high blood pressure, he was surprisingly relaxed.

Butts had no specific recollection of the September 13 and 16 phone calls. He called Bryant many times, he claimed, often "on impulse, for no reason." Of the length of the 67-minute call, he said, "That doesn't impress me." One thing he did recall discussing with Bryant during that period was a new NCAA and SEC policy of tougher enforcement of roughness rules. He had called Bryant about it in July after an NCAA committee meeting in Buffalo. When asked what other topics thay might have talked about, he mentioned almost exactly the same things as Bryant had. Mutual aid between coaches, he said, had accounted for many of his phone calls over the years, and he proceeded to give examples of the kinds of "coaching points" that were commonly swapped. One was to instruct a pass receiver running a sideline route to stay within four yards of the sideline. He had never turned down a fellow coach's request for a coaching point and would never have hesitated to ask archrival Bobby Dodd "exactly how he runs his plays."

Butts's testimony on the Burnett notes sent him to the blackboard several times to diagram plays and formations. Unlike Bryant, Butts was affable and mellow and even permitted himself a good-natured wisecrack now and then. When diagramming the option left pass, he said at one point, "Now, this is a tight line, which is something you gentlemen haven't seen much of in this coaching clinic."

Butts used Schroder and his son, a college student, to help him act out a demonstration of Woodward committing too fast. By this time he was confident and poised.

Like Bryant, Butts asserted that except for Rissmiller, they had never discussed any of the items in the notes in a telephone conversation, and as far as Rissmiller was concerned, they had only talked about how he was recruited, not his play.

"Well-disciplined" was a term Butts said he would not have used to describe Griffith's team at that time. Nor would he have offered a judgment of their discipline because he had not seen the first and second teams scrimmage. To demonstrate what the term *discipline* meant to him, he went to the blackboard and illustrated both the "application of discipline under game conditions" and how a lack of discipline cost Georgia three touchdowns in the Alabama game. This was not intended by Butts to be criticism. "It's hard to start sophomores against Alabama," he said.

In his testimony Butts called the pro-set formation "slot left, right end split," which came very close to the description of it in Burnett's notes.

He said that pulling onside guards on sweeps was not done in the Southeastern Conference; outside the conference it was done only at Missouri and Delaware. If you tried it in the SEC against a "loose-six defense," he said,"you would have extreme difficulty in getting back to the line of scrimmage."

Butts contradicted Bryant on one point, the matter of Woodward committing fast. (Griffith had admitted that Bryant should have known this; Bryant said he did not know it and would have taken advantage of it if he had known.) Butts insisted that "Woodard" (as he called him) was not weak on pass defense and that there was no way to take advantage of him because he might or might not commit early on a given play. Butts claimed he had never seen anyone take advantage of Woodward.

He challenged Burnett's final note by saying that he had never known Bryant to set up a future phone call with him.

Though Butts denied that he deliberately attempted to undermine Coach John Griffith by openly criticizing him, on the stand he was unable to suppress his disapproval of Griffith's coaching. When asked whether he had known in advance which formations Georgia planned to use in the Alabama game, he replied, "No, I did not, and I would like to add to that: I was amazed and surprised that they did not do some other things that they had done well."

He then volunteered still more criticism of Griffith's coaching:

> I had no idea about the game plan or the philosophy to be employed in the game. Football coaches who have coached for a period of time usually develop a football philosophy. They believe in certain phases of the game and emphasize this. To be successful in football, a coach must establish, first of all, something they can do real well. I absolutely have no idea at the present time what the Georgia plan is.

On cross-examination Cody questioned Butts about his reaction to the Burnett notes when he first saw them in Cook Barwick's office. Butts denied making any evaluation of the notes or admitting anything more than that a conversation between him and Bryant might have been overheard. He added that he had been under pressure and did not know what the meeting was about. Cody asked, "But weren't you among friends?" Butts responded, "Do you really want me to answer that?" Cody withdrew the question as laughter in the courtroom brought an admonishment from Judge Morgan.

Cody made two attempts to link Butts to gambling. First, he questioned him at length about his connection with a business associate, Frank Childs of Gray, Georgia. Cody insinuated that newspaper accounts of a raid on a gambling house near Gray had linked Childs to its operation, but Butts denied knowing whether Childs was a gambler. Childs's name never came up again.

Cody then explored Butts's relationship with Frank Scoby, a Chicago beer dealer and business associate. Butts described Scoby as a good friend who had advised him on business matters and who had endorsed a note to help him get a loan from a Chicago bank early in 1962. When the *Post* story broke, Butts testified, Scoby was working on a deal to give him a share of a venture in a new Scotch whiskey. Butts admitted he had made 14 phone calls to Scoby in September 1962, and had charged them to his university credit card. He said he thought the calls would be charged to his home phone. He reimbursed the university after he resigned.

Butts denied that his outside business activities had interfered with his performance as athletic director, though the reason he had given for stepping down in his February letter of resignation was that his business interests were "taking too much time." That letter, he said, had been composed by an assistant to President Aderhold. Butts then admitted that the only business interest requiring his time during that period was the loan company. When asked for his real reason for resigning, he conceded that it was the Butts-Bryant incident.

Butts also admitted that his net worth was grossly falsified in the financial statement he filed with the State of Georgia in order to obtain a license for Instant Loan Company. The values of some assets were overstated, and at least three bank loans were omitted, errors he attributed to his accountant. Although the statement showed a net worth of over $200,000, he testified that he had never been worth as much as $100,000 and was now insolvent.

The most dramatic moment in the trial came on redirect examination of Butts. Schroder read to him the editorial introduction to the *Post* article, emphasizing the words *corrupt* and *fix*, and asked Butts if there was any truth to it. Butts said, "No. And I would like to explain that for a time I hid from people, but not anymore. I am looking them in the eye because it is not true." Then, unable to control himself, he burst into tears. At first he tried to stem his sobs with clenched fists and regain his composure on the witness stand. Failing that, he stumbled from the stand and slumped into a chair at his lawyers' table. Judge Morgan declared a five-minute recess.

Fred Russell described the ensuing scene for the *Nashville Banner*:

> The people in the crowded courtroom showed what they thought by their impressively respectful silence during the five-minute recess. Usually at these periods there is moving and chattering. This time everybody stayed where he was, quiet, some crying, many misty-eyed.

Butts's wife Winnie and his three daughters were among those weeping.

Butts helped his own cause on the stand. He came across as amiable, easygoing, and devoted to Georgia football. The tearful denial at the end was convincing. Could this veteran coach, with years of emotional pep talks behind him, have staged it? At this point, further doubts mounted over the basic truth of the *Post*'s story.

Cody had not yet finished his re-cross-examination of Butts when the court adjourned on Friday. The chance to study a witness's direct examination over a weekend often produces a sharper cross-examination on the following Monday, but Cody showed no sign of having taken advantage of the extra time. Schroder again waived further redirect examination.

The next seven witnesses called to testify had been involved in the game on Georgia's side and included two assistant coaches, the Bulldogs' trainer, and four players. The most notable was former All-American back Charlie Trippi, who became Georgia offensive coach in 1961 and at the time of the trial was on the staff of the St. Louis Cardinals. One of the greatest players in Bulldog history, he certainly must have had the admiration of some of the jurors. Trippi declared with feeling that the Burnett notes contained nothing of value for either offensive or defensive planning. He added, "We give more information to the press every week to promote the game than is expressed in these notes." There was no cross-examination.

John Gregory, Georgia defensive coach, testified much to the same effect, but at greater length. He went through Burnett's notes, minimizing and ridiculing them item by item, conceding none to be worthwhile. He also showed the game film, without interpretation after an early warning by Judge Morgan.

Gregory volunteered the first direct evidence that Butts attended the closed Saturday scrimmage that occurred between Butts's call to Bryant on Thursday, September 13 and Bryant's call to him on Sunday, the 16th. In evaluating a note that might have referred to Georgia's goal line offense, Gregory said, ". . . to my knowledge, the last time that Coach Butts saw Georgia practice was on Saturday, September 15." He added that plans for Georgia's goal line offense against Alabama were not made until the following Monday.

On cross-examination, Cody confronted Gregory with the statement he had signed for Georgia Attorney General Cook, in which he said that the Burnett notes contained "vital and important information that could have affected the outcome of the Alabama-Georgia game." By way of explanation, he testified that he had merely glanced at the notes before signing the statement, which the attorney general had sent to President Aderhold's office as a prepared statement. He feared Griffith would have fired him if he did not sign it, although Griffith had put no express pressure on him. (Griffith fired him immediately after the trial.)

The four Georgia players testified that the team was in poor physical condition for the game. Everyone was "leg weary" because of an unusual Thursday scrimmage, and several key players were hampered by injuries. Captain and left end Ray Clark was injured in the Thursday scrimmage and missed the game completely.

The players also testified that they did not take "a terrible physical beating," as alleged in the article. Alabama was not the sort of team that beat opponents physically, they claimed. The Tide's linemen were small and agile and tended to hit and run rather than stay and fight on the line of scrimmage. None of the four recalled anything unusual about the game, anything that indicated that the opponent might have had special advance information.

Two of the players had a year of eligibility remaining, which added to the significance of their testifying in opposition to their coach. All were impressive.

One player, end Mickey Babb, was questioned about the statement Furman Bisher attributed to him in the article, that Alabama players had taunted them by saying, "You can't run *Eighty-eight Pop* on us." He denied making the statement. (Griffith had already established the fact that Georgia had no such play.) Babb had talked to Furman Bisher in Athens in March but said that Bisher had discussed the 1961 Alabama game with him, not the 1962 game.

Sam Richwine, trainer of the Georgia team, also denied the quote attributed to him in the article. He said Bisher had questioned him only about the physical condition of the Alabama team, which he said was superb in 1962 and had been even better in 1961. Richwine insisted he had said nothing to Bisher about Alabama's knowledge of Georgia's plays.

In questioning these witnesses, Schroder continued a clever ploy he had begun when George Burnett was on the stand. Before cross-examining Burnett, Schroder set up two large, six-feet-high cardboard panels with the text of the *Post* article mocked up on them. As each successive witness identified a statement as inaccurate or misquoted, Schroder asked him to take a crayon, initial that statement, and put parentheses around it. The mockup was now so riddled with marks that it looked more like dart board than a magazine article.

The trial's biggest surprise by far came with the testimony of John Carmichael, who was the opening witness for Butts on Tuesday, August 13, the seventh day of the trial. Contradicting George Burnett, he swore that the notes in court were not the notes Burnett had shown him on September 13. In his earlier testimony for Attorney General Cook's investigation and in two depositions, Carmichael had said that he did not read or handle the notes. He now "corrected" his earlier testimony, saying, "I did not pick them up to read them, but I did read them."

How did the two sets of notes differ? This was the obvious next question, but it was not asked by Schroder on direct examination or by Cody on cross-examination. Finally, at the end of redirect examination, almost as an afterthought, Schroder asked it. Carmichael replied that Burnett was a big doodler and that the originals had many more doodles on them than the notes in court. The first page, he recalled, consisted entirely of doodles and the words *Coach Wally Butts* and *Coach Bear Bryant*. Another page had only doodles, a player's name, and the words *greatest in history*. A third was merely doodles plus an entry about Butts being home Sunday and Bryant calling him back. Nothing else in the notes on hand appeared in the originals, Carmichael insisted with certainty.

Carmichael said he had known Butts personally for 15 years, largely through minor business dealings. He did not feel compelled to inform Butts about Burnett's experience until January 30, 1963, the day Burnett told him that he had taken his notes to officials of the University of Georgia. Carmichael reached Butts by phone at a hotel in Philadelphia and filled him in on what Burnett had done. According to Carmichael, Butts's response was:

"Well, John, I appreciate you calling me, but I'll tell you this. I am sure there is nothing to it, because I don't know whether I called Coach Bryant or not, but I'll tell you this. I talk to a lot of coaches and I don't remember making a call on that particular day, but if I did, I will assure you there was nothing to it, because I would never do anything to hurt Georgia."

Carmichael was not an impressive witness. His contradiction of his earlier claim that he had not read the notes had a hollow ring to it, as did his testimony that he had in fact read all the notes without picking them up. It was odd that the only three pieces of the conversation he could recall from the "original" notes happened to be in the notes on hand, and that although he remembered nothing else from the original notes, he was certain they included none of the other items in the present notes. Quite a remarkable exercise of memory after such a brief and superficial examination of the original notes.

Carmichael's testimony corroborated Burnett's on two notes that both Butts and Bryant had denied having discussed: the "greatest in history" player and the reference to Bryant calling Butts back on Sunday. Did this mean Butts and Bryant were lying?

Bill Hartman, Wally Butts's closest friend and a key figure in his final two years with the University of Georgia, was his next witness. Hartman's intimacy with Bulldog football spanned a 25-year period and was second only to that of Wally Butts. He had been a star running back at Georgia, graduating in 1937. After playing professionally with the Washington Redskins, he returned to his alma mater as an assistant on Butts's first staff in 1939. During World War II he served in the armed forces but resumed coaching in 1946 and assisted Butts for another ten years. Though he then entered the insurance business in Athens, he continued to play a major role in university athletic and alumni affairs.

Since Hartman had been involved in the case in a number

of ways, his testimony ranged over most of the key issues. He was truly a multipurpose witness. On the stand he probably helped Butts more than he hurt him, largely because his apparent willingness to tell both the good and the bad about his old boss added to his credibility. A reliable, "old-shoe" quality came through his soft-spoken, matter-of-fact responses to questions from both sides.

Direct and cross-examination of Hartman centered on five subjects: (1) the Burnett notes, (2) Butts's reaction to those notes when he first saw them, (3) Butts's differences with the athletic board, (4) the causes of Butts's 1960 resignation as head coach, and (5) Butts's open criticism of his successor, John Griffith.

Bill Schroder first used Hartman to rebut J. D. Bolton's damaging testimony concerning the February 22 meeting with Butts in Cook Barwick's office. Bolton had claimed that after Butts read the notes, he had in effect admitted that they were accurate because he said, "No doubt that guy heard what he said he heard."

Hartman recalled it differently. He said that Butts had looked at the first page of the notes and then merely "riffled" through the other pages. Unlike Bolton, he did not think Butts had admitted having the conversation reflected in the notes. Rather, he said, Butts had admitted only that he had talked to Bryant many times and didn't doubt that "a conversation between them was overheard but that it had been 'misconstrued.' "

When Cody cross-examined him about this meeting, Hartman conceded that Butts did not deny Burnett's story. The nearest Butts came to a denial at the meeting was his repeated assertion that he never did anything to hurt Georgia.

Speaking in general about the tendency of coaches to talk to one another, Hartman said that since World War II coaches had developed a common terminology and frequently discussed each other's plays. In particular, he mentioned the annual state high school coaches' clinic, where the Georgia staff gave away the entire Georgia offense every year. Echoing Charlie Trippi's testimony, Hartman observed, "There are no secrets in football anymore."

As for Burnett's notes, Hartman belittled their value to an opponent. He found two items to be inaccurate: the references to Georgia's inability to quick-kick and to team discipline.

The relevance of Hartman's testimony on Butts's long-standing financial difficulties with the athletic board was not clear. He may have been trying to prove that there was a strong anti-Butts bias among many of the board members. But if anything, he seemed to hurt Butts's case by establishing bitterness toward the board as a possible motive for the phone call.

Since Butts himself had testified that he had resigned as coach in 1960 because of high blood pressure, Judge Morgan permitted Cody to cross-examine Hartman on the embarrassing subject of Butts's first resignation. Hartman recalled his meeting with Atlanta alumni, who had approached him to discuss Butts's "Night League" activities, which, according to Hartman, included "appearances in nightspots with girls and so forth." As a result of this meeting, Hartman said, he went to Butts and told him that Atlanta alumni felt he was hurting their recruiting efforts and that if he did not resign, they might go to the athletic board. Butts resigned soon thereafter.

It was clear to everyone in the courtroom that Hartman's role in bringing about Butts's 1960 resignation as coach had cut both ways. It was also apparent that Hartman's loyalty to and admiration for Butts had survived that painful experience.

Hartman admitted that he had heard Butts criticize John Griffith's coaching, but he had also heard him compliment Griffith. On cross-examination he added that he had heard considerable discussion among alumni throughout the state about Butts's criticism of Griffith. Asked about the nature of Butts's criticisms, Hartman said:

Well, his chief criticism was about the techniques. It
wasn't necessarily of Johnny; it was the whole coaching
staff; and I think he felt like maybe Johnny, being in-
experienced on the sideline, was not able to recognize
what was going on.

Describing Butts as a "perfectionist" who had also been critical
of Hartman's own coaching and even of Charlie Trippi's, Hartman
implied that Butts was critical by nature. He likened Butts's
criticisms to those he himself had made over the years, such
as, "I remarked to him many times the way to beat Georgia was
to run wide, run off tackle, and pass in the flat. Nothing traitorous
about that."

Schroder closed his case by returning to the subject of the
writing and editing of the article. The *Post* editors were Butts's
final witnesses, testifying in absentia, as Frank Graham had,
through written depositions taken earlier in New York.

The depositions of *Post* sports editor Roger Kahn and managing
editor Davis Thomas added little to Frank Graham's testimony
about the preparation of the article. Kahn mentioned that he
had wanted to see films of the game but that Furman Bisher
had told him they were unavailable. The reference in Graham's
draft to Rakestraw tipping plays by the position of his feet was
one of the facts that convinced Kahn that the game had been
fixed. Thomas said that the editors were influenced by the fact
that Burnett and his notes had been convincing to Coach Griffith
and to University of Georgia authorities.

The deposition of editor-in-chief Clay Blair, however, provided
some dramatic moments. Sitting in the witness chair, Schroder
played the part of the editor-witness; Lockerman was the questioner.

In the opening exchange of the deposition, Blair established
the *Post*'s declining revenues, its recent personnel shakeups,
and his new policy of "sophisticated muckraking to provoke people, to make them mad." He admitted authoring a memorandum
to the *Post* staff in which he complimented them on their progress

and commented, "The final yardstick—we have six lawsuits pending—we are hitting them where it hurts." Blair testified that the March 23 issue, containing the Butts-Bryant story, was only 25 percent of the way to his goal.

Another part of the deposition concerned the call Blair received from Butts's daughter Jean. And here Schroder was at his best, reading Blair's answers in a particularly emotionless and calloused tone:

A. She wanted—she was trying to find out if we were doing the story, I think, or if we were, when it would be out, something like that. It was a very incoherent conversation because she was very emotional and crying, and I had a hard time determining exactly what her point was here.

Q. The substance of the conversation was a request on her part, was it not—

A. Well—

Q. (continuing)—direct to you?

A. Well, my impression was that she was trying to find out (a) if we were doing an article involving her father, and (b) if we were, when it was coming out. It seemed to me that was what she was trying to get at, but it would be presumptuous here or any other time for me to try to interpret what any woman is really getting at when she talks to you.

Q. Well, you told her (a) that you were going to do an article, and (b) that it was coming out soon, didn't you, or gave her the publication date, perhaps?

A. No, I don't think I did give her the publication date.

Q. Did you tell her an article was going to be published concerning her father?

A. I swear to you, I can't remember. I am not trying to dodge your question. I am—I get a hundred phone calls a day, you know, more or less, and it is hard to remember, but I don't know whether I told her specifically whether we were coming out with this article or not. Definitely, I know I would not have told her when, you know, if I said we were publishing it, because we don't ever give a release as to when we are going to publish something, to anyone.

This was a strange and almost incoherent telephone conversation, where I couldn't really figure out what she was after. She was crying through the whole thing and—

Q. You got the impression that she was asking you not to publish the article?

A. Oh, beyond any doubt, that if we had any—I mean, her whole thing was to try to find out if we were, and certainly the undertones of the thing, all this weeping and crying was that if you—you know—"Please don't."

Curiously enough, after Blair's deposition was read, he showed up at the trial and sat at the counsel table. If his belated presence in the courtroom was designed to mitigate whatever damage his deposition had done, it may well have had the opposite effect. The jurors should have recognized him—newspapers carried a picture of him entering the courthouse—and they may have wondered why he had not testified in person.

Brief portions of Furman Bisher's deposition were also entered as testimony. He denied Frank Graham's testimony that he had furnished the *Post* with quotes from John Griffith or with the information that Butts had lost $70,000 investing in orange groves. He did not recall Roger Kahn asking him to obtain game films.

After hearing Bisher's testimony, Judge Morgan was moved to ask, "What did Bisher do for his money [$1,000]?"

Schroder replied, "He spent one day in Athens."

At another point in the trial, Morgan had said of Bisher, "This man is right here in Atlanta. Why isn't he here in this courtroom?" No one replied.

When Butts's lawyers rested their case, the outcome looked good for him. The weight of the expert evidence indicated that Burnett's notes had little, if any, value to Bryant. There was no evidence that the play of the game had been affected. Proof of a motive on Butts's part to betray his school depended on inferences from ambiguous evidence of bitterness and criticism. The case against the *Post* for its shoddy, reckless journalism was overwhelming. The callous indifference that the magazine had shown for the consequences of its rush to publish a scoop cried out for a remedy.

One could sense a mounting indignation in the courtroom toward the *Post*, both for the way the article had been prepared and for the way its case was being handled. The absence from the courtroom of the key *Post* participants was something of an insult. It seemed as if those in charge of distant, powerful Curtis Publishing Company had simply sent their lawyers down to Atlanta to handle a minor problem not worthy of their attention.

A perceptive sports writer asked at this point, "When is the *Post* going to throw the long bomb?"

The *Post*'s rebuttal took the form of a three-pronged counterattack aimed at: (1) Butts's character, (2) his connections with gambling, and (3) Bear Bryant's credibility.

The assault on Butts's character was based on the testimony of six highly placed men, all connected with University of Georgia athletics for many years. Everyone present in the hushed chamber was embarrassed for Butts as these six impeccable representatives of the university testified on his character and truthfulness.

The first character witness was Professor Harold Heckman, chairman of the department of accounting, and a member of the athletic board since 1946. He testified that in his opinion Butts's general character was bad and that he would not believe him under oath. Heckman's low opinion of Butts was reiterated by R. H. Driftmier, chairman of agricultural engineering, and a member of the athletic board since 1935; Professor Hugh Mills of the education department and member of the athletic board; treasurer J. D. Bolton; and William Bradshaw, the alumni member of the board who had helped to engineer Butts's January resignation. All spoke in a clipped, unemotional manner. They did not seem to relish their task; rather, they appeared to be performing an unpleasant civic duty.

President Aderhold was the final character witness. He was not asked whether he would believe Butts under oath. After testifying that Butts's character was bad, he said, "I would like to make an addition to that." The judge intervened and ruled that he could not qualify his answer. Some surmised that Aderhold may have wanted to say that in his opinion Butts's bad character was a relatively recent development.

The most impressive and damaging of the character witnesses was Bradshaw. He had been recruited as a player by Butts and had played first-string center on bowl teams in 1949 and 1950. His election to the athletic board in 1961 attested to the wide respect he enjoyed among Bulldog supporters. Unlike the other five anti-Butts character witnesses, he had no animosity toward his old coach. He had nothing to gain and, as a rising young businessman, possibly much to lose by alienating Butts's supporters.

Bradshaw had played no part in the running battles between Butts and veteran board members over finances and other matters. His position as a respected neutral was one reason the board's executive committee asked him to join Cook Barwick in urging Butts to resign as athletic director. For Bradshaw this delicate assignment had been a difficult duty, mandated by the best interests of both Wally Butts and Georgia's athletic program. He recounted the painful event as gently as he could in his opening responses to Cody's questions:

Q. In January of 1963, did you have an opportunity to have a conference with Wallace Butts?
A. Yes, sir.
Q. Where did that conference take place?
A. Mr. Cook Barwick's office.
Q. Here in Atlanta?
A. Yes, sir.

Q. Can you pinpoint the date for us?

A. The 18th—I believe it was the day of the Touchdown Club banquet that night. . . .

Q. Was anyone present other than you and Wallace Butts?

A. Mr. Barwick; yes, sir . . .

Q. Do you remember the subject matter of that discussion? . . .

A. It had to do with our bringing it to his attention that it might be wise for him to resign as athletic director of the University of Georgia.

Bradshaw then stated that he and Barwick told Butts of the executive committee's concern about Butts's outside business activities and the adverse publicity his loan company had received. On further questioning by Cody, he admitted somewhat reluctantly that the executive committee had discussed other reasons to oust Butts (the athletic director's open personal indiscretions, no doubt), but added, "We didn't see any sense in bringing them up at this time."

Cody used Bradshaw to confirm John Gregory's earlier testimony placing Butts at the closed scrimmage on Saturday, September 15, 1962. Bradshaw testified that both he and Butts had been invited to attend as members of the athletic board. When asked by Cody whether Georgia practiced the plays that would be used a week later in the Alabama game, Bradshaw answered, ". . . I am sure they must have, but I don't know play-for-play that they did."

On the key questions asked of all six character witnesses, Bradshaw's testimony was terse:

Q. Mr. Bradshaw, would you state whether or not you are familiar with the general character of Wallace Butts?

A. Well, insofar as being associated with him as my coach and then as athletic director, I would to that extent . . .

Q. Do you think you are familiar with his general character in the community?

A. . . . I believe so.

Q. From that knowledge, can you state whether it is good or bad?

A. I would say "bad."

* * *

Q. I'd like to ask you one more question, Mr. Bradshaw. Will you tell the Court whether or not, from the general character of Wallace Butts about which you testified, that you would believe him under oath?

A. I don't believe so.

Bradshaw had testified earlier that at the time he became involved in the athletic board's move to persuade Butts to resign, he had heard nothing of the growing scandal over the Butts-Bryant phone call. So his low regard for Butts had developed completely independently of the much greater indictment soon to emerge against his embattled old coach.

President Aderhold also testified to the circumstances leading to Butts's resignation as athletic director, including the February 22 meeting in Cook Barwick's office when Butts saw Burnett's notes for the first time. He essentially corroborated J. D. Bolton's version of Butts's reaction, recalling that Butts looked at the notes for three to five minutes and then said, "This is just general football talk. . . . I can understand how somebody listening may have made these observations . . . but I had no intention of hurting the University of Georgia. . . ."

Throughout the testimony of the character witnesses, Butts sat stonily, his hands clasped tightly on the table, and looked straight ahead. Not one of them was cross-examined to determine the basis of his opinion. It was a one-sided requiem for the reputation of the once proud Little Round Man.

(Judge Morgan excluded other evidence aimed at Butts's character as irrelevant, including his relationship with Evelyn and

$2,800 in personal phone calls—over 300 of which were to Evelyn—that he had charged to the university.)

The attempt to link Butts to gambling was limited to the deposition of Chicago beer dealer Frank Scoby. It established that Scoby was a gambler and that he had a close relationship with Butts.

Scoby's gambling had been publicized in 1957, when he testified in the federal prosecution of his bookie. In the deposition he admitted that he had bet as much as $50,000 a year on college football games and as much as $2,000 on a single game. He sometimes bet on as many as ten games a week. One of the trial's lighter moments came when Scoby testified that his bets were always picked up by a man known to him only as "Lefty."

Scoby said that Butts often sought his advice on business. On one occasion, however, he took Butts's advice and invested $20,000 in Wolfson's Continental Enterprises. Early in 1962, Scoby recalled, Butts asked him for assistance in obtaining a $10,000 loan. A bank in Chicago agreed to a $6,000 loan with Scoby endorsing the note. Both Scoby and Butts made reference in their testimony to Scoby's interest in buying the rights to a new brand of Scotch Whiskey and in employing Butts as his southeastern representative. Butts said the venture had fallen through because of the *Post* article; Scoby insisted it was still a possibility.

Scoby estimated that he had seen Butts 15 times in the past three years and had talked to him by phone 25 to 40 times in the past year. The most incriminating evidence revealed in Scoby's deposition was the pattern of Butts's phone calls to him. In 1962 there were no calls in April or May, five in June, two in July, four in August, and *fourteen* in September. Two were made the day before the Alabama-Georgia game. (Cody neglected to mention that one of these calls was made immediately before the call overheard by Burnett.) Butts could not explain why the number of calls to Scoby jumped so sharply during football season. Scoby was not asked. He denied ever discussing Georgia's chances in an upcoming game with Butts except perhaps to ask him in general terms, "How do you think you'll do?"

The *Post*'s implication was clear: Butts had made the phone call to serve Scoby's gambling interests. Although Butts and Scoby both denied that Butts knew of Scoby's gambling, they could hardly have been expected to admit it if it were true. It seems improbable that Butts could have been ignorant of Scoby's gambling in view of their closeness and the magnitude of Scoby's habit. It was at least a possibility that pressure from Scoby could have been the motive for Butts's call to Bryant.

The *Post*'s final rebuttal witness was President Frank Rose of the University of Alabama. An unlikely witness against Bryant and Butts, Rose was called to the stand because of the letter he had written to Georgia President Aderhold on March 6, 12 days before the *Post* article appeared.* This letter, which presumably reflected Bryant's explanation to Rose of the Butts-Bryant phone call, contradicted Bryant's testimony that he had no recollection of the contents of his September 13 and 16 telephone conversations with Butts. It stated that the two rivals had discussed new NCAA rules that would penalize Alabama unless the Tide's defenses were changed.

Bryant had denied under oath that he had ever made any of the statements attributed to him in Rose's letter. He accepted responsibility for only one inaccurate detail: George Gardner, head of officials of the Southeastern Conference, did not come to Tuscaloosa as a result of the call; he had visited the week before.

It was impossible for Rose to reconcile his letter with Bryant's testimony. For the most part, he repudiated his letter and denied that it was an accurate representation of Bryant's explanation of the call. The *Post* was counting on the jury's skepticism; would they really believe that a university president faced with such a serious situation could have been so mistaken either in un-

---

* For the full text of Rose's letter, see pp. 76–77.

derstanding his coach's explanation or in relating it to another president?

Dr. Rose was in his sixth year as president of the University of Alabama. He had come there from the presidency of Transylvania College in Lexington, Kentucky, where he had earlier served as chairman of the department of religion and philosophy. For a time he was minister of a church in Danville, Kentucky. In 1954, he was selected as one of the ten outstanding young men in the United States. Although he had no Ph.D., he used the title "Doctor" on the basis of honorary degrees.

On the witness stand Rose cut a very impressive figure. Tall, suave, and handsome, he spoke in poised stentorian tones as he detailed his background. His voice was perfect for the theological career he had once pursued.

Rose said he had dictated the letter hurriedly to his secretary early in the morning before catching a plane at 8:40 A.M. and did not get a chance to read it over after it was typed. His secretary was instructed to let Bryant see the letter before sending it. But he was out of the city, so she signed and mailed it anyway because Rose had also told her the letter was to go out that day.

In his explanation of the letter itself, Rose alluded frequently to his lack of knowledge of football terminology. He agreed with Bryant that all the statements he attributed to his coach about the contents of the alleged phone conversation were erroneous, as were the statements that Bryant specifically remembered the calls of September 13 and 16, and all statements attributed by Bryant to Butts. He said the letter misused the term *plays*; Bryant had spoken instead of offensive "techniques" such as "butt-blocking" and "head-blocking." The entire letter was characterized as his "interpretation" of what Bryant told him.

When Rose testified that his secretary had signed the letter, Judge Morgan asked, "Dr. Rose, did you consider this matter of great importance, the letter you were writing to Dr. Aderhold?" Rose replied that it was one of the most disturbing things that had happened in his 13 years in higher education.

Morgan went on, "But you did let your secretary sign the letter?"

"Yes, sir," Rose answered.

Welborn Cody pursued the doubt he thought he detected in the judge's question. When he resumed his examination of Rose, he walked to the witness stand and asked Rose to step down and put his signature on a piece of paper. The left-handed Rose calmly complied.

Later, after requesting Rose to write his signature twice more, Cody produced correspondence subpoenaed from Georgia Tech files, including a personal letter from Rose to the Tech president. Asked if the signatures on four letters were his, Rose said, "No, they are not. They were signed by my secretary."

All the signatures were then introduced into evidence as proof that the signature on the March 6 letter was Rose's. Law-trained Fred Russell of the *Nashville Banner* may have spoken for many observers when he wrote of that day's testimony that if he were a juror, he would have been bothered by this treatment of Rose:

> If this was a desperate, cheap trick, pulled late in the game here, without any real basis for belief, it was insulting to Dr. Rose, and if a juror I would resent it. If not, a handwriting expert should have been summoned to testify in an effort to establish the truth or untruth of Cody's insinuation that the signature on the letter to Dr. Aderhold was Dr. Rose's.

It was hard to believe that Cody would accuse a university president and former theologian of lying under oath without being sure of himself. It seemed equally unlikely that Rose would have lied about something as verifiable as his signature. This issue was tangential at best, and Cody blew it out of all proportion. (The ploy backfired. Jurors later revealed that the signatures Rose had written in court did not match the one on the letter.)

Rose's testimony completed the *Post*'s rebuttal. The weight of the evidence favoring Butts when his case was rested had been slightly diminished by the testimony on Butts's character, his Scoby connection, and the Rose-Aderhold letter. But none of the rebuttal evidence touched upon the Burnett notes, the playing of the game, or the preparation of the article. Nothing had occurred to stem the sense of outrage in Judge Morgan's courtroom.

The *Post*'s rebuttal concluded on Thursday, August 15, the ninth day of the trial. Arguments to the jury began on Friday and extended into the following Monday. Cody's argument for the *Post* hit hardest on Butts's character and Bryant's memory. He said little about the Burnett notes or the text of the article, except to admit that it contained inaccuracies.

One of Cody's best arguments was an observation about the misspelling of Georgia safetyman Brigham Woodward's last name in Burnett's note. The player himself pronounced the second *w*, as did everyone else who used his name in the trial, with the exception of one witness—Wally Butts. Butts dropped the second *w* and pronounced the name "Woodard," just as George Burnett had written it. This was strong confirmation that Butts had mentioned the player to Bryant, as charged by George Burnett and denied under oath by both Butts and Bryant.

Butts's lawyers pounced on the failure of the *Post*'s editors and writers to testify in person, to "look this jury in the eye and tell you they believed that article." The fact that Burnett's notes were never consulted and that John Carmichael was not interviewed was cited as proof that the *Post* did not want to learn anything that might have deterred them from publishing the article.

Not all of Butts's counsel's argument was limited to the evidence. Allen Lockerman improperly became an unsworn character witness for Butts early in his argument, when, in a voice charged with emotion, he said:

> I probably have known Wally Butts longer than any man
> in this case. I was at Mercer University with Wally Butts

when he played end on the football team there. He was in some respects a small man in stature, but he had more determination and more power to win than any man that I have ever seen in my life. I would not stand before you in this case today arguing in his behalf if I thought that Wally Butts would not tell you the truth when he raises his hand on this stand and swears to Almighty God that what he is going to tell you is the truth.

Bill Schroder followed Lockerman and also strayed from the record by informing the jury that it was "a glowing tribute" to Butts that "his lovely wife Winnie and his three daughters have been seated here with him throughout these two weeks," thus implying that any personal indiscretions had obviously been forgiven.

Schroder accused the *Post* of a policy of deliberately buying libel suits, calling it "libel for profit," and urged the jury to bring in an award of damages big enough to protect the public from such wrongdoing. Summing up on this point, he made an impassioned appeal:

> Somebody has got to stop them. There is no law against it, and the only way that type of, as I call it, yellow journalism can be stopped is to let the Saturday Evening Post know that it is not going to get away with it today, tomorrow, or anymore hereafter, and the only way that lesson can be brought home to them, Gentlemen, is to hit them where it hurts them, and the only thing they know is money. They write about human beings; they kill him, his wife, his three lovely daughters. What do they care? They have got money; getting money for it.
>
> I am looking to you for my protection. Heaven knows, if you let them out of this case for five million dollars or less, and boy, it's been worth it to them, I may be next, because they are not going to stop with that. You

may be next; my wife; my children; yourself. We have got to stop them now, and you are the only twelve in the world that can stop them.

I say, Gentlemen, this is the time we have got to get them. A hundred million dollars in advertising, would ten percent of that be fair to Wallace Butts for what they have done to him? Would a fifty-cent assessment on each of the twenty-three million issues which they wrote about him there, would that be a strain or a burden on them? I think it would teach them that we don't have that kind of journalism down here, and we don't want it down here, and we don't want it to spread from 666 Fifth Avenue any further than that building right now.

When he reached the conclusion of his argument, Schroder paused, then lowered his voice. A hush fell over the courtroom as he said:

My time is up, I have done the best I can. I have lived in agony with this man since I got the first notice that this was what was going to happen, this Post article was coming out. I have seen him deteriorating ever since it came out, and I have lived in agony along with him, and it may be that the personal firsthand knowledge that I have had since almost living with him and his family every day, I may have said some things or done some things or conducted myself in some manner that was displeasing to you. All I can say, I have done my best, and if I have done any of those things, don't hold it against Wallace Butts.

You know, one of these days, like everyone else must come to, Wallace Butts is going to pass on. No one can bother him then. The Saturday Evening Post can't get at him then. And unless I miss my guess, they will put Wallace Butts in a red coffin with a black lid, and he will have a football in his hands, and his epitaph will read something like this: "Glory, Glory to old Georgia."

After a brief recess Judge Morgan carefully read his charge to the jury. First he instructed them that in order for the *Post* to prevail on its defense of truth, it did not have to prove that everything in the article was true but only that "the sting of the libel" was true. The sting in this case was that Butts "rigged and fixed" the 1962 Georgia-Alabama game by giving Bryant information that was calculated to or could have affected the outcome of the game—in other words, that could have caused one team to win or lose or that could have increased the number of points by which the game was won.

The jury was then instructed that if they felt the defendant had failed to make out its plea of truth, Butts was entitled to general damages without proof that he had suffered any particular monetary injury. Since the article defamed him in his profession, it was libelous per se and was presumed to have injured him. The judge defined general damages as funds "intended to compensate a party who has been libeled for the actual damages he has suffered, to make him whole." He added that a person of bad reputation is not entitled to the same damages as a person of good reputation, an instruction undoubtedly requested by the *Post.*

Explaining the plaintiff's right to punitive damages, the judge said that these were entirely within the jury's discretion. Such an award could be made if the jury found that the defendant acted with actual malice, which encompassed the notion of "ill will, spite, hatred, and an intention to injure, or wanton or reckless indifference or culpable negligence with regard to the rights of others."

He said the purposes of punitive damages were to deter the wrongdoer from repeating the trespass, to serve as warning to others, and to express the "ethical indignation" of the community.

At 3:03 P.M., the jurors retired to the jury room, taking with them 63 evidentiary exhibits, and began their deliberations. After a dinner recess, they continued deliberations until 9:45, when they were escorted by U.S. marshals to a nearby hotel to spend the night. Deliberations resumed at 8:20 A.M. on Tuesday, August 19.

At 10:25, a marshal announced that the jury was coming in. Reserved seats were no longer needed, since the overflow crowds that had competed for the 200 public seats throughout the first 12 days of the trial had not returned for the verdict. The jury filed in. The 12 middle-aged white men appeared somewhat self-conscious. The marshal ordered, "All rise." Judge Morgan emerged from his chambers solemnly and walked swiftly to his chair. He glanced around the courtroom to see if everyone was in place, then turned to the jury and asked if they had reached a verdict.

The foreman said, "We have, your honor."

The judge said, "The marshal will receive the jury's verdict."

The marshal walked to the foreman, took a piece of white paper from him, and carried it to the judge. Judge Morgan read it impassively. He then handed it to the attractive, well-dressed woman in the clerk's chair to the right of the bench, saying, "The clerk will read the verdict."

The clerk glanced at the paper, adjusted her glasses, and read aloud without a trace of emotion, "We, the jury, find in favor of Wallace Butts. We assess general damages in favor of Wallace Butts in the sum of $60,000. We find that Wallace Butts is entitled to recover punitive damages from the Curtis Publishing Company. We assess punitive damages in the sum of $3 million dollars."

There was a collective gasp in the courtroom.

Bill Schroder took a deep breath and let it out slowly, staring straight ahead.

For the second time in the trial, Wally Butts broke into tears.

With horror and disbelief on his face, Clay Blair turned to one of his lawyers. "Did she say *three* million dollars?" he asked.

Bear Bryant Compromises

BRYANT HAD SUED Curtis Publishing Company for the *Post*'s "fix" article on March 25, 1963, the same day as Butts, and only two months after suing both Curtis and Furman Bisher for Bisher's brutality article. He did not file suit against author Frank Graham, who apparently did not incite Bryant's wrath the way the despised Bisher did.

At the same time as the *Post*'s Atlanta lawyers began to lay the groundwork for an appeal in Butts's case, pretrial activity was getting under way in Alabama. The *Post* was determined to go to trial against Bryant fully prepared and to avoid the many costly mistakes made in Atlanta against Butts. Philip Strubing's first step was to assign a new lawyer to the case. He chose John Runzer, a seasoned trial lawyer in Strubing's Philadelphia firm. The energetic, Harvard-trained Runzer was determined to follow Bill Schroder's example, not Welborn Cody's; he was going to master the facts and terminology and, in his words, "play football" at Bryant's trial.

Runzer was aided by the aggressive Birmingham firm of Beddow, Embry, and Beddow. Two members of the firm, Eric Embry and Roderick Beddow, Jr., had begun their preparation by observing Butts's trial in Atlanta. For most of it, they sat inside the rail behind the *Post*'s counsel table, but two days before the trial ended, they returned to Birmingham in disgust; they could not bear to watch the disaster they sensed was coming.

Runzer first set out to complete the discovery work at the University of Alabama that had been left unfinished for Butts's case. He subpoenaed all relevant records from the offices of the president and athletic director of the university and unearthed a treasure trove of valuable documents, including an incriminating letter from Bryant to Rose about the overheard phone call, and Alabama's scouting report and defensive records on the game. After studying these new documents carefully, Runzer began to exploit them.

January 8, 1964, must have been a long day for Frank Rose. The "confidential" letter his secretary had failed to clear with Bear Bryant before mailing it to Georgia president Aderhold on March 6, 1963, came back to haunt him. From early morning until midafternoon, with no lunch break, Runzer grilled Rose relentlessly about this brief communication and his earlier testimony concerning it.

Rose had been an admirer of Bear Bryant ever since their paths had first crossed in Lexington, Kentucky, where Rose was president of Transylvania College and Bryant was head football coach and athletic director of the University of Kentucky. Luring Bryant from Texas A & M to Alabama in 1957, just after he became its president, had launched Rose on what appeared to be a euphorically successful tenure in office. The Tide's 1961 national football championship was a jewel in the crown of the Rose administration. It came as no surprise when Rose told Judge Lewis Morgan from the witness stand in August that the Butts-Bryant incident was "one of the most disturbing things" that had happened in his 13 years of college administration; nothing had ever upset him more.

The 140-page deposition that Runzer exacted from Rose in his office on January 8 supplied much more information than Rose's August testimony had about the origins and circumstances of his embarrassing March 6 letter to O. C. Aderhold. It also added considerably to the contradictions in Bryant's and Rose's accounts of the coach's explanation of the phone call.

The former theologian testified that his involvement in the

Butts-Bryant affair began with a telephone call from his Georgia counterpart, President Aderhold, on Friday, February 22, the very day Wally Butts was confronted with Burnett's notes in Cook Barwick's Atlanta office. Disclosing only that an "ethical matter" had arisen, Aderhold asked Rose to meet in confidence with him and SEC commissioner Bernie Moore in the conference's Birmingham office at nine o'clock the following Sunday morning.

The Alabama president drove the 45 miles from Tuscaloosa to Birmingham alone, only to find, much to his surprise, that President Aderhold was accompanied by counsel—Cook Barwick. Rose had not been told that he could bring someone with him. The meeting got off to a bad start when Moore announced that he had just received a phone call from Alabama's old nemesis, Atlanta sportswriter Furman Bisher, who said he had learned of the meeting and wanted to be informed of what transpired. Aderhold seemed as shocked by this as Rose, since the meeting was supposed to have been confidential. Barwick denied that he had leaked news of the meeting to Bisher, though he did admit that he was Bisher's personal lawyer. Rose probably began to fear something of a conspiracy; he admittedly grew suspicious.

Little is known about the meeting except that the Burnett notes were shown to Rose, who took notes of his own during the three-hour session. He later summarized the position of the Georgia representatives:

> They had talked with Mr. Burnett about the matter and felt that Mr. Burnett was telling the truth. I was led to believe either by word or by insinuation that Mr. Burnett was an honorable man. There was no doubt that he had heard everything that they had told me regarding plays, two or three players, and other things relating to the game.

In Rose's words, he was "shocked and stunned" by Burnett's revelations. At the end of the meeting, he agreed to investigate the matter in Tuscaloosa, and both he and Aderhold said they would keep each other abreast of any new information.

Rose pondered his course of action as he drove back to Tuscaloosa, arriving home sometime between noon and one o'clock. He described the balance of his Sunday afternoon in this exchange with Runzer:

Q. What did you do when you got home?

A. Well, I was so upset about the matter that I went upstairs and sat down and thought about it for a while, and then my wife called me down to lunch, and I went down and had a very light lunch and went back up and thought about it some more. Then I decided the best thing for me to do was to take a nap and then think about it when I was more refreshed and relaxed.

Q. And you did that?

A. Yes, sir. After taking a tranquilizer and I slept for about an hour.

Q. Did you take a tranquilizer because of the upsetting nature of the news, or is it your custom to do that?

A. Because of the upsetting nature of the news.

Q. I assume when you awoke you began thinking about this matter again?

A. Yes, sir. I thought about it from about 2:30 to 3 o'clock until about five and I thought of it from every angle that I possibly could. I thought about the people that I should see first, and by 5 o'clock came to the conclusion that the thing for me to do is confront the man that had been accused.

Rose discussed the matter with his wife, and she agreed that he should talk to Bryant about it before speaking to anyone else. Rose then called Bryant at home and arranged to meet him in the president's office at seven o'clock. That Sunday evening meeting between the anguished president and his accused coach lasted about three hours. Rose told Runzer that he explained the general nature of the allegations to Bryant and then went through the notes he had taken in Birmingham to fill the coach in on the details. Bryant's exact response must forever remain uncertain. Rose's first official version of that response was his controversial letter of March 6 to President O. C. Aderhold, which both he and Bryant would repudiate under oath at the trial of Butts's case.

For the next five days, February 25 to March 1, 1963, Rose had to put the subject aside while he attended meetings in Washington and New York. Bryant had agreed to check his telephone records in the meantime to see if he had called Butts on Sunday, September 16, as indicated in Burnett's notes. On Rose's return to his office he found this letter from Bryant:

February 28, 1963

Dr. Frank Rose
President
University of Alabama
University, Alabama

Dear Dr. Rose:

We were able to find a record of only three calls from me to the person in Athens. The first was on September 9th; the second on September 14; and the third on September 16th. He must have telephoned me some during that period because I am sure we talked more than that. As a matter of fact, over the years, I have talked with him by phone some eight or ten times per year. I might add, I have done the same thing with other coaches, Duffy Daugherty, Bud Wilkinson, Darrell Royal, and Bobby Dodd, for instance.

There were two additional calls made to Athens; one from our Publicity Department on September 11 and one by an Assistant Coach on September 27.

I like to think that these calls were fruitful so far as our program is concerned; particularly, the one the middle of September on a Sunday, because I remember very well that this gentleman discussed in detail with me the new interpretation of the piling on rule and warned us to warn our team to be very careful or else we might lose a good player early like LeRoy Jordan or some other aggressive defensive man. On that particular date, we also discussed at length some coaching points on some pass routes that although we were using we had had very little success with. This man over the years had had tremendous success with the passing game; in particular, these two routes and after learning these coaching points we began to use the two particular passes often, including for the clutch Touchdown against Tennessee in Knoxville the third week in October.

Again, I want to say that I have for years discussed football; ours, his, football with this man and like to feel that I would still have that privilege because I have a great deal of respect for his knowledge of the game, particularly the passing game.

Respectfully yours,
Paul Bryant
Director of Athletics

The significance of the letter is obvious. Bryant's words, "I remember very well," in reference to the call to Butts on a Sunday in mid-September, flatly contradicted both Rose's and Bryant's testimony that Bryant had only told Rose what he and Butts *might* have talked about and that he had no specific recollection of any particular call. The letter's claim that Butts helped Bryant by giving him coaching points on pass routes was never mentioned by Bryant or Rose at the trial or in Rose's letter to Aderhold. This information, as well as Bryant's assertion that Butts gave him a tip that helped Alabama beat Tennessee, would surely have raised eyebrows at the trial. If the tips helped the Tide defeat the Volunteers, couldn't they also have helped against the Bulldogs of Georgia?

The letter was also interesting in its disclosure of phone calls from Bryant to Butts on September 9 and 14—the latter occurring between the call overheard by Burnett on September 13 and the 67-minute call on September 16. This made a total of four calls in eight days, three of which were initiated by Bryant— who was not the compulsive and wasteful caller of the two.

After reading the letter, Rose allowed himself three or four days before writing to Aderhold. During this period he had two more meetings with Bryant, in which the February 28 letter must have been discussed, and he talked with key advisors on his own staff and in the athletic department. One person Rose consulted on this and most matters of importance was Jefferson Bennett, the university's administrative vice-president, who was also a lawyer. Rose first brought up the Butts-Bryant matter with Bennett in Washington on Friday, March 1, when the two met there on other university business. After returning to the campus, Rose sought advice from two members of the athletic committee and from Jeff Coleman, business manager of the athletic department. Coleman confirmed that coaches sometimes talked about tickets—one of the subjects Bryant had said that he and Butts might have discussed.

By the time Rose was ready to dictate his letter to Aderhold, then, he had talked to Bryant three times, taking notes on one occasion; he had received a letter from Bryant; and he had consulted with at least four other people. It could hardly be said that he had acted in haste or upon insufficient investigation when he finally sat down to put his findings in writing.

Rose's testimony at the trial that this painstakingly investigated letter did not accurately represent Bryant's statements to him came under sharp attack by Runzer on January 8. In addition to Bryant's letter of February 28, Runzer confronted Rose with other documents that were not used in the Butts proceedings. One was a statement Rose had issued on March 23, 1963, after

Georgia attorney general Eugene Cook had made public the
March 6 Rose-Aderhold letter. In this handwritten statement
the Alabama president had said, "The substance of my letter
is accurate and correct." His only admitted error was that he
should have used the term *techniques* instead of *plays*.

Rose admitted to Runzer that he had consulted with Bryant
before issuing this defense of the controversial letter, but Bryant's
contribution to the statement is unclear, as the following exchange between Runzer and Rose shows:

Q. Now, the statement we just read points out, as I think
   you said, a mistake in the letter in the use of the word
   plays when it should have been techniques; is that correct?
A. Yes, sir.
Q. Who was the one who told you that was a mistake?
A. I believe that was at the time I called Coach Bryant and
   read the letter to him; I am not sure. He said that just
   isn't right. This isn't what I told you. He said we never
   talked about plays. He said we talked about techniques
   and we talked about things that would have been illegal
   in rule interpretation. I believe that that was the day that
   I read the letter to him.
Q. So, it was Coach Bryant that pointed out to you that there
   was a mistake in the letter?
A. I am not sure, but I think it was Coach Bryant.
Q. And there may be others?
A. Could have been. I just don't know. I still continue to
   say plays and I don't know that much difference about
   it.
Q. But whether Mr. Bryant was the first or not, you did
   say he pointed out to you the letter was wrong?
A. Yes, sir.
Q. And was your subsequent statement which appeared in
   the Birmingham Post, March 23, 1963, drafted in reliance

on the information that Mr. Bryant had given you in this recent conversation with him?

A. Partly.

Q. What other basis?

A. On my reading the letter and the information that I had gotten between that time of writing it and what I had and as I said, in consultation with Mr. Bennett.

Q. Now, in discussing this letter with Mr. Bryant, he pointed out to you there was an error in it. Did he still say he was not sure whether they talked about the rule changes?

A. He said to me, Dr. Rose, you really did not understand. I am a damn poor coach to not to be able to keep my president better informed on football than you are. That's a very poor interpretation of our conversation.

Q. Well, was he still saying that he did not recall what was talked about in the conversation with Mr. Butts?

A. He said that. He said to me that he didn't know what he talked to him about. This is what he told me that afternoon. He said, I told you it could have been and tried to explain, but he said, I am a poor coach—

Q. In other words, he was still telling you he did not know specifically what was talked about and that rule changes was one of the things that could have been talked about?

A. Yes, sir, and about which he was really concerned, and that Coach Butts had the knowledge and explanation.

Q. And did he also again repeat he might have talked about the ticket sales and Continental Enterprises or other investments?

A. No, sir.

Q. In other words, he just said we could have talked about rule changes?

A. He didn't—we didn't even discuss that. He was so upset over the poor job I had done answering the letter, we just didn't talk about it.

Q. What exactly did he say then? Maybe I misunderstood you?

A. He said that the letter was wrong, that I misinterpreted what he said to me, and tried to explain that he could understand how I got some of this misinformation, but it was a very poor interpretation of his conversation with me.

It is difficult to square Rose's public defense of his letter as substantially "accurate and correct" with his testimony that Bryant had insisted to him that the letter was "a very poor interpretation" of that conversation.

The circumstances surrounding the dictation and dispatch of the Rose-Aderhold letter accounted for much of the barbed questioning Runzer directed at Rose. He took particularly strong issue with Rose's claims that the letter had been dictated hurriedly and was not corrected by anyone because Rose had to catch an early flight to Washington, D.C. for a meeting.

At the Butts trial Rose had said that he dictated the letter on Monday, March 6. In his January deposition he admitted that he had been mistaken. He had no choice; March 6 fell on a Wednesday. He told Runzer that he was not sure when he dictated the letter, but that his secretary's notes showed that he dictated it on Tuesday, March 5. (This was confirmed by the secretary in her deposition.)

The fact that the letter was dictated on March 5 was corroborated by another revealing document found in Rose's correspondence files—an earlier draft of Rose's letter to Aderhold, *dated* March 5. It reads as follows:

March 5, 1963
Confidential

Dr. O. C. Aderhold, President
The University of Georgia
Athens, Georgia

Dear Dr. Aderhold:

I have spent a great deal of time investigating thoroughly the questions that were raised at our meeting in Birmingham. I have talked with Coach Bryant on at least two occasions and as best as I can ascertain this is the information that I have received.

Coach Butts has been serving on the football rules committee and at a meeting held last summer of the rules committee the defenses used by Coach Bryant, L.S.U. and Tennessee were discussed at length and new rules were drawn up that would severely penalize these three teams unless the defenses were changed, particularly on certain plays.

Coach Butts had discussed this with Coach Bryant and the two were together at some meeting and Coach Butts had told Mr. Bryant that the University of Georgia had several plays that would severely penalize the Alabama team and not only would cause LeeRoy Jordan, an Alabama player, to be expelled from the game but could severely injure one of the offensive players on the Georgia team.

Coach Bryant asked Coach Butts to let him know what the plays were and on September 14 he called Coach Bryant and told him. There was a question about another one of the offensive plays of the Georgia team that could seriously penalize the Alabama team and bring additional injury to a player. Coach Bryant asked Coach Butts to check on that and he would call back on September 16. This he did.

It was then that Coach Bryant changed his defenses and invited Mr. George Gardner, Head of the Officials of the Southeastern Conference, to come to Tuscaloosa and interpret for him the legality of his defenses. This Mr. Gardner did the following week. The defenses were changed and Coach Bryant was grateful to Coach Butts for calling this to his attention.

Coach Bryant informs me that the calling this to his attention may have favored the University of Alabama football team, but that he doubted it seriously. He did say that it prevented him from using illegal plays after the new change of rules.

I have checked into other matters that were discussed and can find no grounds for Mr. Bisher's accusations, and as I understand it he has now decided for lack of information to drop the matter.

Dr. Aderhold, this continues to be a serious matter with me, and if you have any additional information I would appreciate your furnishing me with it as I am not only anxious to work with you, but to satisfy my own mind.

Thanking you for coming to Birmingham to meet with me and for sharing this information, I am

> Most cordially,
> Frank A. Rose
> President

FAR/mhp

A comparison of this draft with the March 6 letter* shows that they do not differ in substance. But the March 5 version comes closer to Rose's secretary's shorthand notes, which she read during her deposition, indicating that there was an intermediate draft between the dictation and the final draft.

The mere existence of this earlier draft establishes not only that Rose's final letter was not the first and only draft, but that someone made several corrections in the second and final draft, ranging from the spelling of LeRoy Jordan's name to the wording of the description of the September 16 call. That person has never been identified. The secretary insisted that she typed the March 6 letter in final form directly from her notes. She also said the letter was dictated "thoughtfully and slowly" and that it was the fifth of 32 letters dictated over a 1½-hour period.

---

* See pp. 76–77.

Having already corrected his earlier testimony on *when* he left town after dictating the letter, Rose then backtracked on *where* he went. First he explained how he happened to be mistaken about both points in his testimony at the Butts trial:

On checking my calendar before leaving here to go to Atlanta [to testify at the Butts trial], I looked at March 6th and saw Washington there on my calendar, and took it that was the destination. The plane leaves here in the morning at 8:40 to go to Washington and New York and other places. But I am not positive that was where I went; I am not positive that I dictated the letter that morning. Now, also in my testimony I said on Monday, Monday is the 4th. But I didn't have my date book at the trial to check the dates, and as I told you, I was going through two crises at that time as far as the University was concerned, and all I did was quickly refer to my calendar and saw that Washington was on March 6th; but that meeting probably had been changed to our Friday meeting in Washington, which I met with Mr. Bennett, or it could have been that I went to Washington. I don't know, but during that period, during the period of January—of February, March, April, May, June—I took many trips to Washington and over the State of which there are no records. Nothing on my calendar to designate that, because many of them were confidential trips to work out some of these problems that we have here at the University.

The two crises Rose was referring to were the Butts-Bryant affair and the impending court-ordered desegregation of the University of Alabama. Governor George C. Wallace had promised that he would personally "stand in the schoolhouse door" to prevent it. This was undoubtedly a matter of great concern to

President Rose and could well have occasioned secret trips of which no record was made.

In any event, it was now settled that the letter was dictated on Tuesday, March 5. Bennett, who was present at the deposition as Rose's counsel, told Rose that he had indeed left town that Tuesday morning. Rose's expense records showed no trips for March 4, 5, or 6.

Near the close of the deposition, Runzer tenaciously returned to the subject:

Q. Doctor, this trip that commenced on the morning of March 5th, do you have any idea how long it took?
A. No, sir, I don't. I can't tell you exactly.
Q. Do you know how you traveled?
A. No, sir.
Q. You do not know where you went?
A. I am not sure where I went.

Since this trip had occurred less than ten months earlier, Runzer was determined to press Rose's seemingly faulty memory. He rephrased the question:

Q. Where do you think you went? What is your best recollection?
A. That has to be confidential.

In the discussion that ensued, both on and off the record, Rose and Bennett took the position that the trip had nothing to do with the Butts-Bryant affair and concerned discussions and persons whose nature and identity were confidential. Runzer was not convinced. He doubted that the answer would be excluded in court under any rule of evidence known to him. He renewed the question:

Q. Dr. Rose, where did you go when you left the University on the morning of March 5th?

Mr. Bennett: Now, at that point, you have been advised by me that you are free to refuse to answer on the grounds that your trip had nothing at all to do with the matter at issue and involves your confidential relationship as President of the University of Alabama.

On his counsel's advice Rose refused to answer that question and several subsequent questions about his March 5 trip except to say that the university did not reimburse him for his expenses and that he paid for them personally.

Runzer was still not satisfied. Seriously doubting that there was a legal basis for any "university president" evidentiary privilege, he took the question to Judge Hobart Grooms, the federal district judge in Birmingham before whom the trial of Bryant's case was set to begin on February 4.

Judge Grooms ruled against Rose's claim of confidentiality. On January 17, Rose's deposition resumed, with Eric Embry asking the questions for the *Post*. After reviewing the final questions and answers of the January 8 proceedings, Embry asked:

Q. Do you have any recollection, Dr. Rose, of where you went on March 5th?

A. Mr. Embry, I don't know what legal term or what a lawyer means by "recollection." If you are talking about a guess, I can make a guess. I have done everything I can, from checking my notes, notebook, my wife's notebook, and talking to members of my staff trying to ascertain exactly where I went that day.

Q. Have you been able to determine in order to form any recollection of your own as to where you did go on that date?

A. I wouldn't say recollection, but if you want me to guess, I can guess where I went.

Q. Well, if you define your best recollection as a guess it is all right with me, just whatever any of us can draw upon in our minds or intellects as we best recall what

we did and when we did it. That is the context I am
asking you this in.
A. Yes, sir. I would guess that I went to Montgomery.
Q. Montgomery, Alabama?
A. Yes, sir . . . I have not found any information that would
tell me definitely where I was that day, but I am having
to guess at it and I would guess that it was Montgomery.

On advice of counsel, Rose then refused to answer any further
questions about the trip, including the mode of transportation,
persons visited, and lodgings. Bennett and Embry disagreed on
the scope of Judge Grooms's order. With the trial only two weeks
away, returning to him for clarification was unfeasible. The issue
would have to be resolved in the courtroom with Dr. Rose on
the witness stand.

This was not to be. A week before the trial was to begin, Dr.
Rose and Bryant's principal lawyers, Winston McCall and Harry
Pritchett of Birmingham, came to see Bryant at his home. In
his autobiography Bryant described them as "very solemn and
serious."

Little is known about this meeting except that Pritchett apparently went straight to the point, saying, "Paul, what would
you settle for?"

Bryant was ripe for the question. In *Bear* he wrote that if he
had been the only one involved, he would have loved to have
gone to trial in the hopes of collecting the full $10 million he
had sued for, but the whole affair was taking a heavy toll on
his family, and he feared it could drag on for years.

Bryant may also have heard that someone had hired private
investigators who were asking ugly questions all over Kentucky
in an attempt to dig up dirt on him. Some feel that he probably
did know about the investigation and that it contributed to his
eagerness to settle out of court. He did admit that he dreaded
the trial partly because of a fear that "they'd bring in some sensational witness who would testify to some lie, that I'd done this,

that or the other." Unbeknownst to Bryant, however, the investigators, who had been hired by Curtis Publishing Company, found nothing of consequence.

The fact that Bryant's own lawyers recommended settlement undoubtedly influenced his decision. It is unusual for a plaintiff's lawyers to initiate last-minute proposals of settlement in cases of this magnitude. And considering Butts's spectacular victory in Atlanta, where he had been held in disgrace, Bryant's recovery might have been unprecedented. The case could not have been prevented from going to an Alabama jury, and unless that jury were presented with a vastly different picture of the facts, they would surely have awarded the state's number-one hero a record-breaking sum. The lawyers' fees for winning this one case could have been greater than many lawyers make in a career.

Was Bryant also influenced by the fact that Frank Rose accompanied the lawyers on this visit? On a symbolic or personal level, the presence of the man who was both a key witness and his superior at the university must have signified to Bryant that settlement was in the best interests of the University of Alabama. The highly publicized accusations of falsehood that were sure to come could only harm the institution.

In any event, Bryant set a figure, and a settlement was quickly reached. He agreed to split $25,000 with Darwin Holt to settle their suits against Bisher and Curtis for the brutality story. For the "fix" story he accepted $275,000 in damages and $20,000 for expenses. The total settlement, then, came to $320,000, of which Bryant netted $196,000 tax-free.

The *Post*'s Birmingham lawyers were disappointed. They wanted to go to trial—they thought they could win. But to Curtis the settlement was "an offer they couldn't refuse." The potential liability was too great. President Culligan personally directed the settlement for Curtis and felt that it saved the company at least $2 million.

There is ground for further speculation on Bryant's decision to settle out of court. He may well have been influenced by the records subpoenaed from his office, which Runzer planned to use against him.* Bryant's testimony at the Butts trial that he was surprised by Georgia's use of the pro-set formation would not have gone uncontested in Birmingham as it had in Atlanta. Runzer would not only have exploited the evidence of the commonplace nature of the formation and Georgia's previous uses of it but would have confronted Bryant with contrary evidence in the coach's own records. The first incriminating record would have been the 1962 Alabama scouting report on Georgia. A highly complex and detailed document, it was prepared by assistant coach Charlie Bradshaw, later head coach at Kentucky. Bradshaw was an exceptionally astute student of the game, and this report attests to his painstaking care in analyzing an opponent's formations, plays, personnel, and tendencies.

Preparing a scouting report for an opening game is a real challenge. The only sources Bradshaw had to go on were the spring intrasquad game, which he himself scouted; Georgia's personnel; and the Bulldogs' tendencies in the previous season. He reported that in its spring game Georgia had run almost exclusively from the slot formation, the simplest variation of the regular tight T formation. (Spring games are purposely kept simple to minimize their value to opposing scouts.) This formation splits one end and puts a halfback behind the slot thus created. In Alabama terminology the slot was called "pro" for slot-right and "con" for slot-left.

Speaking of Georgia's offense in general, Bradshaw said, "Georgia's offense is similar to ours. The formations they like are pro and con. They will use long motion. They will split an end to help their passing game." This explanation describes both the slot and pro-set. Splitting the other end to form a second, wider slot, produces the pro-set formation.

---

* Copies of these documents were furnished to this writer by Runzer in February 1964.

Using diagrams, Bradshaw indicated that he expected Georgia to use the pro-set. These diagrams are reproduced on page 168.

The third diagram, "con-out," is what Georgia would call the "pro-set left formation." The left is the strong side, with the half-back in the slot. The weak side end is split wide. Conversely, "pro-out," the fourth diagram, is "pro-set right" in Georgia terminology.

The first and second diagrams show Georgia's slot-right and slot-left, the other formation used in the Alabama game and described in Burnett's notes. The fifth and sixth diagrams, "pro-wide" and "con-wide," illustrate Georgia's slot-right and slot-left with the end split wider but with the strong side running back still in the slot. It was not used in either the spring game or the Alabama game, though Bryant said in his testimony that it was a formation he had expected.

These diagrams would have been powerful evidence. The *Post*'s new lawyers could have forced Bryant into an embarrassing situation. Could he really have explained why he claimed to be surprised by one of only three formations his own scouting report told him to expect?

Another document found in Bryant's files would have been equally, if not more embarrassing to him. Labeled "Defensive Breakdown," it was prepared by assistant coaches from the game film and from statistics kept during the game. For each Georgia offensive play, it recorded (1) the "situation," including down, yard line, and yards to go for a first down; (2) Alabama's defensive formation; (3) Georgia's offensive formation; (4) Georgia's play and its result; and (5) the "breakdown"—comments on the performance of particular Alabama defensive players.

Reproduced on pages 169–170 is the Defensive Breakdown for the first half. The five plays in which Georgia used the pro-set ("pro-out" and "con-out") are those numbered 6, 11, 12, 13, and 15. It should be remembered that Bryant testified that Georgia used the pro-set effectively until Alabama shifted out of its Bama defense.

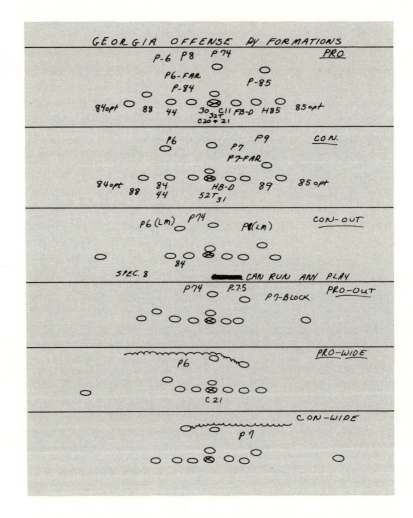

	Situation	Defense	Formation	Play	Breakdown
1.	1-10-G38	Stack	Con M	84 opt + 1	Henry trailed. Sharpe didn't step out. Battle good. Versprille good.
2.	2-9-G39	Bama	Pro	C22 T O	Jordan good. Versprille blocked. Pettee went around block.
3.	3-9-G39	Scissors	Pro M	P84 Int.	Battle nothing. Williamson fair. Versprille intercepted.
4.	1-10-G27	Scissors	Pro M	45 + 7	Henry blocked. Jordan & Hurlbut blocked. Sharpe blocked. Pell makes tackle.
5.	2-3-G34	Directions	Pro	P8 + 6	Battle not tough enough. Stephens should have Int.
6.	1-10-G35	Stack	Pro out M	P8 Inc	Wieseman nothing. Stephens poor position. O'Dell should not drop off. Must contain. Morton trailing, Kearley poor trail.
7.	2-10-G35	Slant	Pro M	22T + 4	Wieseman poor slant. Wilson raise straight up. Kearley poor slant. O'Dell nothing. McGill & Layton makes tackle.
8.	3-6-G40	Stack Ray	Pro	68 + 2	Kearley blocked. Morton miss tackle. Layton blocked. Martin came up too slow.
9.	1-10-G-2	Stack Bullets	Con	QBS	Pettee offsides
10.	1-5-G7	Slant Luke	Con	85 + 1	Kearley poor tech. Hooper good. Jordan good.
11.	2-4-G8	Slant Luke	Pro out M	P9 + 13	Pettee nothing. Henry fair rush. Williamson should have intercepted.

Situation	Defense	Formation	Play	Breakdown
12. 1-10-G24	Slant (Omaho)	Con out M	P8 Inc	Hooper poor contain. Williamson went to inside. McGill should have int. Kearley blocked.
13. 2-10-G24	Slant	Con out M	P8 + 1	Williamson very good.
14. 3-9-G35				
15. 3-17-G32	Scissors	Con out (M)	P8 & Pen.	Got outside of Hopper. Wilson blocked. McGill, Martin, Stephens miss tackle.
16. 3-22-G28	Punt	Punt	Fake Punt & Run	Jordan good. McGill good. Hopper blocked.
17. 4-17-G30	Punt	Punt	Punt	
18. 1-10-G19	Slant Luke	Pro	Fumble	Line good.
19. 3-9-G20	Slant	Pro (M)	85 Opt K-2	Henry must make him pitch. Williamson in fair shape. Jordan very good. Pell good.
20. 4-12-G18	Punt	Punt		Martin great for safety.
21. 1-10-G24	Scissors	Con	P6 Far + 28	No rush by Hopper. Henry good rush. Kearley had hands up. McGill played throw back poorly. Clark did not go for ball.
22. 1-10-A48	Split	Con	RO left + 3	Hopper fooled bad. Kearley poor route to ball. Wilson blocked. McGill made T
23. 2-7-A45	Scissors	Pro	P8 Inc	Poor rush by Hopper. McGill not tough when playing through receivers.
24. 3-7-A45	Bama	Con M	Fake C Trap P Inc	Good rush by Hopper & Henry. Good position by Jordan.
25. 4-7-A45	Punt	Punt	Punt	[End of half]

Here is a summary of the defensive formations and the offensive results for those five plays:

Play	Defense	Result
6	Stack	Incomplete pass
11	Slant luke	Pass for nine-yard gain; should have been intercepted
12	Slant (Omaha)	Incomplete pass
13	Slant	Pass for one-yard gain
15	Scissors	Five-yard penalty against Georgia

Clearly, the Defensive Breakdown does not support Bryant's testimony that the pro-set hurt Alabama. It produced only one Georgia gain of any consequence, nine yards on the eleventh play, and this was on a pass that should have been intercepted. The two incompletions, the penalty, and the one-yard gain can hardly be viewed as effective plays. True, it was said that one of the incompletions should have been caught. It is also possible that on the fifteenth play the pro-set produced a gain that was nullified by a penalty. But even giving Georgia's offense the benefit of the doubt, Bryant's claim that his defense failed against the pro-set can scarcely be justified. Could the use of this formation have possibly thrown Bryant into the quandary he described at the Butts trial?

Just as damaging to Bryant would have been the Defensive Breakdown's record of the defensive formations used by Alabama against the pro-set. At the trial he had testified that he was initially in the Bama formation and was forced to shift from it because of the effectiveness of the pro-set. As the above summary shows, however, the Bama defense was never even used against the pro-set. Is it possible that the savvy coach could have confused one defense with another in his testimony? Unlikely, because a different defense was used in each of the five plays.

Bryant's earlier testimony implied that the defensive adjustment he made against the pro-set after its fifth use by Georgia rendered that formation less effective for the rest of the game.

In his own trial, this claim would have been tested against the Defensive Breakdown for the second half.

This incriminating document (not reproduced here) shows that any diminished success of the pro-set must have been lost on Georgia signal callers. The Bulldogs ran 18 plays from the pro-set in the second half, more than three times as many as in the first. The two halves were about equally miserable for the hapless Georgia offense, which netted 63 yards in the first half and 53 in the second.

Contrary to Bryant's claim, the Defensive Breakdown for the entire game shows that no major defensive adjustment was made by Alabama at any time. The Tide used ten defenses in the first fifteen plays and added only one other thereafter, the "split hard" in the next to last play of the game. Thus, essentially the same defenses were used in both halves, with a heavy reliance on four defenses—slant, stack, scissors, and split—throughout the game. Bama was used only twice.

It is possible that there are mistakes in the Defensive Breakdown. It was, after all, hastily prepared by busy coaches anxious to start planning for the next game. There are discrepancies between the Defensive Breakdown and another Alabama record that summarizes every play of the game. Even taking this possibility into account, however, there is still no explanation for the vast gulf between the record and Bryant's testimony.

Former Vanderbilt coach Art Guepe, an adversary of Bryant during this period, said, "It is hard to believe that a coach who prepares as thoroughly as Bryant would not have been prepared for the pro-set. In an opening game you must be prepared for everything, particularly a formation so widely used as this one." One of Bryant's players who became a coach said to me, "Nobody surprised Bear Bryant."

In retrospect, without game films, it admittedly cannot be said with 100-percent certainty that Alabama was not hurt by Georgia's early use of the pro-set. The Tide really may not have been in the soundest defense against it. A complex football thinker, Bryant could have chosen his early defenses for any number of reasons. The least plausible among them, however, was the one he himself offered at Butts's trial.

Bryant's claim of surprise at Georgia's use of the pro-set was far from essential to his basic contention that he never had the conversation allegedly overheard by George Burnett. Given the choice, he certainly would not have raised the pro-set smoke-screen at his own trial in Birmingham. But he would have had no choice. He would have been stuck with the flimsy "surprise" scenario because of his previous testimony. In the face of all the new adverse evidence Runzer had amassed, the prospect of testifying in Birmingham must have seemed perilous indeed to the awesome witness who had so easily overpowered Welborn Cody from the stand in Atlanta.

9

. . . .

Stopped at the Goal Line

JOHN RUNZER RUEFULLY ACCEPTED the decision to settle Bryant's case out of court, but he did not close his files. He hoped to use them in a retrial of the Butts case. The Curtis lawyers viewed the settlement with Bryant as a sound business judgment, not as an admission of the *Post*'s guilt, and were inalterably opposed to the idea of settling with Butts.

A new trial can come about in either of two ways: the judge can set aside a verdict and order a new trial, or an appellate court can reverse the judge and remand for a retrial. The motion for a new trial is a peculiar legal device. Its main oddity is that it usually seeks a remedy that is contrary to human nature: it is almost always based on alleged errors in the conduct of the trial by the judge who hears the motion. In other words, the judge is asked to confess error and reverse himself. He is asked to undo his own work and that of others. Overworked judges with a backlog of cases on their docket are understandably loath to let the original trial go for naught. It is little wonder that motions for new trials are rarely granted.

The *Post*'s lawyers made three successive motions for a new trial. The first was based on an unusually large number of alleged errors in the conduct of the trial, 24 in all. Judge Morgan ruled on it on January 14, 1964.*

---

* Judge Morgan's opinion is published at 225 Fed. Supp. 916.

Three grounds of the *Post's* motion challenged the Georgia statute authorizing juries to award punitive damages. (State law governs substantive matters when a federal court is exercising jurisdiction based on diversity of citizenship.) The statute was alleged to violate the U.S. Constitution's guarantees of due process and of free speech and press.

The *Post* was raising these issues for the first time. They should have been raised and disposed of as questions of law before the trial. Judge Morgan predictably ruled that these questions were raised too late and summarily rejected them.

Eight grounds of the motion contended that the judge erred in excluding evidence of specific acts of misconduct by Butts. Judge Morgan gave serious consideration to this issue but declined to reverse the rulings he made excluding this evidence at the trial.

Morgan conceded that the *Post's* defense of the article's truth had put Butts's character in issue, causing evidence of his general character and reputation to be admissible, but not particular acts of misconduct. As far as it went, Morgan's opinion was persuasive in justifying his exclusion of the evidence in question, most of which concerned Butts's activities with his mistress and his use of his athletic department credit cards for personal purposes. A plaintiff should not be forced to put his whole life on trial in order to sue for libel.

However, there was a different and much narrower theory of admissibility that Morgan did not address. This was that much of the rejected evidence concerned *official* misconduct by Butts; it contradicted his repeated claims of devotion and loyalty to the university.

Morgan similarly reaffirmed his original rulings excluding evidence offered by the *Post's* lawyers to impeach the testimony of John Carmichael. One piece of evidence concerned a 1933 petty larceny conviction in Ohio. As a matter of discretion, Morgan adhered to his exclusion of this evidence because of the lapse of time since the conviction. The other concerned false statements Carmichael had made to obtain business and liquor licenses. Their exclusion was reaffirmed by Morgan under a rule that a witness generally cannot be impeached on the basis of contradictory statements collateral to his testimony and to the issues of the lawsuit.

Several grounds of the motion were rejected without consideration because they concerned jury instructions, and no objections had been made to them at the trial. Similar treatment was given to a ground of the motion claiming improper arguments to the jury by Butts's counsel. Judge Morgan rejected it on the "elementary principle" that a new trial is not granted on the basis of such misconduct when that issue is raised for the first time on motion for a new trial.

The failure of the *Post*'s lawyers to object to Schroder's and Lockerman's arguments during the trial was compounded by the amount of time they had to do so. Morgan noted:

> Arguments were begun on Friday by both counsel and completed on Monday. Much of the argument of which complaint was made was offered on Friday, and yet on the following Monday, no objection was made on this portion of counsel's summation. Counsel for defendant consisted of numerous counsel, and yet exception was made only on the filing of the motion [for retrial].

In all, the motion complained of at least nine errors in the conduct of the trial to which no objection was made at the time. This was inexcusable, particularly with respect to the claims of allegedly erroneous jury instructions. These instructions are submitted to counsel before they are given to the jury. Rule 51 of the Federal Rules of Civil Procedure expressly requires that objections to them be made at that stage.

Only one issue raised by the motion for retrial troubled Judge Morgan. It was the contention that a new trial should be granted because of the excessiveness of the award of punitive damages.

Morgan reviewed similar awards in state and federal courts throughout the country and found that the largest award of punitive damages ever to be upheld in a libel action was the $175,000 awarded author Quentin Reynolds in his famous suit against columnist Westbrook Pegler. Noting that the jury's punitive award for Butts was 17 times this amount, Morgan concluded that it was "grossly excessive."

Whether this excessiveness alone justified a new trial was not discussed by Morgan. Instead, he considered only the question of how much he should reduce the award by applying the curious legal device called "remittitur."

A judge has no direct power to reduce the amount of damages awarded by a jury. This would undermine the constitutional right to a jury trial. When he feels that a jury's award is too high, however, he may base his denial of a defendant's motion for a new trial upon the condition that the plaintiff accepts a specified lesser amount. The plaintiff "remits" the difference between the two figures as an alternative to undergoing a new trial and possibly losing everything. The remittitur is one of those judicial compromises that satisfies neither party. It is rarely used.

In reaching his decision on an appropriate punishment for the *Post*, Morgan took into consideration the *Post*'s carelessness in the preparation of the article, its many inaccuracies, and its general editorial policies, saying of the latter:

> The jury was warranted in concluding from the foregoing incidents and the persistent and continuing attitude of the officers and agents of the defendant that there was a wanton or reckless indifference of plaintiff's rights.

One example of the attitude of the *Post*'s agents cited by Morgan was the fact that every editor and writer involved with the story testified by deposition, even though two of them, editor-in-chief Clay Blair, Jr., and senior editor Davis Thomas appeared in court. (This confirmed my own impression that the failure of these witnesses to testify in person did not meet with Judge Morgan's approval.)

Describing the article as "clearly defamatory and extremely

so," the judge concluded, without explaining his arithmetic, that $400,000 was the maximum sum that could reasonably be awarded as punitive damages. Morgan's exact order was:

ORDER

Now, this the 14th day of January, 1964,

It is ordered that the motion of the new trial is granted unless the plaintiff, Wallace Butts, within twenty (20) days after the service of this order, shall, in writing filed with the Clerk of the United States District Court for the Northern District of Georgia, remit all the punitive damages awarded above the sum of $400,000.00; the award for general damages in the amount of $60,000.00 to remain undisturbed.

Butts accepted the remittitur. He had no right to appeal. His only other choice was to risk all in a new trial.

The *Post*'s lawyers proceeded to perfect an appeal to the U.S. Fifth Circuit Court of Appeals. Judge Morgan normally would have been finished with the case until and unless his denial of a new trial was reversed by that court or by the U.S. Supreme Court. But Morgan's respite was brief. On February 28, the *Post* filed a second motion for a new trial and in March still a third one. One was based on newly discovered evidence, the other on newly discovered law.

The second motion was based on the evidence obtained by the *Post*'s lawyers in Alabama during their preparation for the trial of Bryant's case. It consisted of Bryant's February 28 letter to Rose, Rose's contradictions of his earlier testimony in the depositions taken by Runzer and Embry, and the deposition of Rose's secretary.

The statement in Bryant's letter that he remembered his call to Butts on Sunday, September 16, "very well" was cited as showing that both Bryant and Rose testified falsely at Butts's trial when they swore that Bryant had no specific recollection of the call.

The motion said Rose had "under oath recanted and contradicted" his earlier testimony concerning the dictation of his letter of March 6, 1963, to Georgia president O. C. Aderhold. Both the deposition of Marion Park, Rose's secretary, in which she testified that Rose had dictated the letter "slowly and thoughtfully" on March 5, and the March 5 draft of the letter itself were cited as proving that Rose testified falsely in the Butts case when he claimed that the letter was "hastily dictated" and "error-laden."

This motion predictably was denied by Judge Morgan under the well-established rule that a new trial will not be granted on the basis of newly discovered evidence that was in existence at the time of the first trial and that could have been discovered and used by the exercise of reasonable diligence. No excuse was advanced by the *Post*'s lawyers for their failure to do for Butts's case what was later done for Bryant's case. Furthermore, the evidence was tangential to the basic issue of the truth of the *Post*'s "fix" story and did nothing to ease Morgan's indignation at the *Post* for its handling of the article and the trial.

The *Post*'s third motion for a new trial gave Judge Morgan more trouble. On March 9, 1964, the U.S. Supreme Court had revolutionized First Amendment law governing libel actions brought by public officials when it handed down its landmark decision in *New York Times Co. v. Sullivan*, 376 U.S. 254.

The *New York Times* case originated with a full-page ad that appeared in that paper in 1960. The ad charged that a wave of terror was being waged in the South against nonviolent civil rights demonstrators. Montgomery, Alabama, was specifically mentioned as a place where the authorities had denied black college students their rights. Sullivan, the Montgomery police commissioner, sued the *Times* and some signers of the ad for libel and obtained a judgment of $500,000 in the Alabama courts. The U.S. Supreme Court reversed the decision, establishing new standards for libel actions by public figures.

Reasoning that debate on public issues should be "uninhibited, robust and wide-open," the Court announced that public officials could no longer recover libel judgments merely because inaccurate statements were made about them. To be libelous, a statement must also have been made with "actual malice—that is, with knowledge that it was false or with reckless disregard of whether it was false or not."

The instructions given the jury in Butts's case were not based on this new standard. Butts's lawyers had only two ways to avoid a new trial under the *New York Times* rule. One was to argue that the *Post*'s lawyers had waived the right to rely on this defense because they had not raised it in their pleadings. The second was to convince Judge Morgan that Wally Butts, as athletic director, was not a "public official" within the *New York Times* rule.

Judge Morgan did not consider the first argument and went directly to the second. Reasoning that Butts was more analogous to a university faculty member or employee than to a public officer, he ruled that Butts was not a public official.

As a final reason for denying a new trial on the basis of *New York Times*, Judge Morgan declared that even if the ruling applied, the evidence against the *Post* would have justified a jury in finding that the defendant acted in reckless disregard of whether or not the article was false.*

With this, the proceedings in Morgan's court ended, and he appeared to be on solid ground in most of his rulings on the motions for a new trial. As the case headed for the federal appellate courts, the excessiveness of the verdict and the *New York Times* argument appeared to be the two major weapons in the *Post*'s tenacious battle for a second trial. On these issues, Butts's reduced verdict was to undergo two close calls by the federal appellate courts. They were as close as such calls can be, two judges to one and five judges to four.

In the Fifth Circuit Court of Appeals, the case was assigned

---

* Judge Morgan's opinion denying the second and third motions for a new trial was issued April 7, 1964, and is published at 242 Fed. Supp. 390.

to a three-judge panel that included two of the more prominent members of the federal judiciary, both particularly respected as veterans of the difficult civil rights cases in the deep South in the fifties and sixties. They were Judges Richard T. Rives of Montgomery, Alabama, and John R. Brown of Texas. The third judge was Adrian A. Spears, U.S. district judge for the Western District of Texas, who was sitting by special assignment. Over a vigorous dissent by Rives, Brown and Spears joined to affirm Butts's judgment.*

The *Post*'s brief assigned 28 specifications of error, far too many for effective argument or full consideration of all of them. They were grouped under ten propositions. The judges disagreed on several issues. In an opinion written by Spears, the two-judge majority agreed with Judge Morgan that the issue of improper argument cannot be raised for the first time on motion for a new trial. Failure to object at the time of the argument was tantamount to a waiver. Judge Spears then gratuitously added that reversal would not be required even if timely objections had been made. His reasoning was remarkable:

> Some of the argument was invited, but the very nature of the case made it virtually impossible to discuss the evidence free of emotion or drama. The editor-in-chief of the Post set the tone and the stage for the attack. He openly boasted that the Post's new policy of "sophisticated muckraking" was the "final yardstick" of editorial achievement since it meant "we are hitting them where it hurts." It was no wonder that the author Graham was equally callous in admitting that he knew that "when this article was published that it was the death of Wally Butts in his chosen profession" and that "Curtis Publishing Company knew that when that article was published it would ruin Coach Butts' career." The policy

---

* The opinions are published at 351 Fed. 2d 702.

of the magazine so bluntly stated was by itself more than enough to inflame the jury. Counsel for Butts could only gild the lily.

The idea that otherwise improper argument of counsel can be "invited" and justified by the pretrial acts of the opposing party is novel. Spears cited no precedents on this point.

By contrast, in his dissent Judge Rives expressed "shock and surprise" at the majority's condonation of appeals to passion and prejudice by Butts's lawyers. Rives felt that the excessiveness of the jury's verdict, following such arguments, showed that the verdict was clearly based on passion and prejudice engendered by the arguments. He contended that such a verdict could not be cured by remittitur but only by a new trial.

The panel divided most sharply on the applicability of the *New York Times* rule. The majority held that the right to raise this issue had been waived by the *Post*'s counsel. Once again the *Post* suffered one of its many losses because of mistakes made by its lawyers.

By the rarest of coincidences, the *Post*'s Birmingham firm, Beddow, Embry, and Beddow, had represented *The New York Times* against Sullivan in the Alabama courts and in the U.S. Supreme Court. They had helped persuade the Supreme Court to adopt the new rule on libel of public officials that the *Post* now vainly sought to invoke. The Fifth Circuit majority held that the Beddow, Embry firm's representation of the *Post* in Bryant's case and their attendance at the trial of Butts's case, combined with Philip Strubing's involvement against both Butts and Bryant, added up to a waiver of the *New York Times* issue. Here is how Judge Spears reasoned:

> A Birmingham, Alabama, law firm, which represented The New York Times in the case brought against it by Sullivan, also, together with Curtis' General Counsel, represented Curtis in a libel suit Coach Bryant had filed against it in the United States District Court at Bir-

mingham, Alabama. A member of this law firm had sent information to Curtis about the alleged telephone conversation between Butts and Bryant, and had talked with the author, Graham, about the matter prior to publication of the story. The same lawyer, together with another member of the firm, sat (as did General Counsel for Curtis) at Curtis' Counsel table throughout the trial of the case.

While it is true that the Supreme Court did not decide the Times case until March 9, 1964, it would be contrary to reason and common sense to assume that there had not been, at all times during the pendency of this case, full communication among Curtis' counsel, particularly concerning trial strategy. The facts more than justify our conclusion that Curtis was fully aware when this suit was instituted, and certainly no later than the beginning of trial, that the constitutional questions it now argues had been for some time, and were still being, vigorously asserted in Times. . . .

. . . For whatever tactical reason Curtis sat back and failed to carry the constitutional torch before verdict and judgment, the fact remains that it was charged with knowledge, through its interlocking battery of able and distinguished attorneys, of the issues involved in the Times case, and was afforded every reasonable opportunity to have those same issues heard and determined by the trial court in the case at bar. . . . Curtis' complete and utter silence amounted to "an intentional relinquishment or abandonment of a known right or privilege."

Judge Rives disagreed on the waiver issue. He believed that mere "silence" could not waive a constitutional right not known at the time, noting that this new right of a libel defendant was not even asserted by counsel who initially petitioned the Supreme

Court for review of the *New York Times* case. Rives felt that *Times* applied and required reversal.

The Fifth Circuit's majority did not dwell on most of the issues raised by the *Post*. It did, however, deal with one contention that Judge Morgan had not discussed, an additional theory for admission of evidence of Butts's particular acts of misconduct.

Butts was asked on cross-examination if he had not said on television, in denying the *Post*'s charges, that he would "never do anything to injure the University of Georgia." Butts admitted that he had. Before Judge Morgan and on appeal the *Post* argued that the excluded evidence was admissible to contradict this statement and impeach Butts's credibility.

The Fifth Circuit properly rejected this "bootstrap" argument, ruling that the *Post* could not interject an out-of-court statement just in order to disprove it. Inexplicably, the *Post* failed to point to similar statements made at the trial in testimony generated by Butts's lawyers. John Carmichael testified that when he telephoned Butts to warn him of Burnett's revelations, Butts's response included a statement that he would never do anything to hurt Georgia. And Bill Hartman testified that Butts had said this repeatedly at the meeting when he first saw Burnett's notes. Yet the *Post*'s brief failed to call the appellate court's attention to this testimony by witnesses for Butts.

Everyone in the courtroom was well aware that Butts had claimed many times that he would never intentionally hurt the University of Georgia. Again, inexcusable errors by the *Post*'s lawyers deprived it of full consideration of its rights.

After the Fifth Circuit's opinion came down, the *Post*'s lawyers did not go to the U.S. Supreme Court immediately. Instead they moved swiftly to counter the Fifth Circuit majority's conclusion that they had intentionally waived their client's constitutional rights under *New York Times*. Eric Embry filed an affidavit that he and Roderick Beddow attended the Butts trial only as "spectators" to prepare themselves for the trial of Bryant's case and that they were never consulted concerning trial strategy or constitutional questions. He also noted that the "actual malice" requirement of the *New York Times* rule was not argued in that case in the courts of Alabama or in the petition for review by the U.S. Supreme Court.

Welborn Cody filed an affidavit confirming that Embry and Beddow were not part of the "trial team" in Butts's case and were not consulted on trial strategy. He added that he was not aware of the constitutional issues being argued in the *New York Times* case and certainly did not intend to waive any constitutional rights of his client.

Philip Strubing also filed an affidavit confirming the spectator role played by Embry and Beddow in Butts's case. He admitted that he had worked actively on both Butts's and Bryant's cases but said of the *New York Times* issue:

> There were no discussions between Messrs. Embry and Beddow and me in regard to the constitutional questions being alleged by The New York Times Company in the case of *New York Times Company v. Sullivan* . . . and there was no suggestion by these attorneys that any constitutional issues be raised in the *Butts v. Curtis* case. . . . I certainly did not intend to waive any constitutional defense of Curtis in the *Butts v. Curtis* case . . . and was not aware of the constitutional defense provided by *New York Times Company v. Sullivan* until that case was decided by the Supreme Court on March 9, 1964, some six months after the trial of the *Butts* case.

The Fifth Circuit panel divided once again in ruling on the *Post*'s position for a rehearing on the waiver issue. The majority adhered to its earlier position on waiver but shifted its factual grounds. It accepted Eric Embry's statement that neither he nor Beddow informed Welborn Cody of the constitutional issues being raised in the *New York Times* case and withdrew its reliance on the Birmingham lawyers' attendance at the Butts trial. Instead, it attributed a waiver solely to Strubing's involvement in both Butts's and Bryant's cases.

The names of Strubing's law firm and the Beddow, Embry firm were on motions filed for Curtis in both of Bryant's cases against the *Post* in Birmingham. Both of these motions included the following passage:

> To subject this defendant to liability in the circumstances complained of would abridge the freedom of speech and press in violation of the First Amendment to the Constitution of the United States, made applicable to the states by the Fourteenth Amendment to the Constitution of the United States.

From the mere inclusion of this generalized defense in Bryant's case, the Fifth Circuit two-judge majority inferred the non sequitur of intentional waiver because of its absence in Butts's case. No logical reason was ever advanced to explain why Strubing might deliberately have chosen to forego known constitutional rights in the Butts case but not in the Bryant case. The generalized First Amendment claim in Bryant's case was thrown into a grab-bag pleading by the Birmingham lawyers, who even added a farfetched claim that Bryant's suit violated the interstate commerce clause of the Constitution.

The unsoundness of the Fifth Circuit majority's reasoning is perhaps best evidenced by the fact that of the total of thirteen federal judges on three courts who considered the question of waiver, only three found in Butts's favor. The third aberrant judge turned out to be the sole member of the U.S. Supreme Court who found waiver; he was also the one who held the controlling vote in narrowly preserving Butts's judgment.

For its appeal in the Supreme Court, the *Post* retained Herbert Wechsler, who had successfully represented *The New York Times* in that court in the case the *Post* was struggling to invoke. Wechsler was a veteran Columbia University law professor and a nationally known expert on constitutional law and Supreme Court litigation. Bill Schroder argued for Butts.

When the decision came down, Wechsler had trounced Schroder soundly on the waiver issue. Schroder had persuaded only one justice. The 8–1 victory on waiver, however, did not prevent a 5–4 loss for the *Post.* The Fifth Circuit was affirmed.*

Four members of the court, Justices Harlan, Clark, Stewart, and Fortas, felt that a modified *New York Times* rule for "public figures" had been satisfied by the evidence of malice and Judge Morgan's instructions on punitive damages. Speaking through Harlan, they found that the evidence supported a finding that the *Post*'s story was "highly unreasonable conduct constituting an extreme departure from the standards of investigation and reporting ordinarily adhered to by responsible publishers."

The four dissenters divided two ways. Justice Black, speaking for himself and Douglas, accused the Harlan group of looking at the facts as if they were jurors instead of appellate judges in concluding that the requisite malice had been proved.

Brennan's dissenting opinion, for himself and White, applied the *New York Times* rule and found that the trial judge's instructions did not comport with the *Times* standard in several ways. One was that the jury was instructed that it could award punitive damages even though it found good faith on the part of the defendant. The opinions of Black and Brennan made no mention of the waiver issue. The four dissenting justices did not even consider the question worthy of discussion.

The Harlan foursome considered the waiver issue but had no difficulty in rejecting Schroder's argument. They said of Strubing's actions that "even a lawyer fully cognizant of the record and briefs in *New York Times* litigation might reasonably have expected the resolution of the case to have no impact on this case. . . ."

With four justices led by Harlan voting to affirm and four led by Black and Brennan voting to reverse, Chief Justice Earl War-

---

* The Court's opinion was announced June 12, 1967, and is published at 388 U.S. 130.

ren became the swing man. He alone accepted Schroder's waiver argument, and joined the Harlan plurality to affirm the Fifth Circuit and preserve Butts's judgment.

Warren's cryptic opinion on the waiver issue verges on the incredible. He did not refer to Strubing at all but relied solely on the involvement of Birmingham counsel, the very theory that the Fifth Circuit had abandoned when it learned that they were merely spectators at Butts's trial. Warren reasoned that the waiver must have been based on "tactical or public relations considerations" of counsel, but he did not suggest any such consideration. This, then, became the final and fatal instance when the conduct of the *Post's* counsel played a key role in the outcome of the case and, ironically, the instance when the lawyers' actions least merited the penalizing of their client.

Thus, a view held by only one of the 13 judges who considered the question cost the *Post* a second trial—and it was a view on a factual issue that was not litigated in the lower courts. Butts won on the rarest of judicial miscarriages. The ultimate irony was that southern segregationist Wally Butts was the beneficiary of the aberrant judicial behavior of Chief Justice Earl Warren, the principal architect of *Brown v. Board of Education*, which laid the foundation for the desegregation of America's public schools.

10

. . . .

Fix or Fiction?

SUPPOSE THE *Post* had been granted the new trial it so narrowly lost. Or suppose Bear Bryant's case had gone to trial. Better still, suppose Wally Butts's case had been tried the first time around without the multitude of mistakes made by the *Post*'s lawyers. Would we now know whether the *Post* article was a true account of a real fix or a fictional account of an innocent phone call? Or does the truth lie somewhere between fix and fiction?

In describing the work of his lawyers, Matthew Culligan, president of Curtis Publishing Company, called the trial a "comedy of errors." The case was a rare combination of mistakes in preparation, strategy, and execution. The mismatch in performances by lawyers was comparable to the mismatch between John Griffith's and Bear Bryant's football teams.

Every lawyer has seen cases go to juries whose picture of the facts is 180 degrees removed from reality. This was one of those rare cases. Such a distorted view of the facts can result from false testimony, lawyers' failures to offer evidence, the judge's exclusion of evidence that has been offered, and various tricks by lawyers. All of these operated to mislead the jury in the Butts case.

No useful purpose would be served by simply cataloging the errors of the *Post*'s lawyers. But an analysis of these mistakes is important in evaluating how far the jury's verdict might have strayed from a determination of truth. Many mistakes caused

189

the jury either to fail to receive evidence that would have assisted its search for truth or to receive evidence or argument that steered it away from truth.

The *Post*'s lawyers felt that they labored under one major handicap not of their own making: they were required to go to trial a little more than four months after Butts filed his complaint. It is usually impossible to schedule a trial that quickly in a federal court, even if the litigants want to, but Judge Morgan insisted upon completing the trial before the 1963 college football season opened and made it clear that there would be no continuances.

Except for Burnett's testimony, the *Post*'s lawyers had nothing by way of proof when they started out. They had a long way to go and—considering that they all had busy law practices and obligations to other clients—a relatively brief period of time to get there. They began by scrambling about the country, taking time-consuming discovery depositions in New York, Chicago, Tallahassee, Birmingham, Jacksonville, Athens, Lexington, and Atlanta. Unfortunately, however, they failed to pursue obvious discovery opportunities in Tuscaloosa, an omission that deprived them of the incriminating documents in the offices of Bryant and Alabama president Rose, particularly Bryant's February 28 letter to Rose and Alabama's scouting report and defensive records on the game. With the services of a large law firm at Cody's disposal, this oversight was inexcusable. He could easily have asked Curtis's Birmingham counsel to explore this crucial source of evidence for possible use in both Bryant's and Butts's cases.

Lacking this evidence, the *Post* went down one blind alley after another trying to link Butts to gambling, looked in vain for usable proof that Butts had betrayed Georgia to other opponents in 1962, and gathered voluminous but ultimately useless evidence of immoral conduct in Butts's personal life. While Welborn Cody was in Lexington, Kentucky, taking depositions of hotel employees on Butts and Evelyn, Bill Schroder and Allen Lockerman were poring over the Burnett notes and the game film with Georgia assistant coach John Gregory.

The discovery proceedings in Tallahassee, Florida, are another example of the precious time wasted by the *Post*'s lawyers. On July 25, 1963, only two weeks before the trial was to open, *Post* lawyers took depositions of Florida State University football coaches about a call Butts had made to Florida State head coach Bill Peterson during the week before the Seminole-Bulldog game in 1962. As it happened, Peterson had been in conference with his staff when Butts called, and they all listened to the conversation. The witnesses agreed that Butts had said that Coach John Griffith was getting smarter as the season advanced because he was using more of Butts's old offense but that he would do even better if he installed two particular plays, the halfback pass and the shovel, or Utah, pass. The Utah pass was in fact then used by Georgia for the first time that season in the Florida State game that Saturday, and it was intercepted by the Seminoles, who went on to win 18–0. Could Butts's call have prepared the Florida team for this play?

Coach Peterson and his staff insisted in their depositions that Butts's call was of no help to them. No defensive changes were made after the call. Georgia's Utah pass was intercepted by a Florida State lineman only because quarterback Rakestraw threw it short. This explanation neutralized their depositions enough to render them useless to the *Post*'s lawyers at the trial.

When a lawyer tries a big case involving a specialized, complex field such as medical malpractice or products liability, his first duty is to master the science and technology of that field in order to meet an expert on his ground and examine him as an equal. At the Butts trial big-time college football emerged as an enormously complex field with a terminology all its own. To relate the Burnett notes to the play of the game and to meet Butts and his witnesses on equal terms required preparation in the technology of the sport. Cody's strategy of virtually ignoring the notes and the game in favor of evidence to smear Butts's character left him unprepared to play football in the courtroom.

Schroder, on the contrary, was prepared to perfection. Building on his football background, he mastered every detail of the game in question and technical aspects of football in general. His preparation produced a classic instance of "massive representation." He exploited every possible line of attack. In retrospect, I can think of no available stratagem or argument that he overlooked. His strategy was much like that employed in an old case deep in the folklore of the common law: An iron pot is borrowed from its owner. When the borrower returns the pot, it is cracked. The owner sues the borrower, alleging that the pot became cracked while in the borrower's possession. The borrower's defenses are (1) he never borrowed the pot; (2) the pot was in good condition when he returned it; (3) the pot was cracked when he borrowed it.

Although taking such flatly contradictory positions is now rare in formal pleadings and violates rules requiring good faith in alleging facts, a lawyer can present inconsistent facts at the trial and let jurors choose. Schroder did this and got away with it. His overall strategy was threefold: (1) Butts and Bryant never admitted that the phone call in question actually happened— they didn't deny it, but they stopped short of admitting it; (2) if the call did occur, they did not have the conversation alleged by George Burnett—they denied ever having a conversation that included any of the items on football in his notes; (3) even if they did have the conversation alleged by Burnett, it was innocent and of no value to Alabama. Cody allowed Schroder to get away with inconsistent positions on important factual issues, such as whether Bryant was surprised by the pro-set and whether Bryant knew that safetyman Brig Woodward committed fast on defense.

In trial tactics, the *Post*'s first mistake was that not a single representative of the company was seated at the counsel table except lawyers. The omission was one of several indicators that the case was not being taken seriously enough by the *Post*.

A much greater blunder was Cody's decision to rest his case without calling the author or any of the editors of the article to the stand. The *Post*'s success hinged on the good faith of these people. Schroder seized on their absence to read the portions of their depositions that most helped Butts's case, particularly on the question of malice. In final argument, Schroder hammered hard on the failure of anyone responsible for the article to appear on the stand, look the jury in the eye, and say he believed the article was true. Nothing prevented Cody from calling them in person after Schroder read their depositions; they should have been called in rebuttal.

The *Post* was also hurt by the failure of its lawyers to call three key witnesses, all of whom were located in Atlanta and had been eyewitnesses to crucial events: Furman Bisher, Milton Flack, and Cook Barwick. Judge Morgan himself was perplexed by Bisher's failure to testify. The malice issue may account for the *Post*'s decision not to call Bisher. Since he was a codefendant in Bryant's pending libel suit based on the brutality article, his incentive to discredit Bryant and lessen Bryant's chances of winning the first suit was undeniable. The *Post*'s counsel may have feared that cross-examination of him by Schroder about his animosity toward Bryant could have aided Butts's case on the question of malice.

Milton Flack's absence was also conspicuous. After the trial Fred Russell interviewed a juror who said that Flack's failure to appear was a factor that influenced him. Referring to the conflict between Carmichael and Burnett, the juror said, "I wondered why the defense didn't bring as a witness the one other man—Milton Flack—who was said to have seen the notes on that day, September 13."

One can speculate on possible reasons why Flack was not called as a witness, but there seems to be no good reason why Cook Barwick was not. The critical February 22 meeting with Butts was held in his office. There was conflicting testimony on what Butts said when he saw the Burnett notes. Butts and Bill Hartman differed from Treasurer Bolton in their testimony on Butts's reaction to the notes. Barwick would have supported Bolton, who claimed that Butts had admitted that Burnett undoubtedly "heard what he said he heard." (At the time, Barwick whispered to me that he believed Bolton was repeating Butts's words verbatim.) Barwick's testimony could have made the difference on this important issue. He apparently preferred not to take the stand, and friends respected his wishes. Lawyers have a peculiar aversion to going to a court either as parties or as witnesses, but Barwick should have joined in defending the fruits of his handiwork for the University of Georgia.*

Without knowing the exact reasons why these three eye-witnesses were not called, it is impossible to be absolutely certain, but it is hard to see how their presence could have harmed the *Post* as much as their absence did.

In addition to the Alabama records left undiscovered in Tuscaloosa, there was still other evidence Cody could have used against Bryant on the pro-set surprise issue. I was reminded of it by an incident in the recent retrial in Rhode Island of Claus von Bülow for the attempted murder of his wife. Midway through the prosecution's case, it offered an expert medical witness who had not been named before the trial. Although the judge denied the defense's motion to disqualify the witness for this reason, she postponed the trial long enough for the defense lawyers to study the expert's books and articles, noting that it is essential and commonplace for lawyers to read an opposing expert's publications in preparation for cross-examination.

Unbeknownst to the *Post*'s lawyers, apparently, three years before the trial Bear Bryant had written a book entitled *Building a Championship Football Team*. It is a remarkably comprehensive work and includes a section called "Our Surprise Defense," which opens:

> We never send our boys into a football game without trying to prepare them for every conceivable situation that might arise during the contest. We must try to anticipate every situation, and counteract with a sound defense. A situation might be very unusual, and we can-

---

* Barwick's sympathies were very much with the *Post*. He wrote to me after the trial, "It looks like the federal government won the lawsuit and the University of Georgia lost it." (The taxability of punitive damages accounts for the reference to the government.)

not actually defense it properly until the coach in the press box tells us exactly what the opposition is doing. Then we can work out the proper defense on the sideline and send it in. In the meantime the boys must have something they can counteract with immediately or the opposition is likely to score with its surprise offense. Consequently our signal caller will yell, "Surprise Defense," when he sees an unusual offensive formation, and the boys will react accordingly. Our rules for covering a spread or unusual offensive alignments are as follows:

1. If one man flanks, our halfback will cover him.

2. If two men go out, our halfback and end will move out and cover them.

These are descriptions of Georgia's two formations—the slot, with one man out, and the pro-set, which simply moves another man out. Bryant goes on to list nine more rules for his team's defensive reactions to unusual offensive formations, including rules for three, four, and five men out. This material would have been devastating in a skilled cross-examination of Bryant, for it establishes his general preparedness for the pro-set.

The *Post*'s lawyers' inability to persuade Judge Morgan to admit evidence of specific acts of misconduct—particularly concerning Butts's affair with Evelyn—was one of their costliest professional miscalculations. The rejected evidence included the records of the more than $2,800 in personal long-distance phone calls charged by Butts to his athletic department credit card between 1961 and 1963. (As already mentioned, Butts paid for these calls upon demand after he left the university.)

The *Post* was also prepared to prove that Evelyn traveled to numerous University of Georgia football games with Butts and was frequently seen with him on these trips by members of the Georgia team. Airline records were offered to show that Butts charged the university for her plane tickets on these and other trips. (Butts later repaid these, too.) They also show that Evelyn often traveled under a false name. Depositions had been taken in Lexington, Kentucky, to establish details of Butts's and Evelyn's trip there for the 1961 Georgia-Kentucky game. Evidence of Butts's nonfootball travels with Evelyn, his public appearances with her in Atlanta night spots, and his gift of a car to her was also presented in vain.

If Judge Morgan was legally correct in excluding this evidence, the *Post*'s lawyers made a serious misjudgment of the law of evidence and wasted much time and energy. If Morgan was incorrect, they failed as advocates by not educating him as to its admissibility. The latter appears to be the case. As indicated earlier, they did not adequately support the soundest argument for admissibility of this evidence—namely, that it contradicted Butts's claims that he would never intentionally hurt Georgia.

The exclusion of the evidence of Butts's official misconduct was the most glaring instance of the *Post*'s inability to use voluminous evidence that it had so painstakingly collected. The value of its use would have been inestimable. It would have shown that Butts could and had done many things that he had to know had injured the university.

Conversely, the exclusion of this evidence was an enormous boon for Butts's trial team; it enabled them to present the jury with a view of Wally Butts that was utterly at odds with reality. He came through as a friendly, mellow little man who had rendered the University of Georgia long and faithful service and was still totally dedicated to it.

The real Wally Butts had certainly ceased to be such a man during the 1960–63 period. Could he really have believed he had done nothing to hurt Georgia? Remember, he resigned as head coach in 1960 after learning from alumni that his "Night League" activities in Atlanta with Evelyn were hurting football recruiting there, yet he continued these public indiscretions as athletic director. Could he possibly have thought that flaunting his young mistress before players, alumni, and the public and misappropriating thousands of dollars of university funds to finance these activities was of no harm to the university?

In my opinion, the evidence of Butts's misconduct that injured the university should have been admitted. The jury then would have seen a more complete picture of the real Wally Butts of recent years—one who was capable of behavior that would have been unthinkable for him before 1959, one who was capable of deliberately doing things that he knew would hurt the university. His bitterness toward the university for having mistreated him, combined with his indiscreet personal life and a possible desire to see John Griffith fail, lent considerable credence to the possibility that he might have been susceptible to turning over Georgia football secrets to Bear Bryant.

Eric Embry, the *Post*'s principal Birmingham lawyer, now an Alabama Supreme Court justice, feels that Cody's biggest mistake was in paying so little attention to the importance of the point spread or betting line. Schroder successfully kept the jury focused on why the game was won by Alabama. The jurors never appreciated the fact that the margin of victory is the critical factor to gamblers. Throughout the trial there was an assumption that "fix" meant improper conduct that determined the *victor*, not the margin of victory. The totality of the evidence about the game and the two teams overwhelmingly established the fact that Alabama had such superior talent and coaching that Georgia would not have won one out of a hundred games between them. One of Schroder's easier achievements was to persuade the jury overwhelmingly that Bryant had no need of a fix merely to defeat John Griffith's team.

In his instructions to the jury, Judge Morgan defined *fix* as including acts that affect the margin of outcome as well as who wins and loses. This was the first time the jurors had heard of this double meaning. By then its importance was probably lost on them.

The double meaning of the term *fix* figured in a rather flagrant violation of rules of evidence. Without objection from opposing counsel, Schroder asked Alabama players whether, in their opinion, a football game could be fixed without the knowledge of the players. They readily answered in the negative. There are at least three reasons why this question was objectionable. First, it was opinion evidence about a subject on which the players presumably were not experts—the fixing of football games. Second, it assumed a fact not in evidence—that they had no knowledge of fixing. Third, the term *fix* was not defined; Cody should have at least demanded that much.

If Schroder's question concerned the type of "fixing" that allegedly occurred when Butts called Bryant, the players were flatly wrong. Players do not necessarily know all the sources of the information their coaches use in preparing them for a game. For instance, if Alabama's defensive coaching had been limited to preparing for the slot and pro-set formations, this could easily have been due to Bryant's receiving information from Butts, and the players would have had no reason whatsoever to suspect foul play. In other words, exactly the sort of fix alleged in the article could have occurred without the players' knowledge. The odds are that Morgan would have sustained an objection to the question had one been raised.

There were many other incidents of defective handling of evidence. For instance, the *Post* did not enter the records of Bryant's long-distance phone calls for the season to show his pattern of short, efficient calls. This evidence would also have revealed that Bryant did not call any other opposing athletic director during the entire season, belying the claim by both Bryant and Butts that they might have been talking about routine business between athletic directors. This claim is also belied by the fact that Butts was never in his office when he talked to Bryant; twice he was at home on Sunday, and once he was in Atlanta.

Better use could have been made of telephone records with regard to Frank Scoby, Butts's one friend whom the *Post* was able to link to gambling. Cody noted the fact that Butts's calls to Scoby increased sharply in September but failed to mention that Butts called Scoby just before he called Bryant on September 13. This fact did not necessarily mean that there was a connection between Scoby and the call to Bryant, but it certainly would have added credence to the possibility.

The factual evidence that the NCAA crackdown on roughness

and Bryant's extensive study of it took place early in the summer of 1962 and that George Gardner approved Bryant's defenses a week before the phone call were not used to refute the claim that Bryant and Butts could still have been talking about these things as late as September 13 or 16.

Cody's challenge to Frank Rose's testimony that he did not sign his March 6 letter to Aderhold was an evidentiary disaster and one that can only be described as a self-inflicted wound. After obtaining signature specimens from Rose and submitting them to the jury for comparison with the letter, Cody simply let the signatures speak for themselves. His expectation was that the jury would find the signatures identical and conclude that Rose was lying on this and other issues. There have been few instances when evidence offered by a lawyer backfired so disastrously.

A juror interviewed by Fred Russell after the trial said of the signatures, "I studied those signatures in the jury room, and in my opinion they definitely aren't the same. There's a difference in the small *A*s and the capital *R*s. So I rejected the inference that Dr. Rose might not be telling the truth."

Having found Rose to be truthful on this overblown issue, the jury apparently believed his testimony on a much more important issue—Bryant's credibility. The *Post* paid a heavy price for its lawyers' failure to consult a handwriting expert.

The signature question was not raised in Rose's pretrial deposition. If it had been, signatures could have been obtained for experts to compare well in advance of trial. The *Post* would then have had the advantage of an expert witness, or would have avoided the issue. This is another instance of fatally inadequate pretrial preparation.

A final instance of the *Post*'s inadequacies of proof is the fact that the importance of secrecy in football was never driven home to the jury. Indeed, the *Post* allowed contrary evidence to go unchallenged, leaving the impression that Butts could not have helped Bryant if he tried. Charlie Trippi declared that Georgia gave more information to the press than was shown in Burnett's notes. Bill Hartman claimed that Georgia disclosed its entire offense at an annual statewide clinic for high school coaches. This testimony aided the aspect of Schroder's strategy that was designed to prove that Burnett's notes contained nothing Bryant would not have known otherwise. The idea that there are no secrets in college football went virtually unrebutted at the trial.

If college teams have no secrets, why do they close practice sessions to the public? Followers of the sport know better today. We hear bizarre stories of efforts to spy on closed practices from distant high positions. A Tulane assistant coach was recently caught in a tree observing Mississippi State's practice through binoculars. Before a recent bowl game, another team practiced with 12 men on the field, one of whom was a decoy; the purpose was to fool any spy who might have been watching for the opponent. In 1962, the Georgia coaches took precautions against their own players. As assistant coach Leroy Pearce testified, they divided the players into three groups—backs, linemen, and ends—and gave each group only its own assignments, so no one player could construct an entire play.

When Tennessee played Iowa in the Peach Bowl in 1982, the Iowa coach was asked by a TV announcer before the game if he feared the quarterback option. He replied that he had no fear because Tennessee had not used it all year. It turned out that Tennessee had installed the play for the bowl game, and the announcer commented again and again on the difficulty Iowa was having handling Tennessee's option. If Iowa had been able to observe Tennessee's secret practices, it would have been prepared for the option.

In 1984, Coach Charlie Pell's Florida Gators were cited for more than a hundred violations of NCAA rules, six of which involved spying on opponents' practices. Florida offered to forfeit all six tainted games. Pell, who had been a protégé of Bear Bryant and a witness at the Butts trial, was ousted in midseason.

Commissioner Bernie Moore, a former coach himself, felt that if Bryant had known that the Bulldogs would use only the two formations described in the Burnett notes—as they did—it would have been of immense value to him in defensive planning.

A problem related to keeping information secret from opponents is that of keeping a team's secrets from gamblers. Robert Barrett, chief investigator for the Southeastern Conference, was recently quoted in the Knoxville *News-Sentinel* on this issue:

> "We're not concerned with bookmakers as such," Barrett explains. "We're concerned with people trying to get information. And we're concerned with players, coaches, managers—anybody connected with teams—being a source of information to give an edge to bettors.
>
> "We're concerned with the guy trying to fix a game."
>
> In the SEC, "We're concerned because of organized crime involvement in illegal sports betting. We're concerned because we don't want any of our athletes put in compromising positions. We're concerned because $25 billion is bet illegally every year."
>
> Consequently, Barrett toots off to visit SEC teams before the football and basketball seasons.
>
> "We tell the kids to be careful and how to handle specific situations," Barrett explains. "It's ridiculous to think it [illegal betting] can be stopped, but we can try and keep it controlled."
>
> Barrett said the gambler's approach to a player is pretty standard.
>
> "He tries to get friendly with the athlete," Barrett explains. "He's low-key, really soft at first. Soon he might toss the kid keys to a car and tell him to use it for his big date. Or, he might give him some money to fill up the gas tank which will already be filled.
>
> "Once he gets the kid in a compromising position then he begins asking questions like: 'How's so and so's ankle . . . How's Bill and his girl doing . . .'
>
> "With some seemingly harmless information that can

affect the way a team plays, the bettor then makes a score."

If a player can unwittingly furnish valuable secret information, a coach is in a far better position to aid an opponent or a gambler. The same secrets that help a gambler decide how to bet can be exploited by an opposing coach. A prime example of a possible fix that both an opponent and a gambler could profit from is the one described in the *Post* story.

"Gambling on professional football is the primary source of income for organized crime," wrote Marvin West in the Knoxville *News-Sentinel* of January 18, 1983. West was discussing the Public Television documentary, "An Unauthorized History of the NFL," which included claims that games had been fixed by a coach, a quarterback, and a leading defensive player working as a team. All were paid six-figure sums by a gambler.

There is probably even more gambling on college football than on the professional sport simply because of the greater number of games. Is there any reason to believe that the college game is less attractive to gamblers or less vulnerable to fixes?

The bottom line is that there are secrets in college football and good reasons for keeping them secret. The very integrity of the game is undermined if a team tries to win by learning what its opponent fairly assumes it does not know. This is true now. It was true in 1962. But Bill Schroder probably convinced some jurors to buy the theory that Georgia had no secrets for Butts to betray.

Finally, the *Post*'s lawyers must be faulted for their failure to raise many issues at the trial that were subsequently raised for the first time on motions for new trial and appeal. These issues range from the *New York Times* ruling to objectionable jury instructions.

The jury very well might have been affected by a timely objection to Schroder's and Lockerman's improper closing arguments. No one in the courtroom could have doubted that the jury was moved. Few lawyers, if any, could have denied that

Butts's counsel vastly exceeded acceptable limits in their appeals to passion and prejudice, expressions of personal opinion, and use of facts outside the record. Judge Rives's position that these arguments alone justified reversal, even though opposing counsel had not objected, is the best evidence of their extreme impropriety.

The record does not begin to convey the eloquence and fervor with which Schroder delivered his verbal assault on the *Post* and its editors. His concluding description of Butts lying in his casket, draped in Georgia colors, vividly reinforced the jury's mistaken belief in Butts's total and eternal loyalty to Georgia. Judge Rives commented that if his dissent served no other purpose, it was worthwhile for preserving for posterity Schroder's final "colorful peroration."

Considering the jury's flawed view of the facts, one is tempted to disregard the verdict for Butts in trying to ascertain the truth about his phone conversation with Bryant. But a unanimous jury verdict cannot be dismissed so easily. It demands consideration.

Just what did the verdict mean? There is speculation that the jury believed that the phone call had not taken place. The jury made no such finding, and none was called for. It is impossible to believe that the jury could have reached such a decision in light of all the conclusive and essentially uncontested evidence that the call occurred and that Burnett overheard it.

The only issue open to question about the call is what was said in the overheard conversation. Did the jury believe George Burnett? As I reported to the Southeastern Conference in November 1963, the jury's verdict was fully consistent with a possible belief that Burnett told the truth. Schroder may have persuaded the jurors of Burnett's truthfulness with his theory that the Burnett notes reflected an innocent conversation in which Bryant learned nothing new or valuable. It is also possible that the jury believed Burnett but felt that the *Post* should be punished for the way the article was compiled and for the excesses it contained. Burnett himself was not on trial, after all. The lawsuit was concerned with the truth of "The Story of a College Football

Fix," not with the truthfulness of George Burnett. And the article went far beyond his notes and testimony. Such items as the reference to "a frightful physical beating," Rakestraw's tipping his plays, the quotations supplied by Furman Bisher, and other admitted inaccuracies were not traceable to Burnett.

The cavalier manner in which the *Post*'s case was presented in court undoubtedly alienated the jury, as it did the judge. Schroder scored heavily with the jury in attacking Frank Graham, Jr., and the *Post* editors for not coming to Atlanta to "look this jury in the eye" and swear that they believed the story to be true.

The *Post*'s new editorial policy, which Clay Blair had dubbed "sophisticated muckraking," also must have antagonized the jurors. When Schroder coldly read Blair's description of the *Post*'s new approach, "the exposé in the mass magazines [is calculated] to provoke people, make them mad," one could feel outrage mounting in the courtroom. Blair's testimony that the Butts-Bryant story fit this new approach and was a "step in the right direction" but went only 25 percent of the way toward his goal incensed those present even more. Blair's boast to his staff about the lawsuits they had generated provided Schroder with his most inflammatory argument; it enabled him to claim that the *Post* was deliberately engaged in "libel for profit" and that only the jury could stop the killing.

The verdict of $3 million in punitive damages and only $60,000 in compensatory damages indicated that the jury wanted to punish the *Post* for its general misconduct, rather than compensate Butts for any wrong done to him. There is reason to believe that the jurors knew that punitive damages are taxable income and that the federal government would get the lion's share.

The award of only $60,000 in compensatory damages showed that the *Post*'s lawyers had been successful in attacking Butts's character and reputation. The jurors apparently felt that his reputation was already so tarnished that the *Post* did him little further injury. The juror interviewed by Fred Russell said Butts "just symbolized any person in the country that a magazine might have charged with 'fixing' or 'rigging' a game and being 'corrupt,' without proving the charges." Another juror told *Time* magazine that they would as soon have given the entire award to charity. The jury might well have believed that Butts was capable of betraying John Griffith's team whether he actually did so or not.

The jury apparently accepted Schroder's argument that the *Post* deserved punishment more for its editorial policies than for what it did to Butts, and should be compelled to change its policies in order to protect the public. In final arguments the issue of George Burnett's truthfulness was almost completely subordinated to the wickedness of the *Post*'s conduct.

The most serious challenge to George Burnett's truthfulness raised at the trial was the testimony of John Carmichael. Either Burnett or Carmichael was lying about the authenticity of the notes in evidence. In my opinion, the preponderance of the evidence supports a conclusion that Burnett told the truth. I so advised the Southeastern Conference in November 1963, and I am even more convinced of it today.

Carmichael died in 1979, before I resumed work on this subject. George Burnett is still alive and went to great lengths to cooperate with me. He had no fear of having the issue of his credibility revived for public scrutiny; indeed, he welcomed the opportunity for public vindication. His attitude has reinforced my confidence in his credibility.

If Carmichael had believed that Burnett overheard and recorded mere innocent "general football talk," why did he take such pains to locate Butts in Philadelphia, call him at midnight, and warn him of Burnett's disclosures? Neither he nor Butts was specific about the content of that call, but Carmichael obviously felt that the nature of Burnett's revelations was such that it signaled serious trouble for his friend. It is doubtful that mere "general football talk" of the sort Carmichael later claimed would have so alarmed him.

In pretrial statements to Attorney General Cook, Carmichael had said that he did not read the notes when Burnett showed them to him. Yet at the trial he testified that five of the seven pages of the notes in evidence contained material that was not in the original documents. When challenged in court about his earlier statement, "I did not pick them up to read them," he qualified it by adding, "but I did read them." This disingenuous effort to reconcile his contradictory claims meant that he had read all of the notes while they were spread on Burnett's desk without handling them, a highly implausible scenario. It is equally hard to believe that he could recall only three items in the original notes and yet claim with certainty that nothing else in the notes in evidence was in the originals.

Did George Burnett replace the original notes, which Carmichael claimed to be innocent, with a fabricated, more incriminating version? If so, he had the help of someone who knew much more about Georgia football than he did, someone so close to the Bulldogs that he knew the two formations Georgia had used and many other facts not found in the newspapers. Who might this have been? I have never heard even the slightest hint that any person close to Georgia football joined Burnett in such a bizarre and dangerous conspiracy.

The notes contain too many inaccuracies, such as the misspelling of Babb as "Baer" and Rissmiller as "Reismueller," to have been the work of an expert. Deliberately misspelling Woodward as "Woodard," the way Wally Butts pronounced it, would have been an act of genius, as well as an act of someone close to Butts. There were also too many entries that were incomplete and meaningless. If the notes had been an expert's work, Coach John Griffith would not have been forced on cross-examination into agreeing with Schroder that the two formations were the only items that would have been helpful to Bryant.

What motive could Burnett have had to fabricate a second and more incriminating set of notes? He had no animosity toward Butts or Bryant. Butts was a director of the company Burnett worked for. A profit motive, like the sale of an exclusive story to the *Post*, can also be ruled out; it is inconsistent with Burnett's voluntary surrender of his only copy of the notes to John Griffith. It is implausible that Burnett would have taken on two figures like Bryant and Butts on the basis of forged documents, risking personal grief if he failed and with at best only a remote possibility of modest pecuniary gain. George Burnett was a middle-aged churchman and family man without the imagination and recklessness required for such a bold and dangerous venture. To speculate on the identity of an expert accomplice from Georgia football circles is utterly impossible. There are no suspects.

Burnett's testimony is corroborated in too many ways for it to have been part of a hoax. He voluntarily submitted to two lie detector tests, the validity of which was better established than that of the tests taken by Butts and Bryant. He offered to take truth serum. His story never varied through the many times he told it. Unlike Carmichael, he was never caught in inconsistent statements. His willingness to admit damaging facts, such as his testimony that he agreed with Carmichael that he would not have known how to bet on the game, also operates in his favor. When there was something in the notes that had no meaning to him, Burnett admitted it. Where the *Post* article inaccurately attributed something to him, such as the reference to Rakestraw's feet, he did not support the *Post*.

Finally, Burnett was a composed and impressive witness on the stand. Fred Russell, who was generally sympathetic to Butts and Bryant, described Burnett as a witness who "speaks slowly, clearly, and looks his questioner in the eye."

By contrast, Carmichael's demeanor on the stand hurt his credibility. His tone was unconvincing when he changed his story about having read the notes. His facial expression and vocal inflection indicated to me that a fierce anger at Burnett for disclosing the notes continued to motivate him. He wanted very much to thwart Burnett. After Carmichael's testimony, a neutral sportswriter said to me, "That guy's lying through his teeth."

During the trial Carmichael was often seen in the company of Butts's followers, and he attended the victory party in Butts's hotel suite after the trial. He seemed quite anxious to ingratiate himself with Butts and his supporters.

At this point it seems appropriate to review the facts in the

Butts-Bryant affair about which we can be reasonably certain:

• Butts and Bryant exchanged an unusual number of long-distance phone calls in September of 1962.

• Their explanations for these phone calls are not believable. The NCAA crackdown on roughness might have been the most plausible, had it not been for the time elapsed since the changes were announced. Bernie Moore, who knew how much the issue had been belabored over the summer, found it hard to believe this explanation of the calls made in mid-September. It was one of the reasons he became suspicious of Butts and Bryant.

• George Burnett overheard a call on Thursday, September 13, and made notes on that call.

• The call included discussion of the Georgia football team.

• The call ended with agreement that Bryant would call Butts back on Sunday.

• Butts observed a secret Georgia practice on Saturday.

• Bryant called Butts back on Sunday, and they talked for 67 minutes.

Given this much corroboration of George Burnett's story, the implausibility of Carmichael's testimony, and the unlikelihood of a hoax attempt, the odds come down strongly on the side of Burnett's truthfulness. There are loose ends and inconsistencies, to be sure, but in reconstructing past events, we often must settle for probabilities and degrees of probability. My personal conclusion is that it is highly probable that Butts and Bryant had the conversation reflected in Burnett's notes.

That the jury did not necessarily reject Burnett's testimony is confirmed by the little evidence we have of the substance of their deliberations. A young associate in Schroder's firm who worked on the Butts case remembers the "office wisdom" on the key to understanding the jury's verdict. The jurors avoided the task of deciding who was lying by concluding that even if the *Post* article told the truth about the phone call, the game simply was not fixed.

Post-trial interviews with jurors revealed that the football witnesses for Butts, particularly the Alabama and Georgia players, convinced them that the game was played and won fairly regardless of the phone call or of what Butts may have said to Bryant. The jurors apparently did not believe that a game could ever be fixed by a mere phone call. The failure of the *Post*'s lawyers to develop the reality and importance of secrecy in football thus turned out to be one of their most fatal blunders.

My own recent conversations with the five jurors who could be located confirm the fact that the jury's reasoning made it unnecessary to consider the conflict between John Carmichael and George Burnett on the authenticity of the notes introduced at the trial. None of them recalls that there was even any discussion of this question.

Whether the Butts-Bryant conversation affected the play of the game is a different question. Alabama's personnel and coaching were so superior to Georgia's that we can be certain that the Tide needed no special information in order to win decisively. Georgia's sophomores, playing from the simplest possible offense, did not belong in the same league with the Tide, which went on to a 10–1 season and trounced Oklahoma, 17–0, in the Orange Bowl. They gave up a total of 39 points, with no opponent scoring more than 7. Their only loss was to Georgia Tech, the controversial game mentioned in Graham's article in which Bryant elected at the last minute to pass rather than go for a field goal and lost, 7–6.

There is no "smoking gun" to show that the play of the Alabama-Georgia game was affected, although the two formations mentioned in Burnett's notes come closest to filling that role. The knowledge that they were to be Georgia's only formations, complete with the exact width of the slots, could well have helped the defense-minded Bryant to coach his team to a shutout.

It is safe to say that nothing Butts told Bryant caused Georgia to lose. And it is unlikely, though not inconceivable, that their conversation was responsible for Alabama's more than doubling the point spread, enabling gamblers who bet on the Tide to win handily.

This does not mean that Bryant would not have listened if

Butts called with information that had any chance of being helpful. Considering Bryant's drive to win games and championships and Butts's bitterness and vulnerability, such a phone conversation was something both men were capable of at that time.

The other calls during this period increase suspicion about the Butts-Bryant connection, especially the 67-minute Sunday call, which was arranged at the end of the call Burnett overheard on Thursday and which occurred after Butts observed Georgia's secret practice on Saturday. Although Butts might not have had ready answers to all the questions Bryant allegedly raised on Thursday, he may well have had them on Sunday.

There is but one hypothesis that is consistent with all known facts. It answers troublesome questions of motive and the effects of the call on the game.

What were the possible motives of Bryant and Butts? Bryant's is easy. His powerful will to win had motivated him on more than one occasion in the past to resort to means less defensible than listening while an opposing athletic director talked about his team.

Might Bryant have gambled on the game? There is no evidence that he did, but such evidence is hard to come by. He needed money and liked gambling in other forms. But there is little need to speculate on gambling as a motive because winning the game and winning it big was reason enough for Bryant.

Butts's bitterness toward the Georgia Athletic Board and John Griffith may have been sufficient motivation for him. Some suspect that he still hoped to regain his coaching job. As for gambling, his financial troubles were severe, and a winning bet would have helped. Still, there is no proof that he bet on the game, and it cannot be assumed. His financial difficulties are the key to another and more likely motive, however. He had received financial help from businessmen all over the country and would have been vulnerable to pressure from them.

It should be remembered that Burnett said Bryant was the aggressor in the conversation. He had opened it by saying, "Do you have anything for me?" indicating that he was expecting the call and that it was for his benefit. For the most part, Butts did not volunteer information; he only responded to Bryant's questions. In the statement recorded in Barwick's office, Burnett said:

> Butts sounded like he didn't like what he was doing. He sounded ashamed. On several occasions he answered, "I don't know." Bryant kept drawing him out. He asked, "What about this defense and this offense?" He also asked where the weakness on the pass defense was.

Though Butts avoided outright denials of Burnett's charges prior to the trial, he repeatedly insisted that he would never do anything to hurt Georgia. When Carmichael called to inform him of Burnett's disclosures, his response was that Georgia had not been hurt by any call Burnett may have overheard. When first confronted with the notes in Barwick's office, he admitted, according to some, that Burnett could have overheard such a conversation but had "misconstrued" information that did no harm to Georgia.

In this regard, there was a part of Bryant's testimony that may not have been fully appreciated at the time. At one point early on, Bryant volunteered, "He is for Georgia, and I am for Alabama. . . . If he would give me something on Georgia, the first thing I would think is they weren't going to use it. . . ." Could this comment have been inspired by what actually happened?

Bryant's clear indication that he was expecting a call for his benefit, his aggressive questions, and Butts's reluctant replies all suggest that Butts was not the principal architect of whatever scheme was at work. Nor is it likely that Bryant would have taken the initiative in approaching Butts for information. Was it possible that a third party who bet on the game had put pressure on Butts to assist Bryant with whatever information he could get on the Georgia team?

Butts called Frank Scoby 14 times in September 1962, once immediately before the call that Burnett overheard. Scoby was the only person the *Post* was able to link to gambling at the trial; he admitted to being a compulsive gambler on college football games. But in preparing for Bryant's case, the *Post*'s lawyers learned, to their satisfaction, that in addition to Scoby, at least two other friends of Butts were bettors on football games. These were but a few of the many people for whose benefit the call might have been placed.

Considering the absence of proof that the play of the game was affected by the call, it is possible that Butts sought to satisfy this third person by furnishing Bryant with such a mixture of valid, commonplace, harmless, and even inaccurate information that he could honestly believe he had done nothing to hurt Georgia. It is also possible that Bryant sensed what was happening and distrusted or disregarded the information; he may even have sympathized with Butts's predicament.

It is not possible to prove the third-party theory with any degree of certainty. It has the advantage of being consistent with all known facts and of exculpating both Bryant and Butts to some extent. It also squares with one of Schroder's three theories—that Burnett's notes reflected a harmless conversation, a view supported by Trippi and Hartman.

Do my conclusions that Burnett was telling the truth and that Butts and Bryant did have the conversation Burnett overheard mean that the jury's verdict was a miscarriage of justice? Would a new trial, without the lawyer's mistakes, have come out differently? Suppose that Frank Graham and the *Post* editors had testified in person; that Bisher, Flack, and Barwick had testified; that Cody had equaled Schroder in his mastery of technical football and his cross-examination of coaches and players; that the patterns in Bryant's phone calls had been used; that Bryant's letter to Rose and the Alabama scouting report and defensive records had been discovered and used; that Bryant's book had been turned against him; that evidence of specific acts of Butts's misconduct had been admitted as evidence; that Butts's and Bryant's explanations of their phone calls had been refuted; that Cody's fatal experiment with Rose's signature had not been attempted; and that Schroder's and Lockerman's improper arguments to the jury had not been allowed. Nonetheless, there would still have been the overriding issue of the flawed preparation of the article. There would still have been the vast gulf between the article and Burnett's notes. But personal testimony by the *Post* editors and writers might have convinced the jury that they believed the story to be substantially true, which they did.

In support of their good faith, the *Post*'s editors had Burnett's affidavit; Graham's belief in Burnett's truthfulness; Milton Flack's corroboration of Burnett; the extreme one-sidedness of the game; Burnett's lack of a motive to lie when he released the notes; the fact that Georgia officials believed Burnett; the first lie detector test; Butts's resignation in the face of Burnett's charges; telephone company records corroborating Burnett; the corroborating quotations supplied by Bisher; and the mistaken assumption that Bisher's *Atlanta Journal* would break the story simultaneously.

The *Post*'s editors certainly did not publish with knowledge of falsity. Their good faith that the article was true, along with all the corroboration of Burnett, should have prevented a jury from finding that they acted in reckless disregard of truth or falsity. If a new trial had been granted, the *New York Times* rule would unquestionably have applied and could well have given the *Post* a victory.

11

. . . . . .

Aftermath

THE LIBEL SUITS against the *Post* were something of a watershed for Bear Bryant. This crisis in his career apparently prompted him to clean up his act. He mellowed in his treatment of players and opponents and was never again the subject of a major scandal. The easing of Bryant's intensity and ruthlessness did not affect his success in coaching, however. He won five more national championships and was named national coach of the year three times. His six championships were amassed in the astonishingly brief period of 19 years. He became a role model for coaches and was unmatched in his ability to get the most out of countless athletes.

In 1982, Bryant broke Amos Alonzo Stagg's record of 314 college coaching victories and raised his total to 323 before retiring at the end of that season.* He died of a heart attack on January 27, 1983.

Herschel Nissenson of the Associated Press opened an admiring eulogy with this reminiscence:

> He smoked too much. If the pocket was Bear Bryant's,
> you could bet it held a crumpled pack of cigarettes.
> He drank too much. When he came to New York a

---

* Bryant's record has since been broken by Eddie Robinson of Grambling State University, an NCAA Division II team.

couple of years ago to address the Associated Press Board of Directors, his attaché case contained a bottle of vodka.

He partied too much. A few Aprils back, when he was hospitalized during spring practice, I asked him what the doctors had diagnosed.

"They said it was 75 percent smoking, 20 percent diet and 5 percent booze and other stuff," he replied.

"I wish," he added almost wistfully, "I wish it had been 75 percent of that booze and other stuff."

Bryant became a wealthy man, reportedly earning more than $400,000 a year from all sources of income. According to *The New York Times*, his salary from the university peaked at $120,000. Ironically, a part of Bryant's income came from doing sentimental TV commercials for AT&T to promote long-distance telephone calls. One example: "Have you called your mama lately? I sure wish I could call mine."

Except for the explanation he gives in his autobiography, Bryant steadfastly avoided any public discussion of his and Butts's cases. When I called him to request an interview on the subject, Bryant quickly said, "No, I wouldn't be interested in that." I later wrote to him in my vain effort to locate a copy of the game film. This was his reply:

July 9, 1982

Mr. James Kirby
Professor of Law
The University of Tennessee
1505 West Cumberland Ave.
Knoxville, Tn. 37916

Dear Mr. Kirby:

We will be unable to comply with your request of July 6 for a copy of 1962 Georgia-Alabama football game because someone either took it or we lost or I had it destroyed. I really don't know which but we are unable to locate it.

I, too, visited in Nashville a couple of months ago with Fred Russell and lot of the Vanderbilt players. It was certainly enjoyable and something I will remember for a long time. As a matter of fact, when I was working as an assistant at Vanderbilt, I think I had more fun than I've ever had in football.

Have a nice summer.

Sincerely,

Paul Bryant

PB/lk

Wally Butts lived an exemplary life until his death at age 68 on January 17, 1973. Although he had been negotiating with pro teams for a job, discussions ceased when the *Post* article came out, and they never resumed. Georgia sportswriter Doc Greene wrote that Butts found that "all doors were closed to him" in the game that had been his whole life.

Butts's next and final job was selling insurance. He founded his own agency in Athens and reportedly was a millionaire at his death. Furman Bisher, still sports editor of the *Atlanta Journal*, was among those who paid lavish tribute to Butts when he died. He dubbed Butts the "Bona Fide Coach" and recalled the *Post* article as a story "stretched beyond all bounds of imagination by a young sports editor just employed by the magazine attempting to break in with a big noise."

George Burnett left Atlanta soon after the trial. He and Foundation Life agreed that it would be in both his and the company's best interests if he relocated to Texas to head a planned new operation there. After he moved his family, the company failed to qualify under Texas law. He found other employment, however, and to this day continues to work in the insurance business in Dallas.

In April 1967, Burnett lost a coveted executive position when *Time* magazine wrongly referred to him as a "convicted check forger" in its story on the Supreme Court's decision. Quite a misnomer for someone whose most serious offense was a few bounced checks.

Of the sons who, according to the *Post* article, were on Burnett's mind at times while he considered exposing Butts and Bryant, one is a graduate of the U.S. Military Academy and the University of Texas Law School and now practices law in Houston. Another is a graduate of the Air Force Academy and, at this writing, is a colonel. A third went to Clemson on a football scholarship; he died after graduation.

Burnett says that he has wished a thousand times that the Butts-Bryant incident had never occurred, but if he had it to do over again, he would do the same thing.

How were the *Post* and Curtis Publishing Company affected by the verdict and its attendant publicity? After the trial *Advertising Age* surveyed 18 leading national companies then advertising in the *Post* and concluded that its revenues would not be affected "in any way." Of some $80,000 in firm advertising orders that the *Post* had taken in just before the trial, the companies surveyed accounted for 58 percent, or approximately $47,000. Here is a sampling of the advertisers' responses:

Frank R. Hawkins, advertising manager, Libbey-Owens-Ford Glass Company, Toledo: "I have felt that the virile articles in the *Post* were good for a reading public which too often has accepted morally wrong situations with a 'nothing-can be done-about-it' indifference. It is hoped that American writers will not be discouraged from writing on controversial subjects when they have facts and not retreat to Pablum journalism."

A top ad official of Coca-Cola in Atlanta, where the Butts libel case was tried: "This does not influence the thinking of Coca-Cola one way or the other."

Robert K. Heimann, assistant to the president of American Tobacco: "We are placing new space with the *Post* and are planning to use the magazine during the next four months for all of our brands."

Maxine Rowland, advertising manager of the toiletries division of Shulton, Inc.: "It certainly won't alter our plans for 1963, and I do not know whether it will affect our schedule for '64."

Rex M. Budd, director of advertising, Campbell Soup, Camden, N.J.: "The libel judgment will not affect our plans with Curtis. I don't see how the case influences an advertising judgment of the merits of *The Saturday Evening Post*—its audience profile, coverage, influence, impact, cost per thousand, or stature as a magazine."

Jack Glasser, manager of trade relations, National Distillers: "No one has taken a final position in the matter; eventually everything will come out in the wash. There's a general feeling of sympathy for the magazine, a feeling that the *Post* has been doing a hell of a good job and got a kick in the pants—but that's without saying whether or not it deserved it. However, this situation is not going to affect the *Post* as far as our advertising is concerned."

The next few years proved *Advertising Age*'s prediction correct. On July 27, 1967, the *Post* had booked for the year to date more advertising pages than it had carried in all of 1966. The number of readers reached 28 million, the highest in the magazine's history. (There were 23 million readers when the "fix" story appeared.) The *Post*'s success story made headlines in the *Wall Street Journal, Fortune*, and *Saturday Review*.

These facts raise questions about whether the Butts litigation contributed to the death of *The Saturday Evening Post* and later collapse of the Curtis Publishing Company. Some 20 books have been written on Curtis's turbulent final years. The demise of the *Post* in 1969 has been brilliantly chronicled by Otto Friedrich in *Decline and Fall.* Both an eyewitness and a participant, he traces the *Post*'s death to many persons and events going back to the forties. Of the Butts case, he writes:

> The intangible damage was hard to assess, but it was substantial. The *Post* had lost a dangerously large part of its reputation for accuracy and responsibility, the reputation on which all its other stories had to rest. The news magazines and newspaper columnists wrote scathingly about the whole affair. Several major advertising executives were equally critical. And from that point on, even the most implausible suit against the *Post* became news, and the news stories surrounded the magazine with an aura of scandalmongering and sensationalism.

There is now a new *Saturday Evening Post.* It is a descendant of the original magazine in name only and is much more conservative than its namesake was during the Blair era.

Whatever damage their work did to the *Post*, the journalists who put together the "fix" story have fared quite well. As I've already mentioned, the talented and durable Furman Bisher is still sports editor of the *Atlanta Journal* and writes some of the finest columns to be found. Clay Blair was dismissed from the *Post* in October 1964. He has since become a successful author. He coauthored General Omar Bradley's autobiography. Roger Kahn, sports editor of the *Post*, wrote the celebrated *Boys of Summer* about the old Brooklyn Dodgers baseball team. His most recent book is *Good Enough to Dream*, the story of the minor-league baseball team he operated in Pittsfield, Massachusetts. Frank Graham, Jr., impressed the *Post*'s editors with his ability to turn out a draft of "The Story of a College Football Fix" in a mere 24 hours and was given a full-time job. He is now field editor of *Audubon* magazine. Davis Thomas, number-two editor of the *Post*, who testified by deposition, is editor of *Down East* magazine in Camden, Maine. Number-three editor, Don Schanche, who participated in the editing but did not testify, is with the Rome bureau of the *Los Angeles Times*.

Graham ends his 1981 book, *Farewell to Heroes*, with two chapters on the "fix" story. In the concluding paragraph he describes an incident he considers the "ultimate irony." A publisher's distributor saw Graham's name as author of a book on conservation and insisted on having it approved by legal counsel. After receiving approval, the distributor sent the publisher the bill for legal fees. The law firm was none other than Pepper, Hamilton and Scheetz—the firm of Philip Strubing.

The lawyers involved in the Butts case were an older group, and many of them have died, including Welborn Cody, Bill Schroder, Allen Lockerman, John Runzer, Cook Barwick, and Eugene Cook. The only survivor among those principally involved is Phil Strubing; he divides his time in retirement between North Carolina and Florida.

Frank Rose left academic life and is now an educational consultant in Kentucky and Washington, D.C. O. C. Aderhold and J. D. Bolton are deceased.

College football easily survived whatever threat to its integrity the Butts-Bryant incident may have posed. The press treated the verdict as a total vindication of the parties and the sport. Few sportswriters had wanted to believe that two giants of the game could have stooped to the level of corruption they were accused of in the *Post*. The trial was followed by little in-depth critical analysis of the evidence or of the possibility that George Burnett may have told the truth.

One exception to the finality accorded the verdict by the press was a piece in the September 2, 1963, issue of *Sports Illustrated*. Entitled "Rx: Preventive Medicine," it questioned the assumption throughout college football that the sport had been "vindicated" by Butts's victory:

Vindicated? College football itself was not charged with anything. Only Butts and Bear Bryant were directly accused. Even so, the coaches were quite right in feeling that their sport would have been grievously humiliated if Butts had lost his suit. The whole is never unaffected by what happens to one of its parts. Some of the mud would have splattered on the football jerseys of boys as far away as Oregon.

But if the coaches had good reason to feel uneasiness during the trial they have no reason to feel utter relief now. Conditions remain as before. The sport is a multimillion-dollar business and a subject of absorbing interest to vast numbers of bookmakers and heavy gamblers. Money of this magnitude makes for greed, and greed often makes for crooked dealing. Yet the colleges have done precious little to protect themselves against scandal. Their recruiting practices have, in fact, stretched the moral principles of amateur sport beyond recognition. And it was shocking to learn that the major effort of the Southeastern Conference to investigate the Butts-Bryant allegations was to assign a man to attend the trial.

The article then went on to say that the NCAA was planning to investigate but was moving ahead at its "usual slow pace." In *Sports Illustrated*'s view, the whole pattern of the sport cried out for "preventive action." Without being more specific, it called for a "stern and universal ethic . . . to guard against a whole range of scandal-raising possibilities in a sport that professes amateurism while raking in the cash."

Contrary to *Sports Illustrated*'s information, the NCAA never conducted even a semblance of an investigation. From the beginning it had deferred to the Southeastern Conference's investigation. Also contrary to *Sports Illustrated*, the Southeastern Conference did more than merely assign a man (this writer) to attend the trial. Both Commissioner Moore and the sole investigator on his staff spent a great deal of time trying to determine the truth about the matter.

My recommendation to the SEC executive committee after the Butts trial was to withhold final judgment on the matter until Bryant's case was tried; I felt certain that a more complete view of the facts would then emerge. The recommendation was readily accepted in the hope that Bryant's trial would make the committee's decision easier.

After Bryant's case was settled, the *Post*'s Philadelphia lawyers invited the conference to send someone to meet with them and examine the new evidence that would have been used against Bryant. They hoped for disciplinary action of some sort. The conference sent me, and I met with Runzer and Strubing for a day and a half, obtaining much of the information reported in these pages.

I then submitted a supplemental report detailing this information to the SEC executive committee. Although the second report was much more unfavorable toward Butts and Bryant than the first one had been, the SEC took no further action. This was understandable. In the face of Butts's verdict and Bryant's settlement, any sanctions the conference decided to impose on Bryant or Alabama would have appeared unsupportable. I had no quarrel with the SEC's decision, despite my deep chagrin that Butts and Bryant would enjoy undeserved vindication in the public eye.

Big-time college football not only emerged unscathed from the Butts-Bryant incident but is more of a national institution now than it was in 1963. Winning continues to be all important. The problems of the game have changed little. Disciplinary sanctions by the NCAA and conferences are on the rise, however. Whether this is the result of increased violations or of tightened enforcement is arguable. A case in point is the severity of the actions taken against the University of Florida football program in 1984. After the NCAA cited Charlie Pell's Gators for massive rules violations, the university voluntarily ousted Pell and offered to forfeit six games. Nevertheless, the Southeastern Conference stripped the team of its 1984 SEC championship, and the NCAA put the team on probation for three years and imposed further sanctions, including cutbacks in football scholarships and TV appearances. These were unprecedented actions, sparked by the heightened concern of conference university presidents.

The most disturbing recent scandal in college sports occurred at Tulane University. Its star basketball player and two other players, along with five other persons, were indicted and charged with a point-shaving scheme to control the outcome of three games in the 1984 season. Although the players denied the charges (the case is still pending as of this writing), Tulane quickly abolished its intercollegiate basketball program.

This and other publicized cases have created the impression that cheating of various kinds in college sports is widespread and that some of it is related to gambling. According to a Media General–Associated Press poll taken in June 1985, seven out of ten Americans believe gambling on college sports encourages athletes to cheat. The poll was a nationwide survey based on 1,402 phone calls to adults. When asked, "Do you think gambling on college sports encourages athletes to cheat or not?" 70 percent said it did, 20 percent said it did not, and 10 percent were unsure. In answer to the question "Do you think the role of sports in college today is overemphasized, underemphasized, or is emphasized about right?" 60 percent said overemphasized, 2 percent said underemphasized, 33 percent said about right, and 5 percent were unsure.

Support is gaining for proposals to pay scholarship athletes cash sums in addition to room, board, books, and tuition. The idea is that $50 to $100 a month in spending money would help players resist being lured into gambling schemes. The College Football Association's coaches committee has recommended a rule that would allow football players to be given $60 a month to cover incidental costs.

There is still considerable resistance to paying college athletes for playing, grounded in traditional notions of amateur sports and more pragmatic concerns about mounting costs of athletic programs. Supporters counter with the argument that other types of scholarships pay more than athletic scholarships. Protecting players from temptation offered by gamblers should eventually tip the balance in favor of the spending-money allowances.

The most dramatic development triggered by the rise in college sports scandals was the June 1985 action of a special convention of the NCAA, which was attended by a record number of college and university presidents. At this meeting, a tough 12-point program was adopted, aimed primarily at limiting abuses in recruiting and academic eligibility. Its most stringent measures include suspension of coaches, loss of eligibility for players, suspensions of entire programs for up to two years, and external financial audits. The new NCAA rules also provide for control of athletic budgets within normal internal university procedures, rather than by separate athletic associations. This could bring about minor revolutions at many universities that have big-time football programs.

Although college football's popularity on major campuses has not subsided, candid criticism of the game's deficiencies has greatly increased. A notable example of a fan turned critic is John Underwood, coauthor of *Bear*.

Underwood's book, *The Death of an American Game*, was published in 1979. Based on a series of articles he had written for *Sports Illustrated*, it is a strong condemnation of brutality, injuries, and other abuses in football. Underwood's examples and statistics dramatically illustrate the failure of the 1963 NCAA crackdown on rough play that Bryant's teams, among others, had provoked. He notes, for instance, that blows from plastic helmets in "butt-blocking" continue to be a major cause of injuries. Underwood cites Dr. Donald Cooper, medical consultant to the NCAA, who places the blame on the coaches:

> There is no question in Dr. Cooper's mind where the blame belongs. He blames coaches, and the "madness" of their desire to "punish the opposition." He thinks the

coaches' belief in the power of punishment is the worst influence on the game.

Underwood considers widespread cheating in recruiting and on academic eligibility to be cancers threatening the life of college football. He blames administrators for allowing coaches to send "functional illiterates" into college classrooms. On the academic level of football players, he comments:

> The percentage of star halfbacks who would break into a cold sweat at the mere prospect of having to deliver a simple declarative sentence is staggering. Even the Big Ten, which sought for twenty-five years to protect the scholar-athlete image by selecting an All-Academic football team, has about given up the ghost. The Big Ten All-Academic is supposed to be made up of players with at least a B average for the year or for their college careers. In 1978, out of a thousand players on conference rosters, only forty-nine qualified—and eleven of those were from Northwestern, the worst team in the league.

But recruiting and academic eligibility violations are not the only forms of cheating undermining college football's health. Unfair play and even spying have also eaten away at the integrity of the sport. Underwood drives home the pervasiveness of cheating by quoting Dan Devine, esteemed coach at Missouri, Notre Dame, and Arizona State.

> Devine does not admit he ever cheated, as Bear Bryant fessed up to doing in order to stay alive at Kentucky and Texas A & M, but he says he understands how the process works: "When you're young, you see what a coach does and you say, 'I'll do anything to win.' So you cheat. You teach win-at-any-cost. Then you get older, and your career is in the balance. You say, 'I'll do anything to stay in.'"

Today, Underwood's pessimistic prognosis for big-time college football may seem greatly exaggerated. Perhaps in part because of such frank criticism as his, the NCAA's tough new policies give reason to hope that some of the sport's ills may finally be receiving real curative treatment.

Libel law has undergone significant change since the trial of Butts's case. The *New York Times* rule has been expanded and refined by the U.S. Supreme Court to the point where it stands as an "awesome barrier," in the words of veteran litigator Floyd Abrams, to any recovery by a public official or other public figure against a media defendant.

If Butts's case were tried today, he would unquestionably be considered a public figure, and the *Post* would get the full benefit of the *New York Times* rule. The attempt of four members of the Supreme Court to apply separate standards to "public officials" and "public figures" died after Butts's case; a single standard for all public officials and figures became the rule. In this sense his case was unique; he won four of his five votes in the Supreme Court under a relaxed *New York Times* test that was never applied in another case.

Under *New York Times* as it has evolved, the *Post* would not have the burden of proving truth. Instead, Butts would have the burden of proving falsity. He would also have to prove "actual malice." An early formulation of the Supreme Court's standard for actual malice was that the plaintiff must prove that the defendant acted with "a high degree of awareness of . . . probable falsity" (*Garrison v. Louisiana*, 379 U.S. 64 [1964]). A more recent formulation is that the plaintiff must prove by "clear and convincing evidence" that the defendant knew that his statement was false or that he "subjectively entertained serious doubt" as to its truth (*Bose Corp. v. Consumers of United States*, 466 U.S. 485 [1984]).

The jury instructions under *New York Times* would have been very different from those given by Judge Morgan, as two justices of the Supreme Court noted at the time. How important are jury instructions? The recent case of former Israeli defense minister

Ariel Sharon against *Time* magazine shows how a conscientious jury can follow jury instructions and find for the plaintiff on falsity but for the defendant on the malice issue. General Westmoreland's libel case against CBS was abandoned when his lawyer learned that the judge planned to give an unfavorable instruction on the weight of the evidence required.

Nonetheless, the fear that juries will ignore evidence and instructions and vote from prejudice has been an inhibiting factor for the press; under such circumstances a media defendant may still be held liable for honest mistakes, despite the *New York Times* rule.

Statistics show that defendants have had a high rate of success in preventing libel cases involving public figures from being decided with finality by juries. In the 20 years following *New York Times*, there were 61 federal appellate court decisions on the adequacy of proof of actual malice. In 41 of those cases, the defendant had won in the lower court and the plaintiff appealed; in only 10 of these appeals was the lower court reversed. In the 20 appeals by defendants, they were successful in 14 cases, a surprisingly high rate of 70 percent reversals.

A study by the Libel Defense Resource Center, a clearinghouse for information in this field, reveals that in approximately 75 percent of libel cases, the case was terminated for the defendant on summary judgment, usually on grounds that the plaintiff's proof did not meet the standards of *New York Times*. Of cases that do reach juries an astonishing 89 percent were found to have been decided for the plaintiffs but, on appeal, almost 75 percent of these verdicts were reduced or, more commonly, reversed.

These statistics led Floyd Abrams, writing in the August 1984 *American Bar Association Journal*, to conclude:

> From the point of view of libel defendants, the libel scene sometimes seems far less sanguine than these figures suggest. The cost of defending libel cases is high. The ability to dispose of weak cases brought to inhibit

the press is limited. Jury reactions to media defendants tend to be unfavorable. The threat of paralyzing punitive damage awards remains real.

Yet in the end the press generally prevails in libel cases, either at their commencement by motion or at their conclusion on appeal.

The high success rate of the press is sure to reduce the number of libel cases filed by public figures in the future.

Since these statistics were gathered, there has been a major development in favor of the press. It greatly reduces the role of juries and increases the power of judges in libel actions by public figures. In the *Bose* case, cited earlier, the Supreme Court dealt with an appellate review of a trial judge's findings in a case tried without a jury. In its decision, the Court announced a new rule applicable to an appellate judge's review of the facts as well as to a trial judge's determination of whether the plaintiff's proof is sufficient to go to a jury.

It is no longer enough in such cases for a judge to conclude that reasonable men might differ or that there is evidence both ways on the malice question. The judge must exercise "independent judgment" and determine whether the evidence establishes actual malice with "convincing clarity." He must be convinced. This makes the judge virtually the trier of fact and imposes a burden of proof just shy of the "reasonable doubt" standard in criminal cases.

Would the evidence in Butts's case satisfy this test? Did it "establish with convincing clarity" that the *Post*'s editors knew the "fix" accusation was false or that they subjectively entertained doubts of its truthfulness? They may have been negligent, hasty, even gleeful, but that falls far short of publishing with genuine doubts about their article's basic accuracy. Thus, there is serious doubt that Butts's case would be allowed to go to a jury today.

If Butts and Bryant had the conversation described in George Burnett's notes and lied about it on the stand, it was an injustice for them to have recovered damages from the *Post*. If the *Post* had been better served by its lawyers and had received its First Amendment rights under *New York Times*, justice would probably have prevailed. The Bear Bryant–Wally Butts scandal put three of America's most revered institutions—big-time college football, the law, and the press—to the test.

All three fumbled.

. . . .
APPENDIX

THE STORY OF A COLLEGE FOOTBALL FIX

A Shocking Report of How Wally Butts and "Bear" Bryant Rigged a Game Last Fall

by Frank Graham Jr.

Not since the Chicago White Sox threw the 1919 World Series has there been a sports story as shocking as this one. This is the story of one fixed game of college football.

Before the University of Georgia played the University of Alabama last September 22, Wally Butts, athletic director of Georgia, gave Paul (Bear) Bryant, head coach of Alabama, Georgia's plays, defensive patterns, all the significant secrets Georgia's football team possessed.

The corrupt here were not professional ballplayers gone wrong, as in the 1919 Black Sox scandal. The corrupt were not disreputable gamblers, as in the scandals continually afflicting college basketball. The corrupt were two men—Butts and Bryant—employed to educate and to guide young men.

How prevalent is the fixing of college football games? How often do teachers sell out their pupils? We don't know—yet. For now we can only be appalled. —THE EDITORS

ON FRIDAY MORNING, September 14, 1962, an insurance salesman in Atlanta, Georgia, named George Burnett picked up his telephone and dialed the number of a local public relations firm. The number was Jackson 5-3536. The line was busy, but Burnett kept trying. On the fourth or fifth attempt, he had just dialed the final number, when he heard what he later described as "a series of harsh electronic sounds," then the voice of a telephone operator said, "Coach Bryant is out on the field, but he'll come to the phone. Do you want to hold, Coach Butts, or shall we call you back?"

And then a man's voice: "I'll hold, operator."

Like most males over the age of four in Atlanta, George Burnett is a football fan. He realized that he had been hooked by accident into a long-distance circuit and that he was about to overhear a conversation between two of the colossi of southern football. Paul (Bear) Bryant is the head coach and athletic director of the University of Alabama, and Wallace "Wally" Butts was for 22 years the head coach of the University of Georgia and, at the time of this conversation, the university's athletic director. Burnett ("I was curious, naturally") kept the phone to his ear. Through this almost incredible coincidence he was to make the most important interception in modern football history.

After a brief wait Burnett heard the operator say that Coach Bryant was on the phone and ready to speak to Coach Butts.

"Hello, Bear," Butts said.

"Hello, Wally. Do you have anything for me?"

As Burnett listened, Butts began to give Bryant detailed information about the plays and formations Georgia would use in its opening game eight days later. Georgia's opponent was to be Alabama.

Butts outlined Georgia's offensive plays for Bryant and told him how Georgia planned to defend against Alabama's attack. Butts mentioned both players and plays by name. Occasionally Bryant asked Butts about specific offensive or defensive maneuvers, and Butts either answered in detail or said, "I don't know about that. I'll have to find out."

"One question Bryant asked," Burnett recalled later, "was 'How about quick kicks?' And Butts said, 'Don't worry about quick kicks. They don't have anyone who can do it.'

"Butts also said that Rakestraw [Georgia quarterback Larry Rakestraw] tipped off what he was going to do by the way he held his feet. If one foot was behind the other, it meant he would drop back to pass. If they were together, it meant he was setting himself to spin and hand off. And another thing he told Bryant was that Woodward [Brigham Woodward, a defensive back] committed himself fast on pass defense."

As the conversation ended, Bryant asked Butts if he would be at home on Sunday. Butts answered that he would.

"Fine," Bryant said. "I'll call you there Sunday."

Listening to this amazing conversation, Burnett began to make notes on a scratch pad he kept on his desk. Some of the names were strange to him—tackle Ray Rissmiller's name he jotted down as "Ricemiller," and end Mickey Babb's as "Baer"—and some of the jargon stranger still, but he recorded all that he heard. When the two men had hung up, Burnett still sat at his desk, stunned, and a little bit frightened.

Suddenly he heard an operator's voice: "Have you completed your call, sir?"

Burnett started. "Yes, operator. By the way, can you give me the number I was connected with?"

The operator supplied him with a number in Tuscaloosa, Alabama, which he later identified as that of the University of Alabama. The extension was that of the athletic department. Burnett then dialed Jackson 5-3536—the number he originally wanted. This time the call went through normally, and he reached a close friend and former business associate named Milton Flack.

"Is Wally Butts in your office now, Milt?" Burnett asked.

"Well, he's in the back office—making a phone call, I think. Here he comes now."

"Don't mention that I asked about him," Burnett said hurriedly. "I'll talk to you later."

Through some curious electronic confusion, George Burnett, calling his friend Milt Flack, had hooked into the call Wally Butts was making from a rear office in Flack's suite. He was the third man, the odd man. But he was not out.

Putting the pieces together

In the next few hours, Burnett tried to piece together what he knew of Georgia football. Butts, a native of Milledgeville,

Georgia, had joined the university coaching staff as an assistant in 1938. A year later he was named head coach. For 20 years he was one of the most popular and successful coaches in the South. Then prominent University of Georgia alumni abruptly soured on him, and on January 6, 1961, he was replaced by a young assistant coach named Johnny Griffith. Butts, filed away in the position of Georgia's athletic director (which he had held along with his coaching job for some years), was outspokenly bitter about his removal from the field.

Burnett knew, too, that Butts recently had been involved in a disastrous speculation in Florida orange groves. Butts had lost over $70,000 because, as someone put it, "you couldn't grow *cactus* on that land." One of his partners in the deal was also an associate of Milt Flack at a public relations firm called Communications International, the office Burnett had been trying to call when he hooked into the Butts-Bryant conversation.

That afternoon Burnett told Flack what he had overheard. Both of them, though only slightly acquainted with the high-spirited, gregarious Butts, liked him, and they decided to forget the whole thing. Burnett went home in the evening and stuffed his notes away in a bureau drawer. He felt a great sense of relief. The matter, as far as he was concerned, was closed.

Eight days later, on September 22, the Georgia team traveled to Birmingham to play Alabama before a crowd of 54,000 people at Legion Field. Alabama hardly needed any "inside" information to handle the outmanned Bulldogs. Bryant, one of the country's most efficient and most ruthless coaches—he likes his players to be mean and once wrote that football games are won by "outmeaning" the other team—had built a powerhouse that was in the middle of a 26-game winning streak. Alabama was the defending national champion, combining a fast-charging and savage-tackling defense with an effective attack built around a sensational sophomore quarterback named Joe Namath. The Georgia team was composed chiefly of unsensational sophomores.

Various betting lines showed Alabama favored by from 14 to

17 points. If a man were to bet on Alabama, he would want to be pretty sure that his team could win by *more* than 17 points, a very uncertain wager when two major colleges are opening the season together and supposedly have no reliable line on the other's strengths and weaknesses.

Bryant, before the game, certainly did not talk to the press like a man who was playing with a stacked deck.

"The only chance we've got against Georgia is by scratching and battling for our life," he said, managing to keep a straight face. "Put that down so you can look at it next week and see how right it is."

The game itself would have been enjoyed most by a man who gets kicks from attending executions. Coach Bryant (he neglected to wear a black hood) snapped every trap. The first time Rakestraw passed, Alabama intercepted. Then Alabama quickly scored on a 52-yard pass play of its own. The Georgia players, their moves analyzed and forecast like those of rats in a maze, took a frightful physical beating.

"The Georgia backfield never got out of its backfield," one spectator said afterward. And reporter Jesse Outlar wrote in Atlanta's Sunday *Journal* the following day, "Every time Rakestraw got the ball he was surrounded by Alabama's All-American center Lee Roy Jordan and his eager playmates."

Georgia made only 37 yards rushing, completed only 7 of 19 passes for 79 yards, and made its deepest penetration (to Alabama's 41-yard line) on the next to the last play of the game. Georgia could do nothing right, and Alabama nothing wrong. The final score was 35–0, the most lopsided score between the two teams since 1923.

It was a bitter defeat for Georgia's promising young team. The 38-year-old Johnny Griffith, who was beginning his second season as head coach, was stunned. Asked about the game by reporter Jim Minter, he said, "I figured Alabama was about three touchdowns better than we were. So that leaves about fifteen points we can explain only by saying we didn't play any football."

Quarterback Rakestraw came even closer to the truth. "They were just so quick and mobile," he told Minter. "They seemed to know every play we were going to run."

Later other members of the Georgia squad expressed their misgivings to Furman Bisher, sports editor of the Atlanta *Journal*. "The Alabama players taunted us," end Mickey Babb told him. " 'You can't run *Eighty-eight Pop* [a key Georgia play] on us,' they'd yell. They knew just what we were going to run and just what we called it."

And Sam Richwine, the squad's trainer, told Bisher, "They played just like they knew what we were going to do. And it seemed to me a lot like things were when they played us in 1961 too." (Alabama walloped Georgia in 1961 by a score of 32–6.)

Only one man in the Georgia camp did not despair that day. Asked by reporter John Logue about Georgia's disappointing performance, ex-coach Wally Butts nodded wisely and set him straight. "*Potential* is the word for what I saw," he said. "Unlimited *potential*."

The whole matter weighed heavily on George Burnett. He began to wonder if he had done the right thing when he had put the notes aside and kept his mouth shut. Now 41 years old, he was still struggling to support his large family. Among his five children were a couple of boys who played football. "How would I feel," Burnett asked himself, "if my boys were going out on the field to have their heads banged in by a stronger team, and then I discovered they'd been sold out?" He began to wake up at night and lie there in the dark, thinking about it.

In one sense Burnett knew it would be easiest to keep the notes in the drawer. While every citizen is encouraged to report a crime to authorities, the penalties against the man who talks are often more severe than those against the culprit. Burnett wasn't worried about physical retaliation. But there might be social and economic ones. Football is almost a religion in the South; the big-name coaches there are minor deities.

Butts no longer had his old-time stature, but many people were still intensely loyal to him (and he was a director of the small Atlanta insurance agency where Burnett worked). Bear Bryant was a national figure who had made impressive records at Texas A&M and Kentucky and had more recently transformed Alabama from pushovers to national champions.

Burnett, protective toward his family, fearful of challenging deities, was troubled by a drive to do what was right. But what was right? To talk? To create furor, perhaps even national scandal? Or should he remain silent, ignoring wrong? That was a safe course, but one that might sit heavily on his conscience for all the rest of his days.

Living in his private misery, he thought about his past. Burnett himself had played high school football in San Antonio, Texas, where he was born. During World War II, he became a group navigator aboard a Martin B-26. On January 14, 1945, when his plane was shot down over Saint-Vith, Belgium, he was the only survivor. He lost part of his left hand and spent the rest of the war in a German prison camp. Articulate and personable, he was now the division manager of the insurance agency.

On January 4 of this year, he sat in his office with Bob Edwards, a longtime friend who was also an employee of the agency. Burnett knew that Edwards had played football with Johnny Griffith at South Georgia, a junior college.

"You know, Bob," Burnett said, after they had talked business for a while, "there's something that's been eating me up for a long while. I was going to tell you about it at the time, and then I decided to keep quiet. But I think you should know this, being a friend of Johnny Griffith."

After Edwards heard the story of the phone call, he asked if he could report it to Griffith. Burnett, still reluctant to get seriously involved, told Edwards to go ahead but to try to keep his name out of it. Powerful men in Georgia might be offended if Wally Butts was hurt, and Burnett did not want to jeopardize his own career just when things were beginning to break nicely for him.

But like so many others, Burnett found that there is no such thing as a little involvement. Griffith pressed to meet him, and nervously Burnett agreed. In the middle of January, he met with Edwards and Griffith in the Georgia coach's room at Atlanta's Biltmore Hotel. Simultaneously a general meeting of the Southeastern Conference coaches was taking place at the Biltmore.

The Georgia-Alabama game had been forgotten by most of the coaches and athletic officials present. A popular topic of conversation was a late-season game between Alabama and Georgia Tech, in which Bryant's long winning streak had been broken.

Alabama, a five-point favorite, had trailed, 7–6, with only a little more than a minute to play. Then Alabama made a first down on the Georgia Tech 14-yard line. Since Bryant had a competent field-goal kicker, the classic strategy would have been to pound away at the middle of Tech's line, keeping the ball between the goalposts and, on third or fourth down, order a field-goal try. (Alabama had defeated Georgia Tech on a last-minute field goal in 1961.) Instead, Bryant's quarterback passed on first down. The pass was intercepted, and Georgia Tech held the ball during the game's waning seconds, thus scoring last season's greatest upset.

During the January conference at the Biltmore, Bryant was frequently kidded about that first-down pass.

Away from the bars and the crowds, in Griffith's room, the talk was only of Georgia-Alabama. Griffith listened grimly to Burnett's story, then read his notes. Suddenly he looked up.

"I didn't believe you until just this minute," he told Burnett. "But here's something in your notes that you couldn't possibly have dreamed up . . . this thing about our pass patterns. I took this over from Wally Butts when I became coach, and I gave it a different name. Nobody uses the old name for this pattern but one man. Wally Butts."

Suspicions confirmed

Griffith finished reading the notes, then asked Burnett if he could keep them. Burnett nodded.

"We knew somebody'd given our plays to Alabama," Griffith

told him, "and maybe to a couple of other teams we played too. But we had no idea it was Wally Butts. You know, during the first half of the Alabama game my players kept coming to the sidelines and saying, 'Coach, we been sold out. Their linebackers are hollering out our plays while we're still calling the signals.' "

Griffith has since spoken of his feelings when he had finished reading Burnett's notes, and Burnett and Edwards had left. "I don't think I moved for an hour—thinking what I should do. Then I realized I didn't have any choice."

Griffith went to university officials, told them what he knew, and said that he would resign if Butts was permitted to remain in his job. On January 28, a report reached the newspapers that Butts had resigned. At first it was denied by Butts and the university. A few days later it was confirmed with the additional news—that Butts would remain as athletic director until June 1 so that he could qualify for certain pension benefits. Rumors flooded Atlanta. One of the wildest was that Butts was mysteriously and suddenly ill and had entered the state hospital at Athens. This was quickly scotched when Georgia University officials maintained that Butts merely went for the physical checkup required for his pension records. Shortly afterward he was seen in Atlanta at a Georgia Tech basketball game.

But if Butts was seen publicly, events involving him remained closely guarded secrets. Burnett was asked to come to the Atlanta office of M. Cook Barwick, an attorney representing the University of Georgia. There he met Dr. O. C. Aderhold, the university president. Burnett's story was carefully checked. He then agreed to take a lie-detector test, which was administered by polygraph expert Sidney McMain, in the Atlanta Federal Building. Burnett passed the test to everybody's satisfaction.

Phone company check

Next an official of the Southern Bell Telephone Company checked and found that a call had been made from the office of Communications International to the University of Alabama extension noted by Burnett on his scratch pad. This information corroborated Burnett's statement that the call had been made at about 10:25 in the morning and had lasted 15 or 16 minutes.

"I jotted down the time when the call was completed," Burnett said. "It was 10:40. This is an old navigator's habit, I guess. For instance, I know that I was shot down over Saint-Vith at exactly 10:21, because when the bombardier called 'Bombs away!' I looked at my watch and wrote down the time. A few seconds later we got hit."

University officials still nursed reservations about Burnett's story because of the fantastic coincidence that had enabled him to overhear Butts's call. Then, during one of the many conferences he attended in attorney Barwick's office in the Rhodes-Haverty Building, a second coincidence, equally odd, cleared the air. Barwick placed a call to Dr. Aderhold at the university. Suddenly, Barwick and Aderhold found themselves somehow braided into a four-way conversation with two unknown female voices. The two men burst into nervous laughter. Burnett's story gained a little more credence.

February 21 was a painful day for George Burnett. He was summoned once more to Barwick's office, because Bernie Moore, the commissioner of the Southeastern Conference, "wanted to ask some questions." On Burnett's arrival he found not only Moore but Dr. Aderhold, two members of the university's board of regents, and another man identified as Bill Hartman, a friend of Wally Butts.

From the start, Burnett sensed a mood of hostility in the air. The ball was carried by one of the members of the Georgia board of regents, who confronted Burnett with a report that he had been arrested two years before for writing bad checks and that he was still on probation when he overheard the conversation between Butts and Bryant.

"Is there anything else in your past you're trying to cover up?" the regents official demanded.

Burnett was frightened and angry. "I didn't realize that *I* was on trial," he said. He went on to say that he had nothing to hide, that he had given university officials permission to look into his background, and that he had taken a lie-detector test, signed an affidavit that his testimony was true, and permitted his statements to be recorded on tape. His notes had been taken from him and placed by Barwick in the safety-deposit vault of an Atlanta bank.

"I *was* arrested on a bad-check charge," Burnett admitted. "I was way behind on my bills, and two of the checks I wrote— one was for twenty-five dollars and the other for twenty dollars— bounced. I was fined one hundred dollars and put on probation for a year. I think that anybody who is fair will find I got into trouble because I've always had trouble handling my financial affairs and not because I acted with criminal intent."

Burnett was shaken by this meeting. He felt that he had been candid with the university but that he had also angered many friends of Wally Butts. He signed a paper at the officials' request which gave the university permission to have his war records opened and examined. He cared about his reputation. He was proud to have been a navigator.

"Dr. Aderhold was always very kind to me at those meetings," Burnett said later, "but I didn't like the attitude of some of the others. I began to feel that I'd be hurt when and if these people decided to make this mess public. That's when I went to my lawyer, and we agreed that I should tell my story to *The Saturday Evening Post*."

Now the net closed on Wally Butts. On February 23 the University of Georgia's athletic board met hastily in Atlanta and confronted Butts with Burnett's testimony. Challenged, Butts refused to take a lie detector test. The next day's newspapers reported that he had submitted his resignation, effective immediately, "for purely personal and business purposes."

"I still think I'm able to coach a little," Butts told a reporter that day, "and I feel I can help a pro team."

The chances are that Wally Butts will never help any football team again. Bear Bryant may well follow him into oblivion—a special hell for that grim extrovert—for in a very real sense he betrayed the boys he was pledged to lead. The investigation by university and Southeastern Conference officials is continuing; motion pictures of other games are being scrutinized; where it will end no one so far can say. But careers will be ruined, that is sure. A great sport will be permanently damaged. For many people the bloom must pass forever from college football.

"I never had a chance, did I?" Coach Johnny Griffith said bitterly to a friend the other day. "I never had a *chance*."

When a fixer works against you, that's the way he likes it.

THE END

······

INDEX

DATE			